Lecture Notes in Computer Science 2232

Edited by G. Goos, J. Hartmanis, and J. van Leeuwen

Springer
Berlin
Heidelberg
New York
Barcelona
Hong Kong
London
Milan
Paris
Tokyo

Ludger Fiege   Gero Mühl   Uwe Wilhelm (Eds.)

Electronic Commerce

Second International Workshop, WELCOM 2001
Heidelberg, Germany, November 16-17, 2001
Proceedings

 Springer

Series Editors

Gerhard Goos, Karlsruhe University, Germany
Juris Hartmanis, Cornell University, NY, USA
Jan van Leeuwen, Utrecht University, The Netherlands

Volume Editors

Ludger Fiege
Gero Mühl
Darmstadt University of Technology
Wilhelminenstr. 7, 64283 Darmstadt, Germany
E-mail: {fiege/gmuehl}@gkec.tu-darmstadt.de

Uwe Wilhelm
T-Nova
Otto-Röhm-Str. 71C, 64293 Darmstadt, Germany
E-mail: U.Wilhelm@telekom.de

Cataloging-in-Publication Data applied for

Die Deutsche Bibliothek - CIP-Einheitsaufnahme

Electronic commerce : second international workshop ; proceedings / WELCOM
2001, Heidelberg, Germany, November 16 - 17, 2001. Ludger Fiege ... (ed.). -
Berlin ; Heidelberg ; New York ; Barcelona ; Hong Kong ; London ; Milan ;
Paris ; Tokyo : Springer, 2001
    (Lecture notes in computer science ; Vol. 2232)
    ISBN 3-540-42878-X

CR Subject Classification (1998): K.4.4, C.2, I.2.11, H.3, J.1, K.6.5, E.3

ISSN 0302-9743
ISBN 3-540-42878-X Springer-Verlag Berlin Heidelberg New York

Springer-Verlag Berlin Heidelberg New York
a member of BertelsmannSpringer Science+Business Media GmbH

http://www.springer.de

© Springer-Verlag Berlin Heidelberg 2001
Printed in Germany

Typesetting: Camera-ready by author, data conversion by PTP-Berlin, Stefan Sossna
Printed on acid-free paper   SPIN: 10845779   06/3142   5 4 3 2 1 0

Message from the Organizers

It is with great pleasure that we welcome you to WELCOM 2001. The Workshop on Electronic Commerce was first held in 1999 as a one-day workshop in conjunction with the 18th IEEE Symposium on Reliable and Distributed Systems (SRDS) in Lausanne. This first workshop proved quite successful for the organizers as well as the authors, a fact that is reflected in the continued participation of at least seven authors. Both the scope and the size of the workshop have been extended for the second event, which was held during two days (November 16-17, 2001) in Heidelberg and featured two invited talks (one of them industrial) as well as a panel on e-services.

This year, 36 papers from 14 countries around the world were submitted for consideration. Of these, the program committee selected 17 papers for inclusion in the workshop. These papers cover a wide range of interesting topics that were grouped under five major headings: Trade and Markets, Auctions, Security and Trust, Profiling, and Business Interaction.

The organizers want to thank the authors and the program committee for their work in preparing the technical program for WELCOM 2001 as well as the presenters of the invited talks, the panelists, and the organizer of the panel for their efforts. Last and foremost we thank the participants for making WELCOM 2001 a successful event.

November 2001

Ludger Fiege
Gero Mühl
Uwe G. Wilhelm

Organization

WELCOM 2001 was organized by Darmstadt University of Technology in cooperation with the German Informatics Society (GI/EMISA).

Workshop Chairs

Ludger Fiege
TU Darmstadt
Darmstadt, Germany

Gero Mühl
TU Darmstadt
Darmstadt, Germany

Uwe Wilhelm
T-Systems Nova GmbH
Darmstadt, Germany

Program Committee

Gustavo Alonso, ETH Zürich, Switzerland
Jan Boluminski, Loyalty Partner, Germany
Alejandro Buchmann, TU Darmstadt, Germany
Clemens Cap, U. Rostock, Germany
Fabio Casati, HP Labs, USA
Peter Fankhauser, GMD-IPSI, Germany
Oliver Günther, HU Berlin, Germany
Stefan Jablonski, U. Erlangen, Germany
Ravi Jain, Telcordia, USA
Christian S. Jensen, Aalborg University, Denmark
Günter Karjoth, IBM, Switzerland
Ramayya Krishnan, CMU, USA
Josef Küng, U. Linz, Austria
Winfried Lamersdorf, U. Hamburg, Germany
Cliff Leung, IBM, USA
Günther Müller, U. Freiburg, Germany
Stefan Noll, FhG-IGD, Germany
Andreas Oberweis, U. Frankfurt, Germany
M. Tamer Özsu, U. Waterloo, Canada
Sachar Paulus, SAP, Germany
Joachim Posegga, SAP, Germany
Krithi Ramamritham, U. of Massachusetts, USA
Mike Reiter, Bell-Labs, USA
André Schiper, EPFL Lausanne, Switzerland
Hartmut Vogler, SAP Labs, USA
Gottfried Vossen, U. Münster, Germany

Main Sponsor

Deutsche Telekom

Supported by

German Informatics Society (GI)
GI Chapter 2.5.2 (EMISA)

PhD Program
'Enabling Technologies for Electronic Commerce'
TU Darmstadt

Table of Contents

Invited Talks

Process Based E-services 1
Amaia Lazcano, Gustavo Alonso

Digital Rights Management - Dealmaker for E-business? 11
Stephan Heuser

Panel

E-services: The Next Wave of Internet-Based Applications 13
Alejandro Buchmann

Trade / Markets

A New M-commerce Concept: m-Mall 14
Jaime García-Reinoso, Javier Vales-Alonso,
Francisco J. González-Castaño, Luis Anido-Rifón,
Pedro S. Rodríguez-Hernández

Building Comparison-Shopping Brokers on the Web 26
Simone C. dos Santos, Sérgio Angelim, Silvio R.L. Meira

Trusted Mediation for E-service Provision in Electronic Marketplaces 39
Giacomo Piccinelli, Cesare Stefanelli, David Trastour

GAMA-Mall – Shopping in Communities............................. 51
Till Schümmer

Markets without Makers - A Framework for Decentralized Economic
Coordination in Multiagent Systems 63
Torsten Eymann

Incentives for Sharing in Peer-to-Peer Networks 75
Philippe Golle, Kevin Leyton-Brown, Ilya Mironov, Mark Lillibridge

Security / Trust

Mobile Payments – State of the Art and Open Problems 88
Konrad Wrona, Marko Schuba, Guido Zavagli

Using Smart Cards for Fair Exchange................................ 101
Holger Vogt, Henning Pagnia, Felix C. Gärtner

Rational Exchange – A Formal Model Based on Game Theory 114
    Levente Buttyán, Jean-Pierre Hubaux

Enabling Privacy Protection in E-commerce Applications 127
    Dennis Kügler

Auctions

FAucS: An FCC Spectrum Auction Simulator
for Autonomous Bidding Agents 139
    János A. Csirik, Michael L. Littman, Satinder Singh, Peter Stone

A Dynamic Programming Model for Algorithm Design
in Simultaneous Auctions 152
    Andrew Byde

Profiling

User Modelling for Live Help Systems 164
    Johan Aberg, Nahid Shahmehri, Dennis Maciuszek

Multidimensional Recommender Systems:
A Data Warehousing Approach 180
    Gediminas Adomavicius, Alexander Tuzhilin

Business Interaction

A Multi-criteria Taxonomy of Business Models in Electronic Commerce . . . 193
    Andreas Bartelt, Winfried Lamersdorf

Integration of Goods Delivery Supervision
into E-commerce Supply Chain 206
    Anke Thede, Albrecht Schmidt, Christian Merz

Scalable Regulation of Inter-enterprise Electronic Commerce 219
    Naftaly H. Minsky, Victoria Ungureanu

Author Index 233

Process Based E-services

Amaia Lazcano and Gustavo Alonso

Department of Computer Science
Swiss Federal Institute of Technology (ETHZ)
ETH Zentrum, CH-8092 Zürich, Switzerland
{lazcano, alonso}@inf.ethz.ch

Abstract. In this paper we describe WiseFlow, a software platform currently being used to provide a variety of electronic services within the maritime industry. WiseFlow lies at the core of an international trading community formed by certification societies, consulting firms, shipyards, steel mills, manufacturers, insurance companies and government agencies. As such, this community revolves around well defined business processes shared among all participants: certification of materials for the shipping industry. WiseFlow supports the daily execution of these processes and implements different business models from several of the participants.

1 Introduction

Maritime certification societies face a daunting inter-enterprise document handling problem. International law requires every part of a vessel, from manufactured components (e.g., engines) to raw materials (e.g, steel plates), to be certified. These certificates are essential to obtain navigation permits and play a crucial role in the insurance and demarcation of responsibilities in case of accidents. During the lifetime of large commercial vessels like oil tankers or container carriers, the number of certificates associated to the vessel can reach several hundred thousands. These certificates need to be maintained, updated, transferred, and consulted as the vessel undergoes repairs, changes ownership, changes its navegability ratings, changes insurance companies, etc. The certification of components and materials is carried out by *certification societies*, internationally recognized as trusted entities in charge of the issuing and custody of the certificates. Historically, certification societies have faced little competition as they tended to be national entities that concentrated in geographically well defined markets. This situation is rapidly changing and, as a result, there has been a mounting pressure to modernize the certification process as a whole. In addition, current practice is based on keeping several hard copies of the same certificate at several places: at the certification society, at the shipyard where the vessel was produced, at the ship owner, and even at the manufacturers of components and raw materials. This is clearly inefficient and opens up significant opportunities for third parties willing to provide electronic services.

In this regard, both the certification process and the handling of certificates are textbook examples of the type of inter-company data exchanges that could

L. Fiege, G. Mühl, and U. Wilhelm (Eds.): WELCOM 2001, LNCS 2232, pp. 1–10, 2001.
© Springer-Verlag Berlin Heidelberg 2001

greatly benefit from switching to an electronic format. The realities of the market, however, make it very hard to come up with solutions that are, simultaneously, cost efficient, usable by all those involved, and complying with existing business procedures. On the one hand, the certification process involves many different participants from different companies, all of them widely distributed geographically. On the other hand, not all participants are *equals* in terms of their ability to implement electronic processes and the rights they have with respect to the overall process. In addition, the process itself has different interpretations depending on the participant, making it very difficult to find the necessary level of consensus to get all those involved to adopt the same technology.

We have tried to address all these issues by deploying the WiseFlow system. WiseFlow is unique in that it not only addresses the typical technological problems associated with e-commerce activities but also covers the business needs of different participants in the certification process. Thus, WiseFlow can be alternatively or simultaneously used as a workflow engine, as an electronic commerce platform for implementing inter-enterprise business processes, and as a tool for providing web and XML based electronic services. This flexibility offers significant advantages, specially in an environment where, as pointed out above, different partners have different interpretations of the process at hand and need different types of support. By providing a unique tool to all users, WiseFlow has greatly helped to reach a consensus on the technological basis. In this, we agree with other authors who see process automation as a foundation for electronic commerce [7,6].

The paper is organized as follows. In Section 2 we define the certification process and describe the different electronic services supported. Section 3 introduces the architecture of the system as well as the different configurations in which it has been deployed. Section 4 concludes the paper.

2   WiseFlow: Requirements for E-services

2.1   The Certification Process

Figure 1 contains a simplified version of the certification process. The real process includes around 80 execution steps. The certification process is started by a customer who orders certified steel. This order is received at the *steel mill*, and analyzed to decide if it can be manufactured. Once the order has been confirmed, the steel mill can start planning its production. A certificate number for this material is issued by the *certification society* on request.

The steel mill tests the manufactured material and includes the results with some additional information in a report. This is quality data that has to be sent to the certification society, but not before the necessary certificate number has been received. The steel mill may generate the quality data either in Edifact or PDF format. In the case of Edifact format, the document is sent to the *consulting firm* for further processing. They apply a series of conversions to the data and make corrections in case of errors. The resulting XML document is then transferred to the certification society.

The certification society receives either a XML or a PDF document. The XML document is used to generate a certificate which is then archived and copies of it distributed among customer, consulting firm and steel mill. If the document received by the certification society is in PDF format, it is directly stored and copies of it are also distributed.

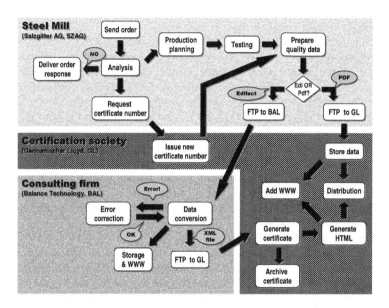

Fig. 1. A summary of the certification process used in the maritime industry

2.2   WiseFlow for a Certification Society

For the certification society, the primary interest is the automation of their (intra-organizational) certification subprocess using a workflow engine. This interest follows conventional wisdom regarding the advantages and benefits of automating business processes [5] [3], [17]. Closely related to the process automation is the problem of document management. Currently, the final certificates are stored in paper, which has both a high overhead and does not make economic sense any more. Automating the process using a workflow tool will immediately allow the electronic storage and management of the certificates, keeping track not only of the certificate itself but also of the process followed to create the certificate (nowadays this information is obtained by following the paper trail of the process).

In addition, certification societies see the automation of their internal certification process as the cornerstone of *trading communities* where they will play an even more central role in the industry and offer their current services in a far more efficient way.

2.3   WiseFlow for a Provider of E-services

The current certification process leaves much room for improvement and offers many opportunities for organizing e-services around it. The two existing services are EDI transcription of documents (acting as a proxy for companies without resources to deal with electronic documents) and storing certificates (mainly at the certification society). WiseFlow has been used to implement these services more efficiently and to create several new ones.

For instance, any participant in the certification process is likely to have several simultaneous processes involving different subsets of participants (steel mills, e.g., often obtain several certificates for the same material, each certificate being issued by a different certification society). To deal with such cases, a trusted intermediary could provide the necessary process support by acting as a process hub in charge of process execution and monitoring but not involved in the process itself. As another example, the coordination between the transport of the material and the delivery of the certificates is a cause of concern. It is not unusual for raw steel to arrive at a shipyard only to sit there unused until the certificates arrive weeks later. An e-service capable of reporting the status of the certification process could greatly enhance the coordination among participants and significantly reduce cost. Naturally, this service can be best provided by the process hub which could charge a premium for accessing this information aside from charging for running the process itself.

Finally, handling the process history can also be an interesting e-service. For any given participant, the certification process contains key information about the way processes are executed. For instance, it can help a steel mill to identify inefficiencies in the delivery process. Or it can help a shipyard to plan their purchases in advance in order to implement a just-in-time operation.

2.4   WiseFlow for Companies Less Committed to Technology

In the certification process, not all the companies have the same computing resources. This is a very important practical limitation that needs to be kept in mind. The certification process usually involves companies in developing or even third world countries, where access to computer and modern networks is limited. Even in Europe, many companies are not willing to make the effort to adopt a large information system. Unfortunately, many of the current B2B (business to business) solutions proposed by industry assume that all participants have a sufficiently large amount of computing and communication resources. From our experience, such systems cannot be used in an environment as heterogeneous as the maritime industry. In fact, the biggest difficulty in implementing an inter-organizational business process are not the big players and compatibility problems between their computing equipment but the smaller players and their lack of computing resources.

This problem was recognized very early on in the design of WiseFlow. Accordingly, WiseFlow allows clients to be connected to the system using a minimal amount of software. All that is needed is a WiseFlow proxy (written in Java) in the client machine. This simplifies the installation procedure as the code can be easily downloaded from a web site. Once the client is registered with the WiseFlow server, it can be used as one more node in the system. Any additional code can be produced on demand by downloading it from the server whenever needed.

3   WiseFlow: The System

WiseFlow has evolved from several systems built at ETHZ. The core of Wise-Flow is OPERA [13,2], a process support kernel that provides the basic workflow engine functionality and a number of programming language extensions (e.g., event handling [10], exception handling [12], spheres of atomicity [9], and high availability [11]). OPERA was first extended to build WISE (Workflow based Internet SErvices) [1]. WISE supports trading communities that interact based on *virtual business processes* [15]. WISE incorporates a commercial process design tool (IvyFrame [14,16]) that has been redesigned to work both as a process definition interface and a monitoring tool. In the MariFlow project (an EU project), the WISE system became WiseFlow once it was adapted to the needs of the maritime certification process. This adaptation includes logging capabilities, more sophisticated interfaces and API for handling documents, the ability to work across corporate firewalls, security, and the ability to arbitrarily combine WiseFlow servers in different locations to form a meta-server. These features are currently being extended as part of the INVENT project (Infrastructure for VIrtual ENterprises).

3.1   Architecture of WiseFlow

A WiseFlow server can be seen as a modular workflow engine that can recursively call other WiseFlow servers to execute subprocesses. WiseFlow is organized around three service layers (Figure 2.b): *database services, process services* and *interface services*.

The database service layer acts as the storage manager. It encompasses the storage layer (the actual databases used as repositories) and the database abstraction layer (which makes the rest of the system database independent). The storage layer is divided into five *spaces*: template, instance, object, history, and configuration, each of them dedicated to a different type of system data. Templates contain the structure of the processes. When a process is to be executed, a copy of the corresponding template is made and placed in the instance space. This copy is used to record the process' state as execution proceeds. For each running instance of a process the instance space contains a copy of the corresponding template. Storing instances persistently guarantees forward recoverability, i.e., execution can be resumed as soon as the failure is repaired, which solves the problem of dealing with failures of long lived processes [19,8]. In addition, the instance space is the basis for e-services based on notification of the status of a process. Objects are used to store information about externally defined data.

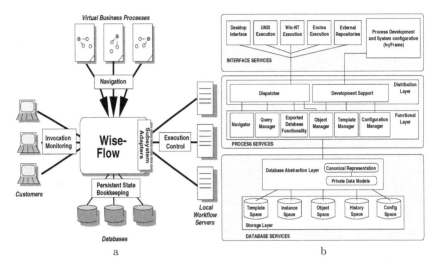

Fig. 2. a) General architecture of WiseFlow, b) Internal organization of the engine

They allow WiseFlow to interact with external applications by acting as a proxy containing the information indicating how to access external data [4]. The history space is used to store information about already executed instances (as in, for instance, [18]). It contains a detailed record of all the events that have taken place during the execution of processes, including already terminated processes. Currently we use Oracle for this purpose as the history space constitutes the basis for several e-services. Finally, the configuration space is used to record system related information such as configuration, access permissions, registered users, Internet addresses, program locations, and so forth. The database abstraction layer implements the mechanisms necessary to make the system database independent.

The process service layer contains all the components required for coordinating and monitoring the execution of processes. The most relevant components for the purposes of this paper are the *dispatcher* and *navigator* modules. The dispatcher deals with physical distribution and acts as resource allocator for process execution. It determines in which node the next step will execute, locates suitable nodes, checks the site's availability, performs load balancing, and manages the communication with remote system components. The navigator acts as the overall scheduler: it "navigates" through the process description stored in the main memory, establishing what to execute next, what needs to be delayed, and so forth. Once the navigator decides which step(s) to execute, the information is passed to the *dispatcher* which, in turn, schedules the task and associates it with a processing node in the cluster and a particular application. If the choice of assignment is not unique, the node is determined by the scheduling and load balancing policy in use. The dispatcher then contacts the *program execution client* (PEC); this is a small software component present at each node responsible for running application programs on behalf of the WiseFlow server. The PEC is responsible for invoking the application program that will complete the computational step. It is written in Java and, thus, it is platform independent, allowing WiseFlow to work with heterogeneous nodes. The PEC contains all the mechanisms that allow WiseFlow to interact with applications in different hardware and software platforms. The small size of the PEC allows providers of e-services to easily attach remote nodes (in the companies using the e-services) to their own WiseFlow server for those cases where user input maybe required. Users interact with the system via *desktop interfaces*, which are also used to inform the user of any activity that they need to execute as part of a process (similar to worklists in workflow engines).

Processes are created using a commercial tool, *IvyFrame* [14,16], which is internally based on Petri-nets and supports not only the modeling of business processes but also sophisticated analysis of its behavior (bottlenecks, average execution times, costs, delays, what if analysis, etc.). Using the process definition tool, it is possible to perform *process creation* and *configuration management*. The configuration management allows users to specify the hardware and software characteristics of the computer infrastructure to be used in the execution of a process (IP addresses, type of OS, CPU specifications, etc.).

WiseFlow uses internally a language called *Opera Canonical Representation* (OCR) [13] to describe processes. The graphical representation is compiled into an OCR text file that is used to create process templates. In OCR, a process consists of a set of *tasks* and a set of *data objects*. Tasks can be *activities*, *blocks*, or *subprocesses*. The data objects store the input and output data for the tasks and are used to pass information around a process. More details of OCR and the internal data structures of OPERA can be found in [13].

3.2   Additional Functionality: High Availability

Since the state of a process instance is persistent, WiseFlow can resume the execution of a process at the point where it was left off when a failure occurred. However, in certain cases it should even be possible to resume execution before the failure is repaired by using a reliable backup strategy. WiseFlow provides such a mechanism [11], implemented using application semantics to optimize the exchange of information between the primary copy and the backup. There is no dedicated backup, and instead databases will act as both primaries and backups depending on the particular process instance. This backup mechanism is also used to dynamically migrate processes as they execute from one server to another. Such functionality is of great help to balance the load on a large system.

3.3   Deployment Options

WiseFlow can be used as stand alone engine or as a cluster of engines over a wide area network. In stand alone mode, it works as a workflow engine capable of controlling remote (across the Internet) clients. From the point of view of an e-services provider, this capability opens up interesting opportunities as it allows designers to link up several companies into a single process deploying only the PEC. Communication across and through firewalls is achieved through a proprietary communication protocol implemented in WiseFlow. The protocol offers a variety of possibilities, including RMI tunneling through HTTP to get through firewalls without compromising security. The protocol also supports encryption, digital signatures and authentication so that system designers can implement the level of security appropriate to each case.

As a cluster of WiseFlow servers, the system allows the implementation of trading communities through a network of interrelated business processes that are combined to form a virtual business process. The system is based on a number of WiseFlow servers acting as clients of each other. Needless to say that controlling this execution has a significant potential as an e-service. Using this approach, the e-services provider runs a skeleton of the certification process activating subprocesses or activities at different companies as needed. The provider does not need to know the details of these subprocesses (which is proprietary information in most cases), it only needs to know where they fit within the overall process (which is known to all participants). The same protocol mentioned above is here used to allow communication across servers located behind firewalls. The provider can therefore act as both a coordinator for the overall process and a proxy for companies that cannot run electronic processes.

3.4   Data Storage, Notification

Keeping track of the execution of a process lies at the center of several e-services around the certification process. Typically, there are many activities that depend on the status of the process and it is a great advantage to be automatically notified when the process has reached a given state. For instance, the steel is sent to the shipyard only when a certificate has been issued, or production does not start until all certificates for a batch of steel have arrived. Such dependencies can be implemented in several ways [3]. If these are dependencies between processes, WiseFlow provides an event propagation mechanism that allows a WiseFlow server to send events to other servers that have subscribed to those events [10]. Since a WiseFlow process can raise events at any point in time, this allows designers to interconnect different business processes. In addition, to expand the number of potential users for such a notification service, WiseFlow combines its instance space with trigger functionality. The triggers are used to implement different notification services (web pages, e-mail messages) according to each user.

WiseFlow also provides an interface that allows to monitor in real time the progress of a given process. This interface is based on the same application as the process definition tool. The novelty of the approach used in WiseFlow is that this interface is entirely written in Java and can be downloaded as a Java applet, thereby allowing the remote monitoring of a process. This functionality is crucial to companies that outsource the execution of their part of the certification process. In spite of not owning the server and not driving the execution, such companies can keep track of their processes by using the WiseFlow interface.

3.5 Performance and Dependability

After extensive testing, the WiseFlow system has proven to meet the requirements of the maritime community. The most important of these requisites is that the system should be able to support 3000 certifications per month. WiseFlow has been shown to tolerate four times that load using a single server.

To increase the scalability of the system one needs only additional Wise-Flow servers and implement the certification process as a skeleton that invokes subprocesses at the different sites. Since load is distributed among the servers, this allows the system to support many more process instances. The e-services provider could coordinate the overall process and offer process monitoring, as well as process history analysis as an interesting e-service. Among the requirements stated at the beginning of this project were a list of typical queries: What is the status of a particular certificate, what is the average processing time of a particular step, list all my certificates, list all the processes of last year, etc. Our current process history based on Oracle supports this and can provide all this important information related to process execution.

4 Conclusions

The maritime industry is one of the many business domains where the different companies involved can benefit enormously from the modernization of their shared business processes. The specific characteristics of this environment offer also a good opportunity to all those interested in providing electronic services to participants in the trading community. In this paper we have presented Wise-Flow, a system that can be used in this context as a platform for implementing intra- and inter-enterprise business processes, as well as a tool for providing e-services.

References

1. G. Alonso, U. Fiedler, C. Hagen, A. Lazcano, H. Schuldt, and N. Weiler. Wise: Business to Business E-Commerce. In *Proceedings of the IEEE 9th International Workshop on Research Issues on Data Engineering. INFORMATION TECHNOLOGY FOR VIRTUAL ENTERPRISES (RIDE-VE'99). Sydney, Australia, March 23-24, 1999.*, March 1999.
2. G. Alonso, C. Hagen, H.J. Schek, and M. Tresch. Distributed Processing over Stand-alone Systems and Applications. In *Proceedings of the 23rd International Conference on Very Large Databases (VLDB'97)*, Athens, Greece, August 1997.
3. D. Baker, D. Georgakopoulos, H. Schuster, A. Cassandra, and A. Cichocki. Providing customized process and situation awareness in the collaboration management infrastructure. In *Proceedings of the Fourth International Conference on Cooperative Information Systems*, 1999.

4. Stephen Blott, Lukas Relly, and Hans-Jörg Schek. An open abstract-object storage system. In *Proceedings of the ACM SIGMOD International Conference on Management of Data*, Montreal, Canada, June 1996.

5. Fabio Casati and Angela Discenza. Supporting workflow cooperation within and across organizations. In *Proceedings of the 2000 ACM Symposium on Applied Computing,*, Villa Olmo, Como, Italy, March 2000.

6. Fabio Casati, Ski Ilnicki, LiJie Jin, Vasudev Krishnamoorthy, and Ming-Chien Shan. Adaptive and dynamic service composition in eflow. In *12th International Conference CAiSE 2000*, Stockholm, Sweden,, June 2000.

7. Fabio Casati and Ming-Chien Shan. Process automation as the foundation for e-commerce. In *Proceedings of the International Conference on Very Large Databases (VLDB)*, Cairo, Egypt, September 2000.

8. U. Dayal, M. Hsu, and R. Ladin. A Transaction Model for Long-running Activities. In *Proceedings of the Sixteenth International Conference on Very Large Databases*, pages 113–122, August 1991.

9. C. Hagen and G. Alonso. Flexible exception handling in the OPERA process support system. In *Proc. of the 18th Intl. Conference on Distributed Computing Systems*, Amsterdam, The Netherlands, May 1998.

10. C. Hagen and G. Alonso. Beyond the black box: Event-based inter-process communication in process support systems. In *Proc. of the 19th Intl. Conference on Distributed Computing Systems*, Austin, Texas, USA, May 1999.

11. C. Hagen and G. Alonso. Highly Available Process Support Systems: Implementing Backup Mechanisms. In *18th IEEE Symposium on Reliable Distributed Systems*, Lausanne, Switzerland, October 1999.

12. C. Hagen and G. Alonso. Exception Handling in Workflow Management Systems. *IEEE Transaction on Software Engineering*, 26(9), September 2000.

13. C. Hagen. *A Generic Kernel for Reliable Process Support*. Ph.D. Dissertation, ETH Nr. 13114, 1999.

14. IvyTeam. Structware'98 Process Manager. Available through http://www.ivyteam.com, 1998.

15. A. Lazcano, G. Alonso, H. Schuldt, and C. Schuler. The WISE approach to Electronic Commerce . *International Journal of Computer Systems Science & Engineering*, September 2000.

16. H. Lienhard. IvyBeans - Bridge to VSH and the project WISE. In *Proceedings of the Conference of the Swiss Priority Programme Information and Communication Structures, Zürich, Switzerland*, July 1998.

17. Peter Muth, Jeanine Weißenfels, Michael Gillmann, and Gerhard Weikum. Integrating light-weight workflow management systems within existing business environments. In *Proceedings of the 15th International Conference on Data Engineering, 23-26 March 1999, Sydney, Austrialia*, pages 286–293. IEEE Computer Society, 1999.

18. Michael Gillmann Peter Muth, Jeanine Weissenfels and Gerhard Weikum. Workflow history management in virtual enterprises using a light-weight workflow management system. In *Proceedings of the Ninth International Workshop on Research Issues on Data Engineering: Information Technology for Virtual Enterprises*, Sydney, Australia, March 1999.

19. B. Salzberg and D. Tombroff. DSDT: Durable Scripts Containing Database Transactions. In *Proceedings of the 12th International Conference on Data Engineering*, New Orleans, Louisiana, USA, February 1996.

Digital Rights Management - Dealmaker for E-business?
Invited Talk

Stephan Heuser

T-Systems Nova, Technologiezentrum Darmstadt / ITC Security
Stephan.Heuser@t-systems.de

The technical development during the last years empowered the exchange of electronic data using the network which became known as the World Wide Web. Especially the development of new compression algorithms allowed a reduction of the amount of data in multimedia content by a factor of 50 or even more – in most cases without an audible or visible reduction of quality! Additionally, the development and mass deployment of broadband technologies also for residential users made an exchange of large files much more comfortable than in times of the good old 9,6 kBd modem. These developments went hand in hand with the deployment of more and more powerful PCs and improved storage technologies (e.g., Gigabyte harddisks or CD-burners).

Economic data shows the trend that there is a new sport: burning of CDs. In Germany in the first half of 2001 there were sold more CD-Rs than recorded CDs. The German Phonographic Association estimated a loss of about 770 Mio. in 2000, regarding only audio.

One of many examples is Napster. It was easy to use, the service and the content was offered for free – and that made it very attractive for a lot of people who used it very frequently. It is assumed, that about 3 billion titles were exchanged in February 2001 which was the last month before the content filters had to be installed. After that the attractiveness of Napster for the users went down, which triggered them to switch to other file sharing communities. According to the numbers given by analysts of Webnoize about 3 billion titles were exchanged in the four of the most frequently used communities in August only.

In the meantime there are several reactions from governments on the one hand and content providers or owners on the other in order to enable the e-business with electronic data. Legal reactions are the adoption of the Digital Millennium Copyright Act (DMCA - Oct. 1998, USA) and the directive 2001/29/EC of the European Parliament on the "Harmonisation of Certain Aspects of Copyright and Related rights in the Information Society". Both try to protect the copyright of electronic data by prohibiting the circumvention of technological measures controlling the access to works protected under the relevant title. The DMCA is already in use whereas the European directive is only the framework for national law. It has to be adopted within the next 12 months.

Several content owners and also platform providers saw the chances and took the challenge to use the newly developed technical systems of several companies to offer a legal variation of music download. These new technical systems allow the owner or the service provider to define several use cases for each offered content. These use

L. Fiege, G. Mühl, and U. Wilhelm (Eds.): WELCOM 2001, LNCS 2232, pp. 11-12, 2001.

cases are controlled individually at each customer by the technical systems, i.e., a special client software. Examples for use cases are "allow to burn on CD", "allow to use one time" or "allow to use three times within the next 5 days but not to burn on CD".

Deutsche Telekom already offers an audio-on-demand service (see: http://www.audio-on-demand.de/mod/) the use of which is restricted due to copyrights only to users within Germany. About 70.000 audio files are available for downloading, most of them individually some of them only in a bundle (i.e., a complete CD). After installing the MoD client software a user may download the music on his PC and do what he is allowed to by the implemented Rights Management system.

A very important issue is the question of payment – independent from the question whether customers are willing to pay for such a service. Deutsche Telekom as a quoted company wants and has to earn money when offering such a kind of service. Therefore, a payment system had to be implemented. Currently the customer has to register for the service, receives his login and his password and may then use the service. For the payment itself the telephone account is used. Additional clearing functionalities have to be implemented for all relevant parties.

Especially in Germany privacy concerns have to be considered very carefully in order to avoid problems with the authorities and – more important – with the customers. One severe or at least massively published mistake could destroy the whole business.

Concluding it can be said that Digital Rights Management is an important facet of e-commerce when dealing with electronic data. It is a basic necessity for a service provider to get premium content and for the content provider to ensure that his copyright is not violated. This is valid not only for the WWW, it becomes more and more important for physical data transmission using CDs or DVDs, too.

E-services: The Next Wave of Internet-Based Applications

Alejandro Buchmann

Darmstadt University of Technology
Wilhelminenstr. 7
64283 Darmstadt, Germany
buchmann@informatik.tu-darmstadt.de

E-services (or their close relatives, Web-services) are defined as self-contained, modular applications that can be described, published, located, and invoked over a network. E-services enable an application developer who has a certain need, to fulfill it by using an appropriate e-service that has been published, for example, on the Web, rather than developing the code from scratch.

Simple e-services, such as delivery of business information (airline schedules, stock quotes, status of an ongoing auction) and basic transactional services (hotel reservations, single site purchases, bidding in an auction) have been available for some time via web browser interfaces. Most of these simple e-services represent the first generation of B2C e-commerce applications.

B2B process integration requires complex e-services that provide support for work ows and process integration among different businesses. Complex e-services are state-preserving and must be composable in the sense that services provided by independent organizations can be combined to provide an added value. It is particularly important for these services to be properly described and that the parties involved in providing and consuming the service can negotiate the terms and conditions of use.

This panel will address the challenges faced by e-service providers. It will present the results of a companion panel on the technical platforms for e-services held as part of the Middleware 2001 Conference and will then concentrate on the challenges for value-added services: standardization, composition, integration, context specification, brokering, reliability, security and privacy, transactions, pricing, accounting, and contracting. These are the challenges that must be addressed for the vision of value-added e-services to become a reality.

L. Fiege, G. Mühl, and U. Wilhelm (Eds.): WELCOM 2001, LNCS 2232, p. 13, 2001.
© Springer-Verlag Berlin Heidelberg 2001

A New M-commerce Concept: m-Mall

Jaime García-Reinoso, Javier Vales-Alonso, Francisco J. González-Castaño,
Luis Anido-Rifón, and Pedro S. Rodríguez-Hernández

Departamento de Ingeniería Telemática, Universidad de Vigo, ETSI
Telecomunicación, Campus, 36200 Vigo, Spain
{reinoso, jvales, javier, lanido, pedro}@ait.uvigo.es

Abstract. In this paper, we propose a new m-commerce concept, m-Mall. Its users are walking individuals that shop in stores nearby, or interact with the stands in an exhibition. m-Mall servers know user location in real-time, by means of an auxiliary Bluetooth network, and push information into user handhelds, regardless of their technology. Network-side location allows the implementation of new services that cannot be supported by previous m-commerce solutions, where users were responsible of providing their position.

1 Introduction

m-Commerce [1] from cell phones or personal digital assistants (PDA) [2,3] has a promising future. For example, Datamonitor [4] predicts that the US m-commerce market will grow 1,000 percent up to 1.2 billion US$ by 2005.

In this paper, we propose a new m-commerce concept, m-Mall, which satisfies the following constraints:

1. The terminals are carried by walking individuals, which move around a space (the *mall*) covered by any wireless data network and a secondary wireless location network.
2. The customer connection is permanent.
3. The service knows the location of all mobile terminals in real-time *without client participation*, with enough precision to discriminate different commercial entities (for example, the stores in a mall).
4. The service may push information into the mobile terminals at any time.
5. The customers may use any wireless handheld device with an IP connection: WLAN PDAs, GPRS phones, UMTS phones, etc.

In order to satisfy constraint 3, the mall provides the users with a small, cheap location *badge* (like a wireless buzzer for restaurant queues). The customer must access the mall Web site from his handheld, and enter his badge number. The server side associates the client's IP address to its badge number, for all subsequent transactions.

A secondary mall-scale wireless location network monitors badges. It receives location information in real-time, and transmits it to the mall server. Its wireless

L. Fiege, G. Mühl, and U. Wilhelm (Eds.): WELCOM 2001, LNCS 2232, pp. 14–25, 2001.

technology must support "store-scale" location precision. No matter the number of badges, their location is known in real-time, without user participation.

By satisfying constraints 1-5, m-Mall admits m-commerce services supported by previous systems. However, server-side (user-independent) location determination allows the implementation of new services. We will propose a sample in section 5.

The paper is organized as follows: the next section describes the background. Section 3 discusses wireless location alternatives. Sections 4 and 5 propose a practical wireless location network and diverse m-Mall services, respectively. Section 6 describes a m-Mall prototype. Finally, section 7 summarizes our contributions and presents some open research lines.

2   Background

2.1   Location-Oriented M-commerce Companies

Among the most recent initiatives, we can cite:

- Sonata Inc. [5] has a platform that offers targeted mobile advertising and coupons, on any mobile or wireless device. Sonata is based on user-provided location information (i.e. does not satisfy constraint 3 above), although it is claimed that an auxiliary GPS can also be used. Unfortunately, GPS demands a highly specialized terminal (violating constraint 5) and is not valid indoors.
- GeePS.com portal [6] uses WAP [7] and GPS technologies to notify wireless users about stores and sales nearby. It has been assumed that WAP was going to be the key technology for m-commerce. However, WAP is a poor alternative in the long run, due to the small low-resolution displays, the text-only constraint and the low transfer speed. In general, it is limited to short, pull-like interactions. As an alternative to GPS, WAP statistical location procedure is rather inexact indoors.

2.2   Indoor Systems: CoolTown

CoolTown [8] is a Hewlett-Packard distributed architecture, for mobile PDAs with a wireless LAN interface and an infrarred/scanner port. The latter receives signals transmitted by location beacons. The network pushes URLs into a terminal daemon, which displays the corresponding Web pages. Although CoolTown is quite close to our concept, it does not guarantee permanent knowledge of user position. Therefore, it does not satisfy constraint 3 in section 1. Also, CoolTown terminals must have two communication interfaces, which makes them too specific, violating constraint 5.

3 Wireless Location Technologies

From the description in section 1, the wireless technology to implement m-Mall badges must be cheap, have low energy consumption, and, more important, implicit user location determination.

The obvious choice -GPS- is technologically infeasible for indoor locations.

In section 1 we stated that the system should coexist with any client terminal. If we relax this assumption for a moment, either GSM-GPRS or UMTS seem good alternatives, due to the high-precision statistical location service [9]. However, these solutions are not desirable, for two reasons:

- GSM-GPRS/UMTS location service has been considered for sporadic user-initiated queries, and not for permanent network-side location determination.
- The m-Mall location service would require the collaboration of all possible operators. The complexity, cost and overhead imposed by such architecture would be unaffordable.

Next, we focus on two wireless technologies for LANs, and evaluate them as auxiliary location networks.

3.1 Bluetooth

Bluetooth (BT) [10] is a short-range wireless technology. The maximum separation between devices is 10 m [11]. It has been designed for applications such as wireless headphones and computer-to-peripheral communications.

A BT network is composed of *piconets*. A piconet is a spontaneous network whose configuration changes when a BT device enters or leaves its range. A piconet has one master and up to seven *active* connected slaves [10].

It is also possible to create *scatternets*. A scatternet is a net of piconets. In a scatternet, the master of a piconet could be a slave in another piconet. In this scheme, inter-piconet communication is allowed. Note that the position of a given slave can be determined with 10-m precision in a scatternet, in the worst case.

From our point of view, the main advantages of this technology are its low power consumption ($\sim$ 1 mA standby and $\sim$ 60 mA peak) [15], small modem size (1 cm^2) and low cost previsions ($5-$10) [16,17,18,19,20]. Note that this cost would allow the installation of a large number of piconets in a mall.

3.2 WLAN (IEEE 802.11)

IEEE 802.11 is a cellular architecture, where a base station (*access point*) manages connections between the mobile devices and the backbone (usually, an Ethernet LAN). The base station range is 100 m. The main advantage of this technology is that in many cases it will be present anyway, to carry client IP communications. We could assume that a terminal is located near its base station. Unfortunately, in order to achieve enough precision, we need to increase the number of base stations, which are much more expensive than a BT modem [12, 13]. Also, the cost and power consumption of a WLAN badge would be higher: 35 \$ [14], $\sim$ 10 mA standby and $\sim$ 400 mA peak [15]. From the previous experience, note that Hewlett-Packard CoolTown uses WLAN for communications but needs auxiliary location systems [8].

Consequently, BT seems a good alternative to deploy an auxiliary wireless network for the m-Mall system. In the next section we propose a specialized BT location architecture. Nevertheless, it should be understood that m-Mall services could be implemented over any wireless networks satisfying constraints 1-5.

4   BT Wireless Location Network

The auxiliary wireless location network is composed of mobile and static BT units (badges and static nodes). Static nodes (SN) are arranged in a network that covers the whole mall area.

Hexagonal tiling is a typical solution in cellular network planning, which we have adapted to our case (figure 1). As a case study, we suppose the system is installed in a large mall with an area of 40,000 m^2.

Network infrastructure: every two neighbor SN are 10 m apart. Each cell has an area of 86.55 m^2. Thus, the location network has $\frac{40,000}{86.55} < 463$ SN (if we ignore edge errors). Assuming a cost of 20 \$ per SN (BT modem plus control logic), the cost of the wireless location network is less than 9,260 \$.

Badge detection: SN units scan their surroundings periodically, by means of BT inquiry calls [10]. Figure 1 shows a radial scatternet arrangement, around a "big" master node, SN0, connected to the central mall server (not shown). The remaining SN are ordered in "circular" layers around SN0. Our example shows the six cells in the first layer, SN1-1 to SN1-6, and two cells in the second layer, SN2-1 and SN2-2. In general, the SN are interconnected in a wireless binary tree topology (except for the root, which has six children). Each inquiry takes up to 10.24 s ([10], pag. 110). The inquiry process scans all frequencies to collect all badges nearby. Badge units respond with a FHS packet ([10] pag. 56), which includes their BT address.

The SN control logic has a circular buffer to store BT addresses. If the BT address in the incoming FHS packet is already in the memory, the packet is simply discarded. Otherwise, the BT address is stored and a location packet is sent to the "big" master SN0, as described below.

Routing: all badge responses are routed to SN0. The location protocol is extremely simple. If a badge with BT address x is detected by SN2-1, whose BT address is y (figure 1), the control logic creates a [x,y] location packet and transfers it to its master. All subsequent SN simply forward location packets to their master. The packet will reach SN0 after 2 hops. In general, a location message transfer needs n hops, if originated in layer n. If the mall is approximately square, it is enclosed in a circle with radius 142 m. Thus, the maximum

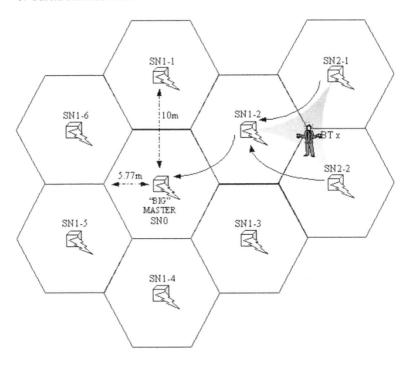

Fig. 1. BT wireless location network

number of hops is $142/10 < 15$. Once the packet reaches SN0, the m-Mall server resolves x as the IP address of the user terminal (remember that the first action of a m-Mall user is entering his badge number in the m-Mall site, via his mobile terminal).

Packet delay calculation: to implement the routing protocol above, we need to transmit two 8-byte BT addresses. We propose to use a DM1 packet ([10], pag. 60), because it can carry our 16-byte payload and has a FEC field ([10], pag. 67). The whole packet has 366 bits, with a 160-bit payload: 16 bytes for $[x,y]$, 1 byte for control, 1 byte for payload header and 2 bytes for CRC. The transfer rate is 1 Mbps ([10], pag. 27). Thus,

$$T_{hop} = 366\mu s$$

BT uses 625 μs-slot time division ([10], pag. 41). A slave needs a transmission token to access the channel. Figure 2 shows a scenario where only two slaves are connected to the master. Slave 2 must wait for token 2 and, once it receives it, wait again for the adjacent time slot $(\frac{3T}{2}\text{-}2T)$.

Next, we will calculate the average waiting time for slave i when N slaves are connected to the master, $\overline{T}_{wait}$. Let T be a slave slot ($T = 2 \times 625\mu s$), and z the time when slave i decides to transmit.

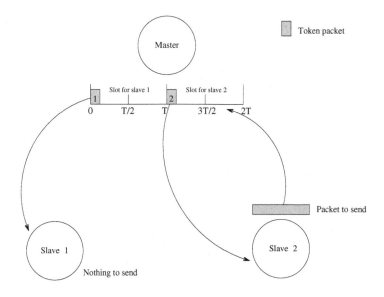

Fig. 2. Transmission slots

$$T_{wait} = \begin{cases} (i+0.5)T - z & \text{if } z \le iT, \\ (NT - z) + (i+0.5)T & \text{if } z > iT. \end{cases} \tag{1}$$

$$\overline{T}_{wait} = E\{T_{wait}/z \le iT\}P(z \le iT) + E\{T_{wait}/z > iT\}P(z > iT) \tag{2}$$

If we assume that z is uniformly distributed in $[0, NT]$,

$$\overline{T}_{wait}(N) = \frac{T(1+N)}{2} \tag{3}$$

For SN units in the second layer and beyond, in the worst case, there are 2 slaves per master, $N = 2$. If the transmitting SN is one of the six slaves of SN0, $N = 6$. In the worst scenario of our case study, for the outermost SN (15 hops away), and discarding local processing time, there is a packet delay of:

$$\overline{T}_{total} = 10.24 \text{ s} + 14 \times \overline{T}_{wait}(2) + \overline{T}_{wait}(6) + 15 \times T_{hop} < 11 \text{ s}$$

Although most people are relatively static when shopping, if we assume a walking speed of 0.8 m/s, a person placed at a SN needs 12.5 s $> \overline{T}_{total}$ to escape from its range. In larger or irregular malls, it is possible to reduce $\overline{T}_{total}$ by linking diverse big masters in a LAN.

Location: user badges are located in the intersection of as many circular sectors as SN units nearby. For example, figure 1 shows the worst case to determine the position of badge BT x. The badge is somewhere inside the intersection of three circular sectors, associated to three neighbor SN units, which will eventually send location packets containing x. The position can be further refined by noticing that other surrounding SN units do not send location packets. The m-Mall server uses SN BT addresses as "outer" points of a boundary defining badge placement. In figure 1, for BT x, if we approximate the intersection of detection sectors as an equilateral triangle, its area is only 43.3 m^2. The best case takes place when a badge is in the same position of a SN unit. The badge is also detected by the six surrounding SN units, and the m-Mall server can calculate its location almost exactly.

Survivability: the system is robust against several SN failure arrangements. As mentioned in section 3.1, there can be up to seven active slaves per SN (seven-slave boundary). All SN but SN0 have up to two slaves. In case of SN failure, its slaves can be assigned to an alternative neighbor SN.

Scalability: BT badges are only expected to identify themselves when requested, but will never enter active (transmission) state. Only SN units will enter it, to route location messages towards SN0. Therefore, the seven-slave boundary does not limit the number of badges.

We must remark that the seven-slave boundary is not strict (the slaves do not have to transmit at the same time).

5   m-Mall Services

So far, we have presented the m-Mall concept and the wireless infrastructure for the location network. In this section, we will enumerate some possible m-Mall services, without being exhaustive. These services are based on three core features: (1) customers carry a handheld terminal, (2) the m-Mall system knows customer location in real-time and (3) customer profiles may be used to adjust the services offered. The examples below assume a particular customer profile (figure 3). A profile is composed of personal data, technical data, preferences information, tracking data and relationship with other profiles (e.g. relatives).

We classify m-Mall services into two main categories according to whom (customer or m-Mall system) initiates the communication. Typical system-initiated services are advertisements, notifications, etc. Users may request services such as guidance through the mall, product searches, etc.

5.1   System-Initiated Services

1. **Advertisements**. Besides of advertisements addressed to all customers, it is also possible to select addressees according to customer profiles and/or current location inside the mall. For instance, tracking data can be used to send offers similar to previous purchases (e.g. advertisements for new *spring01* fashion jackets would be delivered to Mr. Smith once he enters the

Personal data

Name	John Smith
Age	34
Sex	Male
Phone number	555-1234
E-mail	john.smith@nowhere.com
Billing Address	Nowhere St. 1, Springfield, CA
Delivery Address	Nowhere St. 1, Springfield, CA
PDA type	PocketPC 1.0
Pref. net	W-LAN
Browser	Pocket IE

Preferences data

Sports	Soccer, basketball, baseball.
Music	Hip-hop, opera.
Furniture	None
...	...
Books	Art, painting, sci-fi.
Restaurants	Fast food, Chinese, Thai.
Clothes	Jeans, sport wear, Italian design.

Relations

profileId	87655432	
	Name	Mary Smith
	Kind	wife
profileId	8765433	
	Name	Lisa Smith
	Kind	daughter

Tracking data

Type clothes.jacket[a]
Model	*spring01*
Color	*Green*
Size	*XL*
...	...
Brand	*Lacostly*
Store	*Petit Camps*
Price	*140 USD*
Date	*2001.04.21*

.
.
.

Type restaurant.fast.hamburger
People	*2*	
Meal	*cheese burguer,*	
	chicken burger,	
	French fries	
Drinks	*water, cola*	
...	...	
Store	*Krusty Burger*	
Price	*18 USD*	
Date	*2001.04.21*	

---

[a] Taken from m-Mall products taxonomy. A Taxonomy entry determines the following elements.

Fig. 3. Profile example: Mr. Smith

mall). Special restaurant offers could be sent to customers nearby. This criteria can be combined with customer preference data (e.g. this advertisement would only reach Mr. Smith's terminal if the restaurant offers Chinese, Thai or fast food).

2. **Notifications**. General notifications can reach customers via their PDAs (e.g. mall closing time). Profile and location information may be used to filter all notifications but those that must reach a particular addressee (e.g. "Mr. Smith's wallet found in the parking lot"). There are also location-dependent notifications (e.g. "10 minutes to close" will only reach persons that are less than 200 m away). Finally, combined profile/location notifications are possible: Mr. Smith will be notified that a soccer legends exhibition is 20 m away.

3. **General services**. This category comprises other services that cannot be included in the categories above. For example, credit account status, menu for the restaurant the customer has just entered (location dependent), vegetarian menu for the same restaurant (location and profile dependent), etc.

5.2   User-Requested Services

1. **Search services**, to locate a particular product in the mall stores. Searches can be general or profile and/or location-driven. A profile-driven search uses the customer's preference data (e.g. Mr. Smith's book search would present art, painting and sci-fi books first). Location-driven searches use the current customer location (e.g. a location-driven search for restaurants would present those that are close to the customer). Finally, a profile/location-driven search uses both types of information: Mr. Smith's restaurant search would present fast-food, Chinese and Thai restaurants that are close to Mr. Smith.
2. **Purchase/reservation services**. Mall products can be bought from the customer's PDA. Pre-payment systems can be embedded to guarantee the purchase. For those products that impose a waiting time (e.g. a restaurant table), the m-Mall system includes a reservation service. The system generates the corresponding notifications: the restaurant table is ready, the movie will start in five minutes, etc.
3. **Guidance services**. The m-Mall system offers a guidance service from the current customer location to the store selected. It can be triggered by a purchase/reservation request or by the restaurant management service.

5.3   Mr. Smith Wants to Have Dinner. Two Scenarios

Mr. Smith-Initiated. Mr. Smith is feeling hungry, and he decides to look for a convenient restaurant in the mall to have dinner. He requests a restaurant nearby according to his preferences. The m-Mall search service suggests a Chinese restaurant, Great Wall, which is 150 meters away from his current position. Then, Mr. Smith accesses the Great Wall page, examines its menu and decides to request a table. Unfortunately, the restaurant is full at the moment. It is expected to have a non-smoking table available in 25 minutes. Mr. Smith decides to make a reservation for four people and continues shopping in the meanwhile. 25 minutes later he receives a notification on his PDA: his table is ready. Then, he uses the m-Mall guidance service to obtain the shortest path to the Great Wall restaurant.

System-Initiated. Mr. Smith is walking around when he receives a Krusty Burger advertisement on his PDA (a restaurant nearby where he had dinner the last time he was in the mall). K. B. has a special offer: two cheeseburgers for the price of one. The restaurant is only 20 meters away from Mr. Smith's current position, and he decides to go there. The system detects his arrival, and sends a customized page to him including today's menu, that highlights new oriental specialties. The K. B. site admits electronic orders. Mr. Smith makes his selection on his PDA, which is charged in his mall account. When the order is ready, a notification is sent to the PDA. Mr. Smith's dinner is ready at the counter.

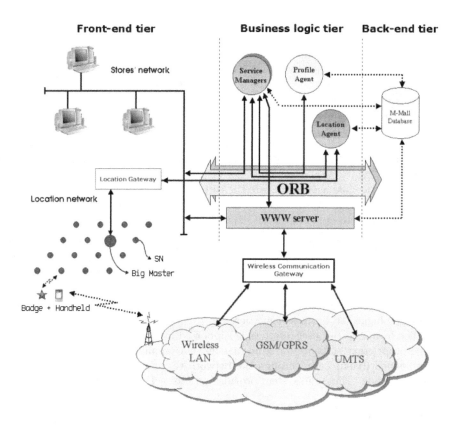

Fig. 4. m-Mall architecture

6   m-Mall Prototype

This section proposes a m-Mall architecture. We have followed a three-tiered architectural design. (1) The back-end tier stores all system data: dynamic location data, shopping info, offers, customer profiles, etc. (2) The business logic tier is responsible for feeding the back-end tier and using its data to offer actual services to customers. (3) The front-end tier receives data from (2) and presents them on the user interface.

Figure 4 shows the architecture. The supporting middleware is CORBA [21], because the authors have thoroughly tested its capabilities to implement interaction between heterogeneous applications [23,24]. Other middleware choices are perfectly possible.

The back-end tier is based on a distributed database management system that stores all persistent data. m-Mall management activities in the business logic tier are divided into three core applications:

- The profile agent manages user-specific data. Users feed preference information through a Web interface. Tracking data, which eventually may evolve into preference information, is dynamically created by the m-Mall service according to customer actions, purchases, etc. m-Mall services request profile information to this agent through a predefined service interface.
- Location agent. The BT network forwards location information to this agent through a dedicated gateway. The agent maps BT location data into m-Mall location-sensitive information. Whenever a customer enters a new m-Mall context cell (BT and m-Mall shopping cells may differ), the location agent submits an event to the service manager agents using the CORBA event service [22].
- The service manager agents are the core of the m-Mall system. There exists a different agent for each service. Each agent may use profile data or location information to enhance service capabilities.

Both customer accesses from a PDA and stores' accesses from desktop computers are possible thanks to the combination of HTTP-based services and the previous CORBA-based applications. The former require a HTTP server with some gateway applications to access CORBA elements. The underlying communication infrastructure for customer terminals is accessed through a dedicated gateway plugged to business logic tier.

The front-end tier user interface is supported by common Web browsers and some proprietary software for store management applications. Java applets are downloaded dynamically through the network to manage data presentation at the client side. Thus, the system provides an interactive full-featured customer interface [25].

7   Conclusions

In this paper, we have presented a new m-commerce concept, m-Mall, where user location is determined at server side, without user participation. To achieve this goal, we propose an auxiliary Bluetooth network. Future research is directed towards optimizing the topology of this network, enhancing the location algorithm, and developing new families of m-Mall services. Also, forthcoming work will evaluate (i) the use of Bluetooth handhelds both as badges and as user terminals, capable of interacting with m-Mall services (ii) alternative low-cost wireless technologies, such as SPIKE [26] (iii) survivability protocols for self-diagnosis and transparent reconfiguration in case of SN failures.

References

1. m-Commerce world. http://www.m-commerceworld.com/
2. Varshney, U., Vetter, R. J., Kalakota, R.: Mobile Commerce: A New Frontier. Computer. **10** (2000) 32–38
3. Darling, A.: Waiting for the m-commerce explosion. Telecommunications International. **3** (2001) 34–39

4. Datamonitor: mCommerce Infrastructure in the U.S.
   http://www.datamonitor.com
5. Sonata. http://www.sonata.com
6. GeePS.com. http://www.geeps.com
7. WAP Forum. http://www.wapforum.org
8. Kindberg, T., Barton, J.: A Web-based nomadic computing system. Computer
   Networks. **35(4)** (2001) 443–456
9. ETSI: ETSI document TS 122 071 V3.2.0
10. Bluetooth SIG: Specification of the Bluetooth System-Core v1.0B. December 1999
11. 10meters.com. http://www.10meters.com/blue_802.html
12. DoD Scientific and Technical Information Program: 1999 Congressional Report.
    http://www.dtic.mil/dust/cgr/army00cgr.htm
13. Enterasys Networks.
    http://www.enterasys.com/products/performance/pdf/interweek_2000320.pdf
14. Techweb. http://www.techweb.com/wire/story/TWB20000918S0005
15. Lansford, J., Bahl, P.: The Design and Implementation of HomeRF: A Radio Fre-
    quency Wireless Networking Standard for the Connected Home. Proc. IEEE. **88**
    (2000) 1662–1676
16. GSMBox. http://uk.gsmbox.com/news/mobile_news/all/19304.gsmbox
17. Journaldunet. http://solutions.journaldunet.com/0103/010307inventel.shtml
18. Transfert.
    http://www.transfert.net/fr/revue_web/article.cfm?idx_rub=94&idx_art=285
19. Security-informer.
    http://www.security-informer.com/english/crd_bluecore01_209282.html
20. Casira. http://www.csr.com/options.htm
21. Common Object Request Broker Architecture, OMG Web Site.
    http://www.omg.org
22. OMG: Event Service Specification version 1.1.
    http://www.omg.org/technology/documents/formal/event_service.htm
23. González-Castaño, F. J., Anido-Rifón, L., Vales-Alonso, J., Fernández-Iglesias,
    M. J., Llamas-Nistal, M., Rodríguez-Hernández, P. S., Pousada-Carballo, J. M.:
    Internet-Based Access to Real Equipment at Computer Architecture Laboratories
    using the Java/CORBA Paradigm. Computers & Education. **36** (2001) 151–170
24. González-Castaño, F. J., Anido-Rifón, L., Pousada-Carballo, J. M., Rodríguez-
    Hernández, P. S., López-Gómez, R.: A Java/CORBA Virtual Machine Architec-
    ture for Remote Execution of Optimization Solvers in Heterogeneous Networks.
    Software, Practice and Experience. **31** (2001) 1–16
25. Anido-Rifón, L., Llamas-Nistal, M., Fernández-Iglesias, M. J.: Developing WWW-
    based Highly Interactive and Collaborative Applications. Software, Practice and
    Experience. **31** (2001) 845–867
26. SPIKE. http://www.spike-wireless.com/main.html

Building Comparison-Shopping Brokers on the Web

Simone C. dos Santos[1,2], Sérgio Angelim[2], and Silvio R.L. Meira[1,2]

{scs, srlm}@cin.ufpe.br, saos@cesar.org.br

[1] Centro de Informática
UFPE – Universidade Federal de Pernambuco
Caixa Postal 7851, Várzea, 50732-540 Recife-PE Brazil
http://www.cin.ufpe.br – Phone: +55-81 3271.8430
[2] CESAR – Centro de Estudos e Sistemas Avançados do Recife
Caixa Postal 7115 – Areias, 50780-350 Recife-PE Brazil
Phone: +55-81 3272.4700 – Fax: +55-81 3272.4701
http://www.cesar.org.br

Abstract. Comparison-shopping brokers can create value to transactions between consumers and vendors by aggregating services and product information that were traditionally offered by separate vendors, thus reducing search costs and contributing for efficiency on Web electronic markets. Specifically in retail markets where the diversity of product data is greater, it is not always easy to find what a consumer is looking for on the Web. This paper presents an architecture for comparison-shopping brokers that provides precise information about products and vendors to consumers, retrieving this information in unstructured sources like the Web and heterogeneous business data on online stores. We also present and discuss a case study of this architecture in use, the WhereBuy broker, detailing its product comparison process.

1 Introduction

Web-based information systems can serve as intermediaries between consumers and vendors, thus creating *electronic marketplaces*. They play a central role in the economy: matching consumers and vendors with increased effectiveness and lower transaction costs, and facilitating the exchange of information, goods, services associated with market transactions. One of the unique features of such systems is that they reduce the search cost on the consumer side, thus decreasing the time the consumer spends to find what he or she wants. This reduction results from the easier access to information about products and services and from price comparison among several vendors [1, 2].

Specifically in retail markets, it is not always easy to find what a consumer is looking for on the Web. Since the Web is large and the consumer-to-business applications are growing, it is difficult to browse the Web looking for diverse products and services. Besides, buying and selling is a particularly time-consuming activity and often includes additional steps such as price comparison or other features.

L. Fiege, G. Mühl, and U. Wilhelm (Eds.): WELCOM 2001, LNCS 2232, pp. 26-38, 2001.

The buying/selling process is composed of three main steps: pre-sale – need identification, product/vendors searching and negotiation, sale – purchase and delivery, and post-sale – support services and evaluation. In order to boost e-commerce activities, electronic intermediaries such as *information brokers* are needed to help consumers in each of these steps where they can absorb transaction and time costs.

Information brokers can be implemented by several Internet-based technologies: hierarchical directories (like Yahoo!), generic tools (like Google), or specialized agent-based tools (such as Bargainfinder or Jango) [3, 4]. In particular, the personalized, continuously running, semi-autonomous nature of agents makes them well suited for mediating those consumer behaviors involving information filtering and retrieval and real-time interactions. Nearly always, these roles correspond to the activities of the pre-sale step, which involve greater information interchange:

- *Product searching* (help users decide which product to buy);
- *Comparison shop* (identify vendor information to help determine whom to buy from by creating a rank of vendors based on appropriate criteria such as price, availability, delivery time, etc.);
- *Product evaluation* (find product specification and reviews);
- *Product recommendation* (make products recommendation that are likely to fit consumer needs);
- *Negotiation* (how to settle on the terms of the transaction);
- *Promotion notice* (inform relevant special offers and discounts).

Agent-based information brokers can play an important role on all the activities listed above by organizing electronic marketplaces that promote efficient production and consumption of information. To be of any information value, the products and services data must first be retrieved, organized and processed, providing some structure and consistence. Information brokers have begun to put some organization to the Web commerce content. They can accomplish the process of retrieving and filtering information, showing only what is relevant to the parts involved [5].

Unfortunately, the Web is less agent-friendly than we might hope. Although Web pages are written in HTML, this language only defines how information is to be displayed, not what it means. Moreover, the Web is decentralized, dynamic and diverse, and despite initiatives such as the XML[1] and UDDI[2] standards, most Web-commerce applications have their own specific implementation, Web page styles and business data organization. In consequence, gathering information about them can be a challenge.

The objective of this paper is to propose an architecture for information brokers based on agent technology that retrieves business data from e-commerce Web sites, providing information about products and vendors to consumers with focus on com-

---

[1] The Extensible Markup Language (XML) is the universal format for structured documents and data on the Web (W3C definition).

[2] UDDI (Universal Description, Discovery and Integration) is a framework for Web services integration, containing standards-based specifications for service description and discovery.

parison shopping (item 2 previously mentioned). This architecture preserves the following features:

- *Modularity* in terms of representing an information search process and information sources;
- *Extensibility* in terms of adding new information agents and information source;
- *Flexibility* in terms of selecting the most appropriate information sources to answer a query;
- *Efficiency* in terms of minimizing the overall execution time for a given query;
- *Adaptability* in terms of being able to track semantic differences among the information source and search models.

This paper is organized in six sections. Section 2 discusses the characteristics of real-time comparison-shopping on the consumer and vendor's perspectives, as well as the environmental aspects of information retrieval on the online stores. The following sections present in detail the proposed comparison-shopping architecture for agent-based brokers. We also present and discuss a case study of this architecture in use, the WhereBuy[3] system, and add concluding remarks and comments on related and future works.

2   Analyzing the Web-Commerce Scenario

The intensive price competition promoted by electronic marketplaces on the Internet results in higher vendors' efforts to enhance business advantage in either cost or differentiation of products. The improvement of each value chain activity to design, produce, market, deliver, and support products, reducing costs or adding efficiency, results in higher profits. Seeking to obtain this advantage, vendors can use information brokers as business channels. In fact, vendors may face search costs in locating qualified buyers for their products, such as market research, advertising and sales calls. So this type of intermediaries can be used to attract potential demand and determine what group of consumers a vendor should focus on, in order to maximize his or her sales potential [6].

Despite the existence of different buying profiles and behaviors, consumers select their purchases from the available product offerings after considering factors such as price and product characteristics [4]. In obtaining and processing this information on the Web, consumers face costs related to the time spent searching on the online stores. Agent-based information brokers on the Web can assist the consumers in finding a product more adapted to their preferences. Such intermediaries can offer more precise information, especially when they aggregate products of several vendors. Since they are repositories of information, the intermediaries can make the information easily accessible to consumers. They can also filter information, showing only what is relevant to the parts involved.

---

[3] http://www.wherebuy.com.br.

Defining the main context of this paper as the role of these brokers in matching consumers and vendors, some considerations about the Web-commerce environment and the characteristics of comparison shopping need to be exposed.

2.1 The Web-Commerce Environment

The Web-commerce environment has to grow over both regularities and irregularities. The lack of information standards among vendors has a direct influence on the information retrieval and extraction process carried out by the information agents. Specifically in the comparison-shopping context, the lack of uniformity at vendors' business data represents a critical problem. By business data we mean the information about business entities (e.g., product catalogs) or activities (e.g., payment systems) that is stored in some media and represented by text, database formats, and specialized file formats [7].

In particular, product data are stored in structured sources such as databases and become available on online catalogs through dynamic HTML pages. Therefore, data structures for company and product profiles should not be fixed. Very often, these catalogs are built with human intervention without a nomenclature standard and are susceptible to typing errors. These characteristics become more evident on the retail commerce, which in most cases doesn't have standard product identifications (except the book segment, through the widely used ISBN code). Due to the product diversity it is difficult to adopt a well-formed catalog based on product models, using for example, product ontology as cited in [7] and [8]. This paper presents an architecture to deal with these issues (Section 3), including an intelligent matching algorithm (Section 4).

On the other hand, there are several regularities that are usually obeyed by online vendors, allowing the construction of real-time and mobile agents [9]:

- *Online stores are designed so consumers can find things easily.* Most stores include mechanisms to ensure easy navigation from the store's home page to a specific product description. In general, these mechanisms are available through search tools based on keywords. In other cases, the business data are organized in sections links that can be browsed forward for more detailed information.
- *Vendors attempt to uniform their business data presentation.* Although stores differ widely from each other in their product description formats, vendors describes all their stocked items in a simple and consistent formats, with little or no variations.
- *Catalogs use some delimiter to facilitate consumer comprehension of product information.* In general, the information about several products are presented in tables, with the columns containing the products attributes such as name, price, availability, and the rows representing a single product. Usually the information uses the "white space" character as a vertical separation.
- *Detailed information about a product is presented in a single and dedicated HTML page.* In general, product specification is presented in the second level page, frequently accessed by a link from the product name presented in the first level. This page contains all information about a specific product necessary to buying decision.
- *One big search results list is partitioned in many numbered pages.* When the search results contains a big list of product names, the results are partitioned in pages, di-

viding the information in several levels. Access to these levels is realized from numbered links, corresponding to the respective pages.

These regularities allow agent-based brokers creation on the online stores, allowing knowledge base construction through the domain and information source models of the online vendors. These models form the starting point for the development of information retrieval mechanisms.

2.2 Understanding Comparison-Shopping

The comparison-shopping task can be requested in two different buying situations. In the first case, the consumer doesn't know what specific product to buy, i.e., his or her needs are based on some criteria that matches several alternatives for both products and vendors. In this paper, this type of comparison is referred to as *product/vendors brokering*.

In the second situation, the consumer knows exactly what product to buy, so he or she only needs to decide whom to buy from. The buying decision is carried out by a rank of vendors based on appropriate criteria such as price, availability, delivery time, etc. This type of comparison is more precise and is referred to as *comparative buying*. It is important to note that, in this type of comparison-shopping, product/vendors brokering is a preliminary step, and the results from this step are processed to generate the final results.

Comparative buying involves more complexity than product/vendors brokering. In the products and vendors brokering, the information retrieval mechanism only needs to collect all products that match the search parameters informed by the user (e.g., keywords, price range, etc.) and present them without a previous selection process or product mapping. In the comparative buying process, the information retrieval mechanism collects the prices and other relevant data about a single product. For this, the mechanism needs to be intelligent enough to identify this specific product in several online catalogs, which have their proper business data description. In this paper, we focus on the comparative buying process.

3   An Architecture for Real-Time Comparison Shopping Brokers

The comparative buying process can be divided into two main search processes: identifying a specific product, through an attribute set, and finding the web vendors' offers for this product. Figure 1 illustrates these processes.

In the first search, the consumer performs a query based on keywords and accesses the respective product catalog organized by business segment (music, books, computers, etc.). After choosing a specific product, the second search based on agent technology is activated. The agents carry out the information retrieval process, through the creation of several agent threads one for each specific vendor, which are registered with the broker. These agents work in parallel and collect product data by metasearch (using several search engines simultaneously), using a knowledge base composed of product keywords, resulting from the first search as well as vendors' description.

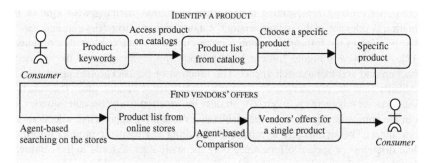

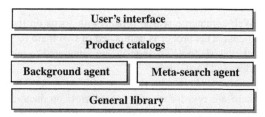

Fig. 1. The comparative buying process

In the sequence, the information of metasearch results retrieved by each agent pass through a comparison process, filtering the previous selected product. Finally, all information gathered by the agents are integrated, filtering the relevant parameters (like title, price, producer, etc.), ordering the offers based on the selected criteria, and summarizing the vendors' offers presented to the consumer.

The architecture presented in Figure 2 shows the structure of the comparative buying broker into five levels: 1) user's interface, 2) product catalogs, 3) Agent-based search engines, and 4) general library.

User's interface
Product catalogs

Background agent	Meta-search agent

General library

Fig. 2. An architecture for comparative buying brokers

The user's interface contains all forms for the queries and the formatting of their results. This level should be generic enough to implements different web interfaces, besides HTML, including, for example, mobile devices interface for WAP applications.

Considering that a user needs to choose a specific product before searching it into several online vendors, the architecture must include enough information about products so that a query can be built, making the agent system able to identify a specific product coming from different information sources. This information is static data, i.e., product attributes that do not change over time, such as name, brand, producer, etc. It's worth to emphasize that each business segment in the agent search domain needs only a single product catalog to represent it. This product information is stored in a local database, which is loaded by a background agent, which is part of the agent-based engine level.

The agent-based search engines represent the information retrieval process [10]. This process involves the following steps: representing the information need (e.g., the consumer profile); representing the information source, defining what kind of information is relevant in the online vendors' catalog and how to retrieve it; and searching the profiles in the information source representations from vendors descriptions [11, 12]. As showed in Figure 2, there are two kinds of search engines in the architecture: background and meta-search agents. The function of the background agent is to periodically feed the product catalogs from a restrict set of vendor sites. The function of the meta-search agents is to retrieve product information from consumer queries, carry out the comparison process on the results and present the appropriate selections to the consumer. The architecture is capable of handling any dynamic product information, like discounts or special offers, since only the static data is stored in the catalog. It is worth to emphasize that a vendor site of a search domain should provide a searchable index or a search tool. Some online stores, especially ones with smaller inventories, that provide no index, won't be in the search domain. In [13], the architecture of these agents is presented in detail. The comparison process is discussed in Section 4.

The general library level contains functionality that is used by upper levels, such as handlers (HTTP, cookies), query caching (for breaking results among pages and store frequently searched results), data fusion (for appropriate presentation) and interface widgets.

4   Case Study: The WhereBuy Broker

WhereBuy is a Web-commerce search broker with focus on the pre-sale step of the buying/selling process. This broker is composed of two main tools: a shopping search tool, and a market analysis tool. These tools are integrated to provide useful information for both vendors and consumers.

The shopping search tool provides the user with shopping information from several virtual stores. There are two information categories: product/vendors brokering and comparative buying. In the first case, the tool collects all products that match the search criteria informed by the user, e.g., keywords, price range, etc. During comparative buying, the tool collects the prices and other relevant data about a single product, which was previously selected by the user and includes precise information, like full price, shipping data, etc.

The market analysis tool provides vendors with information about consumers' behavior, and includes information such as visiting statistics, most searched products, most visited stores, etc. Vendors may use this information to design marketing strategies [14]. In this section, we are going to focus on the architecture of the shopping search tool, more specifically, on comparative buying.

WhereBuy is an implementation of the architecture described in Section 3. The comparison-buying tool is available to Web browsers and WAP-based mobile devices (wap.wherebuy.com.br). The independence of the user interface level and the information precision of this tool made it possible to extend the application for WAP interfaces, which usually have very limited display space. This system was developed using Java™ agents technology, Oracle™ database, HTML (for the Web browsers interface), WML (for the WAP interface) and Servlets™.

4.1 The WhereBuy Information Retrieval Process

In WhereBuy, keywords are used to define the consumer profile. Business sections were created to organize the searching process, so the user selects the business segment where he wants to look for product offers. WhereBuy offers comparative buying for three sections: CDs, books and DVDs, with approximately 30 virtual stores. For these sections, the user can perform queries on specific parameters, for example, title, artist and track title for CD section.

Each business segment in WhereBuy has a product catalog. The background agent periodically fill the product catalogs from a restrict set of vendor Web sites into these segments. The choice of these vendors' Web sites is based on the conformity, quantity and diversity of their catalogs. The catalog updating is realized once a week, retrieving only recently released products.

Table 1. An example of extraction language use

Syntax	Semantic	
FWRD (*aNumber*)	Forward the cursor *aNumber* times.	
FIND (*aTerm*)	Find an expression equivalent to *aTerm*.	
EXTR (*endTerm, aVar*)	Extract the term from the current position until *endTerm*, and stores in the variable *aVar*.	
An application source	**A program extraction**	**An extraction result**
<table><tr >	FIND Price</b></td></tr>	
<td ><b>Product</b> </td>	FWRD 8	var.name = 'One'
<td ><b> Price</b></td></tr>	EXTR </td> var.name	var.price = '20.00'
<tr><td >One</td>	FIND <td>$	
<td>$20.00</td></tr>	EXTR </td> var.price	
</table>		

WhereBuy is limited to collecting and processing HTML documents. These documents are formatted using the HTML standard. As HTML documents are specialized documents formed by structured text, it also includes JavaScript structures.

This broker uses meta-search to collect information from the relevant stores. There is an agent for each department store, which handles the search URLs and the parameters needed to execute a search on the vendor's site search tool. A program written on a simple extraction language defines the agent knowledge base. Table 1 presents some commands and an example of its use.

Through a set of parse commands, this metalanguage provides flexibility enough to retrieve any information on HTML documents [13], making new vendors acquisition an easy and scalable task. The definition of the extraction program process is carried out with human intervention, i.e., a person needs to analyze the page source and write the respective extraction program. However, this process (that basically consists of analyzing candidate forms and identifying product information) is simple enough so that any person with HTML code familiarity can be able to do it. This human intervention does not cause a scalability problem, since it is related to the number of new stores on the market and not the number of users of the system. It is important to note that the inclusion of new stores to the search domain is not a mass process, and stores included can be used by different instances of the system.

Due the dynamic nature of Web sites, we developed a notification agent that informs to the system when the page changes. In contrast, there are cooperative vendors as well as vendors that adhere to standards, that significantly reduce the work of updating extraction rules.

In the selection phase, the page resulting from the meta-search executed by the agent is obtained. After this first result, each agent carry out the extraction of relevant data for the comparison process, detailed in Section 4.2. The final presentation shows a uniform result from each searched store. This result is cached for a configurable "time to live", so that new requests for the same query will not start the retrieval and comparison process again.

After the selection phase, the agent organizes the presentation so that consumers find clearly and easily the information to help an optimal purchase decision. In addition, WhereBuy allows some degree of customization according to the user needs. For example, it is possible for the user to select ordering criteria as well as to apply filters to previously collected information. These filters collect all products that match the search criteria informed by the user such as keywords (results that contains this word or don't) and price range.

4.2 The WhereBuy Comparison Process

The comparison process in WhereBuy involves the similarity verification between two product descriptions: one generated by the user query and one gathered on the vendor catalog from the meta-search agent. These two descriptions are formally represented by p_c and p_v, respectively, so that:

$$p_c, p_v = <term> [<term>]* \tag{1}$$

where a term represents a character sequence and the "*" symbol between brackets represents one or more terms.

Before starting the comparison process between these descriptions, it's necessary to filter each description, extracting the irrelevant terms, and to generate the appropriate structures that will support this process. Figure 3 illustrates the steps followed by WhereBuy to process product descriptions in order to allow comparison.

The first step is to eliminate punctuation from the product description text. After that the *irrelevant* terms contained in the description are also eliminated. By "irrelevant" we mean terms that do not carry meaning to the comparison, like articles, prepositions, etc. In this step WhereBuy also eliminate subtitles that add little or no information to the description. After these steps, two lists of terms are generated. In the following step terms are looked up on a synonym dictionary, which is defined to get around differences between the WhereBuy catalog and the vendor's catalog. This dictionary contains common abbreviations, synonyms widely used on the shopping domain, etc. The ordering step takes into account the semantic of the description. If the description being compared is the title of the book, for example, ordering is preserved, whereas in the case of the name of an author, it is usual to have the last name before the first name, so this case has to be correctly treated.

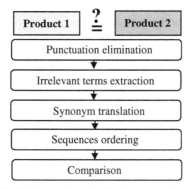

Fig. 3. The product description processing

The effective comparison is initiated through the two lists previously generated, l_1 and l_2, containing the terms of p_c *and* p_v and respecting the following pre-condition: the number of terms in the list l_1 must be smaller or equal to the list l_2. Two other lists are necessary, l_i and l_j, so that:

1. The terms that belong to both lists are stored in the list l_i and
2. The terms that belong to the l_1 and do not belong to l_2 are stored in the list l_j.

The comparison process is based on two metrics: precision and reliability rates. The precision rate represents how much one product description *is* similar to other. While the reliability rate represents how much the product description *needs to be* similar to other for the comparison system. The precision rate is defined by the lists previous described:

$$precision = 100 * size(l_i) / (size(l_j) + size(l_2)) \qquad (2)$$

From an analysis based on diverse real search and comparison data, the comparison system of WhereBuy chooses to work with a reliability rate of 75%, which proved to be satisfactory considering the irregularities found on the product descriptions.. This ratio may be easily tuned to new catalogs. This rate showed to be adequate for the marketplace where WhereBuy is today. An example of such calculation is showed on Table 2.

Also from the experience of dealing with many different catalogs, we identified that it is very common to find stores that include the name of the author on the title of the book (or the artist on the title of a CD). For example, it is common to see a product title like "The Beatles – Revolver", which should be correctly equated to the tile "Revolver" from the artist "The Beatles". WhereBuy was optimized to deal with a few very common cases (although specific to certain domains), like the one just described.

5   Related Work

Today, most of the agent-based Web-commerce brokers focus on product/vendors brokering instead of on comparative buying, in which the information must be more precise to really contribute with the consumer's buying decision. In this section, we compare the WhereBuy broker with related agents that provide some kind of comparison and tolerate unstructured information sources.

Table 2. Reliability calculation example

Descriptions	Lists	% Precision
Segment: CDs Attribute: Title Pc = "Ao vivo – volume 1" Pv = "Ao vivo Vol. 2"	L1 = {"ao", "vivo", "vol","1"} L2 = {"ao", "vivo", "vol","2"} Li = {"ao", "vivo", "vol"} Lj = {"2"}	$(100 \times 3) / (1 + 4)$ $= 60\%$
Segment: Books Attribute: Title Pc = "Cadernos de Lanzarote" Pv = "Cadernos de Lanzarote 1"	L1 = {"cadernos", "lanzarote"} L2 = {"cadernos", "lanzarote", "1"} Li = {"cadernos", "lanzarote"} Lj = {}	$(100 \times 2) / (0 + 3)$ $= 66\%$

BargainFinder, the first shopping agent for on-line comparisons, offers valuable insights into the issues involved in price comparisons in the on-line world. Its domain application was limited to CD segments, and the comparison process was uniquely based on price, instead of on other shopping characteristics such as product availability, delivery time and costs, which are very important to the consumer's buying decision. Moreover, BargainFinder is not an AI application, while WhereBuy relies on AI techniques (pattern matching, information retrieval, and statistical methods), allowing it to scale to different product domains and to be robust to changes on the vendors' sites and their product descriptions.

There are other related works in this area, like Jango and Express, which perform the shopping search role on Excite and Infoseek, respectively [15]. Specifically, Jango results allow a consumer to compare vendor offerings uniquely on price, like Bargain-Finder.

ShopBot is other example of a comparison-shopping agent [9]. Its differential is that it automatically learns how to shop at online vendors and how to extract product descriptions from their Web pages. However, the algorithm that learns what the product description are requires previous, time consuming analyzes of vendor pages. This analysis is necessary for identifying the attributes of products in this domain, defining the regular expressions for recognizing attributes and obtaining a description set of several products, which are used as seed knowledge to support the learning process. Thus, these previous procedures represent equal or more effort than the simple shop description process in WhereBuy (discussed in Section 4). Besides, ShopBot performance is linear with the number of vendors it accesses, while the WhereBuy architecture, based on multi-agents system, allows it to perform simultaneous product searches in an acceptable time.

A detailed analysis about these and other related work will be presented on [16].

6 Conclusions

Comparison-shopping brokers can create value to transactions between consumers and vendors by aggregating services and product information that were traditionally offered by separate vendors, so reducing search costs and contributing for efficiency on Web electronic markets. In general, these brokers are implemented by agents due to their personalized, continuously running and semi-autonomous nature. These characteristics make agents suitable for information filtering and retrieval and real-time interactions.

Despite the irregularities of the Web content and the vendors' non-standardized business data, the structure of HTML pages and the electronic catalogs organization allow the agent-based mechanisms to collect, filter and display precise information about products and vendors, so that consumers can make shopping decisions based on comparative buying capabilities.

In this context, we proposed an architecture for comparison-shopping brokers construction based on agent technology. The architecture preserves modularity in terms of representing the information search process and information sources, so that to shop a new product domain, it simply needs a description of that domain and the correspondent attribute mapping. Extensibility in terms of adding new information agents and information sources is achieved because the architecture is based on scalable acquisition of new vendors and business segments. Flexibility in terms of selecting the most appropriate information sources to answer a query is possible due to the generic profile of a search agent and the interface level isolation, allowing the resulting information to be customized according to the application needs. In addition, the general library level implements cache functions so that frequently retrieved or difficult to retrieve product and vendors information can be cached toward better time results, including the efficiency aspects in terms of minimizing the overall execution time for a given query. Finally, this architecture is adaptable in terms of being able to track semantic differences among the information source and search models, achieving generality across product domains and allowing appropriate consumer search parameters update.

As a case study we presented WhereBuy, an agent-based comparison-shopping broker which implements the architecture proposed. WhereBuy is not limited to the comparison-shopping task. Today, this broker offers product searching and evaluation (finding product specifications). Moreover, WhereBuy is being extended to include product recommendation and reviews, based on consumer search behaviors. The conception of a framework that includes all these aspects is our next future work.

References

1. Bakos, Y., 1998. The Emerging Role of Electronic Marketplaces on the Internet. Communications of the ACM, 41(8).
2. Egev A., Gebauer J. and Farber F., 1999. Internet-based Electronic Markets. Haas School of Business, Berkeley.

3. Guttman R. H. and Maes P., 1999. Agent-mediated Electronic Commerce: a Survey. MIT, Media Laboratory.
4. Maes P., Guttman R. H. and Moukas G., 1999. Agents that Buy and Sell: Transforming Commerce as We Know It. MIT Media Laboratory. Cambridge, MA.
5. Arens Y. and Chee C. Y. et all, 1993. Retrieving and integrating data from multiple information sources. International Journal on Intelligent and Cooperative Information Systems, 2(2):127-158.
6. Porter M. E. and Millar V. E., 1985. How Information Gives You Competitive Advantage, Harvard Business Review.
7. Jeusfeld M. A., 2000. Business Data Structures for B2B Commerce. Tilburg Univesity, Infolab, The Nertherlands.
8. Albers M., Jonker C. M., Karani M., and Treur Jan, 1999. An Electronic Market Place: Generic Agent Models, Ontologies and Knowledge. University of Amsterdam, The Nertherlands.
9. Doorenbos R. B., Etzioni O., and Weld D.S, 1996. Scalable Comparison-Shopping Agent for the World Wide Web. Technical report UW-CSE-96-01-03, University of Washington, Seattle, WA.
10. Oard D. W. and Marchionini G., 1996. A Conceptual Framework for Text Filtering. University of Maryland.
11. Knoblock C. A. and Ambite J. L., 1996. Agents for Information Gathering. In J. Bradshaw, editor, Software Agents. AAAI/MIT Press, Menlo Park, CA, in press.
12. Knoblock C. A. and Ambite J. L., 1994. Reconciling agent models. In Proceedings of the Workshop on Intelligent Information Agents, Gaithersburg, MD.
13. Simone C. dos Santos, Sérgio Angelim and Silvio R. L. Meira , 2001. A Framework for Web-Commerce Search Brokers, International Conference on Internet Computing, Agents for e-Business on the Web section. Las Vegas, EUA.
14. Simone C. dos Santos and Silva F. Q. B., 2000. Electronic Intermediaries as Marketing Agents, International Conference on Enterprise Information Systems. Staffordshire University, Stafford UK.
15. Almeida V., Meira W., Ribeiro V., Ziviani N., 1999. A Quantitative Analysis of the Behavior of a Large Non-English E-Broker. Depto. of Computer Science, Universidade Federal de Minas Gerais, Brazil.
16. Simone C. dos Santos and Meira, Silvio R. L, 2001(in development). Um Framework para Intermediários Provedores de Informação em Mercados Eletrônicos (*A Framework for Information Intermediaries in Electronic Marketplaces*), PhD. Thesis, Centro de Informática, Universidade Federal de Pernambuco, Brazil.

Trusted Mediation for E-service Provision in Electronic Marketplaces

Giacomo Piccinelli[1], Cesare Stefanelli[2], and David Trastour[1]

[1] Hewlett-Packard Laboratories
Filton Park – Bristol (UK)
Ph.: +44-0117-3129610 – Fax: +44-0117-3129250
giacomo_piccinelli@hp.com

[2] Dipartimento di Ingegneria, Università di Ferrara
Via Saragat, 1 – Ferrara – Italy
Ph.: +39-0532-293831 – Fax: +39-0532-768602
cstefanelli@ing.unife.it

Abstract. From a commercial viewpoint, the Internet is evolving from a collection of web sites for advertising products to an open and distributed environment for service provision. Electronic marketplaces represent the mediation contexts where service providers and service consumers can interact to carry out their business transactions. In electronic business relationships the issue of trust becomes central, and its enforcement is a fundamental value that electronic marketplaces can offer to their members. The paper focuses on trusted contract enforcement in the context of an electronic marketplace infrastructure. In particular, it describes the model and the component for mediated service delivery developed at the HP labs in Bristol. The presented solution is based on the concept of externalisation for service consumer views of the business processes of service providers.

1 Introduction

The Internet offers a global and ubiquitous platform to support the deployment and provision of electronic services (e-services). Electronic marketplaces (e-marketplaces) and e-services are among the main drivers of the Internet evolution, from both a business and a technology perspective [15].

E-services are about business assets made available over the Internet to drive new revenue streams and to create new efficiencies. E-marketplaces are the virtual context where to find the match between the customers' demand for services with the set of service offers. The process of negotiation between service consumer and service provider produces a contract that captures and formalises the agreement between the parties. The contract embeds the rules for the interaction between service consumer and service provider. As it happens in normal business contexts, service delivery follows contract acceptance by both parties.

Negotiation and contract formation tend to follow standard patterns, largely independent of traded services. The automation of the negotiation process is therefore relatively easy, when compared to service delivery and contract enforcement. It is not uncommon for existing e-marketplaces to support negotiation and contract formation,

L. Fiege, G. Mühl, and U. Wilhelm (Eds.): WELCOM 2001, LNCS 2232, pp. 39–50, 2001.

while contract enforcement is usually beyond their scope and technical capabilities [1]. Second-generation e-marketplaces will progressively take on the role of trusted mediators, to validate the actions of the parties against the agreed contract [3], [6], [7]. In basic versions of the model, the parties drive the interaction and the mediator just monitors its consistency. Extensions of the model define a more proactive role for e-marketplaces in the orchestration of the parties.

In the context of the second-generation e-marketplace developed at HP Labs, we have designed a model for mediated e-service delivery based on the externalisation of the interaction processes between business parties. Service providers and service consumers make available this information to the e-marketplace infrastructure through the electronic contract. The model has driven the design and the implementation of the E-Service Shield (ESS) component, which is responsible of service mediation in the HP e-marketplace infrastructure.

2   Lifecycle of an E-marketplace Mediated Interaction

E-marketplaces can be involved in all stages of the lifecycle of an end-to-end transaction. An e-marketplace infrastructure should provide the support services and tools required for the provision of e-services, from their advertising, through their negotiation, to their actual delivery.

However, open e-marketplaces in the Internet push for the dynamic creation of business partnerships with previously unknown companies, with possibly a low level of trust. In fact the trust element deriving from long-term relationship is weakened, and the control measures that companies may have to consider can substantially erode the overall benefits of using e-marketplaces. The model and related infrastructure components presented in this paper permits to the e-marketplace to guarantee the behaviours of participants in a business transaction. Let us briefly outline the contribution that e-marketplaces give to a business transaction.

- **E-service advertising.** The e-marketplace is the virtual place where service offers and requests are stored and made available to the members. Advanced directory services or automatic pattern matching facilities are the main mechanisms provided by e-marketplace infrastructures.
- **Negotiation.** In addition to basic pattern matching between offer and demand, the e-marketplace can provide support for different types of negotiation processes. Beyond the initial contact, the objective is to provide support for all the interaction leading to the formation of a mutually satisfactory contract between the parties [5] [strobel]. Common market mechanisms involved at this stage are auctions, exchanges, catalogues, and request for quotes. In addition to basic price-related parameters, there are other important issues related to payment procedures, delivery processes, and service level agreement.
- **Contract management.** The negotiation process produces a contract that captures and formalises the agreement between service consumer and provider. The rules for parties interaction derive from this legally bounding agreement. The e-marketplace support to the definition and formalisation of the electronic contract is considered a critical issue [12]. The trustworthiness of the e-marketplace has a

strong impact on the level of involvement the parties are willing to accept in terms of mediation, and on the level of control the parties impose to each other.

- **Service delivery.** Usually neglected by first-generation e-marketplaces, a more direct involvement in the contract execution and service-delivery phase is the focus of second-generation e-marketplaces [13]. Acting as a trusted entity, the e-marketplace can guarantee that both parties involved in the e-service transaction respect the agreed contract. To this purpose, the e-marketplace can exploit a monitoring component to control the interaction, in order to assume a more active role in the business interaction processes [11].

- **Accounting.** In its role of trusted mediator, an e-marketplace is required to perform several operations also after the actual delivery of the e-service and the conclusion of the contractual relationship between the parties. The information collected about the behaviour of the companies, together with service-level related data, are the basis to prepare the profiles of market members.

Second-generation e-marketplaces, such as the one developed at HP Labs, provide infrastructure-level support for all the phases of the business transaction lifecycle. In this paper we focus on the e-marketplace mediation role in service delivery.

3 Mediated E-service Delivery

An e-service encapsulates the overall business activity behind the delivery of a product (good or service) to a customer. For example, in the case of the sale of freight space there are specific business processes dealing with the collection of the goods, the exchange of the appropriate paperwork, the flow of notifications between the sender and transport provider, payment procedures, etc. The e-service model requires to represent the whole interaction process between service provider and consumer in a format automatically tractable. The interaction process can be captured and formalised in the electronic contract, and the parties map it on their internal processes in order to satisfy their contractual commitments (see Figure 1). Information about financial history, customer/supplier rating, brand, and other forms of credentials represent an important added value for the negotiation process within e-marketplaces.

In terms of business interaction processes, two main aspects to consider are process flow and data flow. The process flow specifies aspects like the sequence and causal order for the interaction activities between the parties. For instance, in the freight example the process flow may indicate that only after receiving the notification from the customer that goods are ready for collection the transport provider has to collect them. The interaction can evolve along parallel threads and adapt to external requirements. While the goods are travelling the transport provider can be required to inform the customer of potential delays, as well as sending standard progress reports. Depending on the purchased service options the customer may or may not be entitled to ask for certain type of reports, or the reports can be requested only at specific stages of the service. For example, the request for payment is possible only if the invoice has been sent.

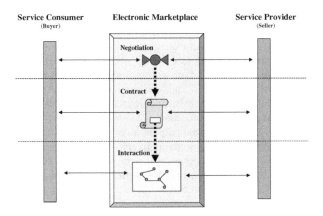

Fig. 1. Mediated cooperation model

Closely interdependent with the process flow, the data flow involved in a business interaction relates to the actual data exchanged in the various steps of the process. The focus is on document types and possibly on the actual content of the documents. The assumption is that the documents are in electronic format, or at least that an electronic description is available. Back to the example, notification messages might need a specific formatting [4], [14]. Raising the level of complexity, the amount filed in the invoice has to contain the same value as the pay filed in the bank order.

The e-service model promises to be very powerful in terms of automation of end-to-end transactions, but the implementation of the model requires some considerations. Despite the flourishing of technologic and standardisation activities around e-services and related paradigms, it is not reasonable to expect companies to reconvert their enterprise resource planning and administration systems in the short term. As it has happened for commercial web sites, e-service technology will have to be deployed on top of existing business information systems. An extra layer of protection and service management provided by a trusted e-marketplace can simplify operational models and technical infrastructure required internally by companies.

Companies can clearly benefit from the offloading to a trusted e-marketplace of the interaction processes management, once agreed at contractual level. The initial effort for the definition of the agreement and the reliance on a trusted e-marketplace to enforce it can streamline the internal structure of the company. To this purpose, we propose to extend the mediation role of e-marketplaces to the execution aspects of the e-service delivery contract.

4 The Mediation Component in the HP E-marketplace

The mediation model described in the previous section is embodied in the E-Service Shield (ESS) component. Integral part of a prototype of second-generation e-marketplace developed at HP Labs, ESS is the system component in charge of validating the interaction between service providers and service consumers. In the first part of this section, we give a brief overview of the overall e-marketplace infrastructure. We then concentrate on the internal architecture and implementation of the ESS component.

4.1 The HP E-marketplace Prototype

The main purpose of the e-marketplace developed at HP Labs is the investigation of the relations between negotiation, service composition, and electronic contracts. A lot of research has been done in each of these areas individually. The challenge is to integrate existing results into a comprehensive solution. The aim is to sustain entirely new business models. For example, we envision the possibility for a service provider to acquire dynamically the resources (services) needed for each service instance it sells. Service providers can interact depending on the evolution of the service delivery process, which is in itself an object of negotiation. The business agreement resulting from the negotiation is captured in a format that makes it automatically enforceable, as well as legally binding.

The architecture of the e-marketplace is depicted in Figure 2. The lower layers (communication and execution) provide the standard execution environment for an e-commerce system. The service management layer provides advanced access services and process management facilities. In particular, it provides a cluster of Web facing services together with functions for membership management (e.g. authentication and profiling) and service-session management. Process management provides the foundation for electronic management of contractual agreements. The solution management layer provides the core facilities for second-generation e-marketplaces, namely service composition, negotiation support, and contract management. The service composition engine defines the requirements for service providers needed to support a specific service request. Requirements are in terms of operational capabilities (e.g. move containers), as well as service delivery processes. The negotiation engine deals with classic auction-based price optimisation, as well as complex contractual issues (namely service delivery process). The contract manager provides monitoring and execution support for electronic contracts. The focus of the contract manager is on the business interaction that derives from contractual agreements.

From an implementation perspective, the prototype has been built by using a wide range of technologies. At one end of the spectrum, we have used off-the-shelf products like HP Process Manager, BlueStone application server, and the negotiation engine from a major e-marketplace vendor. At the other end, we have re-used a number of research prototypes already existing (especially in the area of policy-management), and developed entirely new components, such as the ESS one.

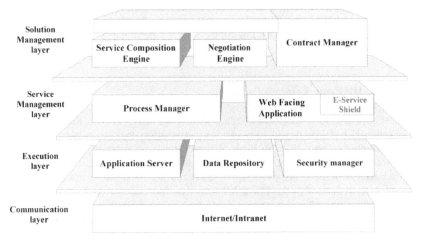

Fig. 2. Architecture of the HP second-generation e-marketplace

4.2 The E-service Shield Component

The purpose of the ESS component is to support the enforcement of the contractual agreement between companies in terms of interaction processes. The contractual communication flow between service providers and service consumers goes through the e-marketplace, which acts as a trusted third party. The first version of ESS is mainly reactive, and focuses on the verification of the communication flow with respect to the stage of the service delivery process at which it occurs. The parties can be confident that incoming requests from their business partners are controlled by ESS, and are compliant with the contractual processes they have agreed upon.

The type of interaction policies enforced by ESS is based on a two-layer approach. The idea is that there are two types of conditions that determine the validity of a specific action. Some conditions depend on general characteristics and capabilities of the actors. For example, only the account manager for a company can send an invoice to that company. Some conditions depend on the stage of the interaction process at which the action occurs. For example, an invoice can be sent to the customer only after it has received the goods. These two types of conditions derive from different business policies. They are orthogonal by nature, but their joint use is fundamental to fully capture a business interaction model. On the one hand, we propose that keeping this separation is beneficial for both the design and the enforcement of contractual agreements. On the other hand, we insist on the importance of a service-driven coordination between the two types of policies. The ESS component represents our initial attempt to address these issues.

The approach adopted in ESS is to blend process management with authorisation management, since the use of only one of them becomes extremely complex to deal with in practice. For instance, an authorisation policy can express conditions on the state of a process, but it then needs to be changed for each process. In the previous example, the fact that the invoice can be sent only when the goods have arrived could be modelled as an extension of the policy that allows only the account manager to send it. If the company now agrees with a different customer to send the invoice before the goods, a new policy needs to be created re-stating also the fact that only the account manager can send it. If the company then decides to allow also the sales representative to send the invoice, all the policies may need to be redesigned. Similar problems occur when everything is modelled as a process.

The methodology supported by ESS implies the coexistence of two layers of policies. In the lower layer, atomic authorisation policies deal effectively (and efficiently) with conditions that are independent of the evolution stage of a service instance. In the higher layer, easily customisable processes capture the execution logic of the service. These processes rely upon specific lower level policies depending on the state of execution. A complete example is given in the following section.

The architecture of the ESS component is based on a foundation layer including a process engine, a cryptographic engine, and an authorisation server (see Figure 3). The need for both process management and authorisation management capabilities derives from the type of policies enforced by ESS. The cryptographic engine is used for basic validation of the message flow. On top of this basic layer, two main components deal with the dynamic validation of the message flow and the management of the overall system. The request validator verifies that the interaction process specified in the contractual agreement is followed by the parties. When a message is received, the source is verified using standard techniques for digital signatures. The message is then validated against the agreed service delivery process. Finally, the authorisation levels required for the entities involved at the specific stage in the delivery process are verified. Most of the activity for the request validator focuses on the coordination of lower-level components. The policy and process manager component deals with the lifecycle management for the two layers of policies deployed in ESS.

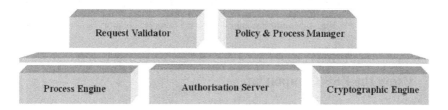

Fig. 3. The architecture of the ESS component

Concerning the implementation of the ESS component, we have used a number of different technologies. For the process engine, we have used HP Process Manager [8]. For the authorisation server we have used ACSIS [2], which is a research prototype allowing dynamic reconfiguration for policy specification. We have developed the remaining components on top of the Bluestone J2EE platform and an Oracle database. A view of the monitoring interface for the request validator is presented in Figure 4.

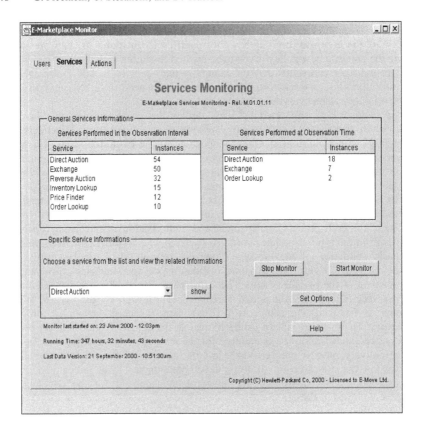

Fig. 4. Monitoring interface for the request validator

5   Using the ESS Component

To describe the impact of the ESS component on business transactions, let us introduce an example in the context of catalogue-based sale of physical goods. The chosen example is from a traditional context, in order to show the impact that ESS would have even on simple e-services.

Figure 5 contains a section of the XML document that describes the specific part of the process with the rules of interaction for catalogue browsing. In particular, when the customer requires an information page, the seller has to provide both the data concerning the product and a sale offer. The customer can then decide to accept the offer, in which case it will have to send both an acceptance notification and a purchase form. However, the customer can decide to decline the offer, but it has to send explicit notification of the fact. The whole procedure has been negotiated in the form of a contract. In this particular case the service "CatalogueBrowsing" was probably offered to the customer at no cost, provided he accepted to comply with the interaction processes proposed by the seller.

```xml
<?xml version="1.0" encoding="UTF-8"?>
<!DOCTYPE process SYSTEM "interaction.dtd">
<process name="CatalogueBrowsing">
  ...
<sequenceProcess name="sequence13">
  <action name="action131" authorisation="Catalogue-
                DetailsSelection">RequestPage</action>
  <parallelProcess name="parallel132">
     <action name="action1321"authorisation="Catalogue-
                SendSaleInformation">Send_Page</action>
     <action name="action1322"authorisation="Catalogue-
                SendSaleInformation">Send_Offer</action>
  </parallelProcess>
  <orProcess name="or133">
  <parallelProcess name="parallel1331">
     <action name="action13311"authorisation="Catalogue-
                DetailsSelection">Accept_Offer</action>
     <action name="action13312"authorisation="Catalogue-
                DetailsSelection">Purchase_Form</action>
  </parallelProcess>
  <action name="action1332" authorisation="Catalogue-
                DetailsSelection">Decline_Offer</action>
  </orProcess>
</sequenceProcess>
  ...
</process>
```

Fig. 5. Interaction process in ESS

In more detail, the action names (e.g. Send_Offer) in a process node are references to data structures called action cards. An action card contains three types of information related to the specific action: user notification, data type, and content constraints. The user notification is a description of the action itself that is provided to the user in order to understand the other two parts of the information in the node. The content can be a human readable description or some sort of action code for use in automatic systems. This information is added to the business data if the request is valid, and the whole structure is sent to the intended receiver. If the request is not valid, the information on user description is returned to the sender of the message. The information on data type gives indications on how to validate the XML structure of the message. The slot for content constraints can be used to capture conditions to be evaluated on the content of the message itself. The constraint specification language supported by the current version of ESS has been kept very basic, but an extension based on XQL is under development.

The attribute name in the process node contains internal references used by the execution infrastructure. The attribute authorisation is instead the link with service-class policies, and the ACSIS authorisation server [2]. Service-class policies embed service-independent authorisation rules associated to the execution of a process step. In our example, the details of the rule `Catalogue-DetailsSelection` are presented in Figure 6.

The first part of the name is an indicator of the library the policy belongs to. The policy itself specifies the constraints that the user has to satisfy. The constraints are defined in terms of the information the authorisation server can gather from different components of the e-marketplace infrastructure. In the example, the authorisation server gathers information from both the connection manager and user profiler. As an aside, the fact that a service-class policy can be reused in different context raises the problem of naming. In Figure 5 we can see how the name "DetailsSelection" policy is of no immediate association with action names.

```
<Service>
  <ServiceName>Catalogue</ServiceName>
  ...
  <Functions>
  <!--........FUNCTION DETAILS_SELECTION.............-->
    <Function>
    <FunctionName>DetailsSelection</FunctionName>
      <Conditions>
        <!-- WHO can use DetailsSelection -->
        <Condition>
          <ConditionContent>
            <![CDATA[CONTEXT.hasRole("customer")]]>
          </ConditionContent>
        </Condition>
        <Condition>
          <ConditionContent>
            <![CDATA[CONTEXT.hasAuthenticationLevel(
                                "financial-action")]]>
          </ConditionContent>
        </Condition>
      </Conditions>
    </Function>
  ...
  </Functions>
</Service>
```

Fig. 6. Action-level policy in ACSIS

6 Related Works

The relevance of electronic contracts to e-service provision has triggered a number of initiatives in both academia and industry [12]. Main points of interest regard contract specification, contract lifecycle, and contract execution. Contract specification is usually approached from a very pragmatic angle. Initiatives such as ebXML and RosettaNet [4], [14] adopt a bottom-up approach, and starting from message-oriented ontology they are moving up towards the formalisation of cooperative business processes. In terms of electronic contract lifecycle, the COSMOS platform well exemplifies the type of requirements that management infrastructures have to meet, especially in order to support the contract formation phase [5]. Process management emerges as central, in both the formation and the execution phase of the contract. Focusing on contract execution, Open Flow, Cross Flow, and RABBIT exemplify how different assumptions on the service provisioning model impact on the infrastructure requirements [9], [11], [16].

The above-mentioned initiatives present many similar features at different levels (e.g. service model, architectural choices), but the central role played by processes is the main common theme. The need for automatic support to business interaction processes is a key issue for second-generation e-marketplaces [6] [10].

7 Conclusion

Trust is both an issue and a source of opportunities for e-marketplaces. The speed of electronic transactions, the broad space of potential business partners, and the potential for price optimisations are just some of the motivations that attract businesses to e-marketplaces. Still, the absence of the proper level of trust between the members of an e-marketplace can dramatically impact on the benefit they can achieve. Trust-related services become crucial components of any e-marketplace infrastructure.

In the scenario of the second-generation e-marketplace developed at HP Labs, the paper proposes a simple model for mediated service provision involving the e-marketplace in the role of trusted third party. The model is based on specific views of the business processes underpinning service provision, and active mediation of the communication flow between service providers and service consumers. The electronic contract captures the business interaction processes between the parties, and the ESS infrastructure component enforces the compliance between contractual agreements and the behaviour of the companies. The paper discusses the position of ESS in the HP e-marketplace infrastructure, and it describes also the main architectural choices related to the ESS component implementation.

References

1. Blodget, H., McCabe, E.: The B2B market maker book. Merrill Lynch & Co. (2000)
2. Casassa Mont, M., Baldwin, A., Goh, C.: POWER Prototype: Towards Integrated Policy-based Management. NOMS-2000, Honolulu, USA (2000) 789-802
3. Casati, F., Ilnicki, S., Jin, L., Shan, M.C.: An Open, Flexible, and Configurable System for Service Composition. Workshop on Advanced Issues of E-Commerce and Web-Based Information Systems (WECWIS 2000), IEEE Computer Society, San Jose, USA (2000) 125-133
4. ebXML, http://www.ebXML.org
5. Griffel, F., Boger, M., Weinreich, H., Lamersdorf, W., Merz, M.: Electronic Contracting with COSMOS - How to Establish, Negotiate and Execute Electronic Contracts on the Internet. Proc. 2nd Int. Enterprise Distributed Object Computing Conference (EDOC'98) (1998)
6. Gipson, M., Runett, R., Wood, L., Clawson, P.: The Electronic Marketplace 2003: Strategies For Connecting Buyers And Sellers. Simba Information Inc. (1999)

7. HP, Hewlett-Packard E-service initiative. http://e-services.hp.com (1999)
8. HP, Hewlett-Packard Changengine www.hp.com/go/Changengine (2000)
9. Klingemann, J, Wäsch, J., Aberer, K.: Adaptive outsourcing in cross-organizational workflows. Proc. 11th International Conference on Advanced Information Systems Engineering (CAiSE'99), Heidelberg, Germany (1999)
10. Ludwig, H., Whittingham, K.: Virtual Enterprise Co-ordinator - Agreement-Driven Gateways for Cross-Organisational Workflow Management. Proc. International Joint Conference on Work Activities Coordination and Collaboration (WACC'99) 29-38. ACM Software Engineering Notes, Vol. 24, No. 2 (1999)
11. Marton, A., Piccinelli, G., Turfin, C.: Service provision and composition in virtual business communities. Proc. 18th IEEE Int. Symposium on Reliable Distributed Systems, Int. Workshop on Electronic Commerce. Lausanne, Switzerland (1999) 336-341
12. Milosevic, Z., Bond, A.: Electronic commerce on the Internet: what is still missing? Proc.5th Conf. of the Internet Society (1995)
13. Reilly B., Block, J.: Next-generation E-Commerce processes and systems. Electronic Commerce Strategies Report, GartnerGroup (1997)
14. RosettaNet, http://www.rosettanet.org
15. Shim, S., Pendyala, V., Sundaram, M., Gao, J.: Business-to-Business E-Commerce Frameworks, IEEE Computer, Vol. 33, No. 10, IEEE Computer Society (2000) 40-47
16. Shrivastava, S.K., Bellisard, L., Feliot, D., De Palma, N., Wheater, S.M.: A workflow and agent based platform for service provisioning. Proc. 4th International Enterprise Distributed Object Computing Conference (EDOC'00) (2000)
17. Ströbel, M.: Communication Design for Electronic Negotiations on the basis of XML schema. Proc. 10th World Wide Web Conference, Hong Kong (2001) 9-20

GAMA-Mall – Shopping in Communities

Till Schümmer

Technical University of Darmstadt and
GMD – German National Research Center for Information Technology
IPSI – Integrated Publication and Information Systems Institute
Dolivostr. 15, D-64293 Darmstadt, Germany, +49-6151-869-4856
schuemme@darmstadt.gmd.de

Abstract. In this article, we consider market places as social places. Social places provide social presence and interaction. Virtual market places often lack in these social factors. Community support tools, such as chat systems or newsgroups try to fill this gap. We argue that a new architecture is needed that brings together customers with common interests. We propose a combined system called GAMA-Mall based on a spatial representation of the shop, which implements this architecture.

1 Introduction

During the last years, virtual presences of shops, so called virtual market places, have grown rapidly (e.g. virtual bookstores such as www.amazon.com or internet shopping malls such as shopping.yahoo.com). The design and the implementation of these shopping places has primarily focused on the process of exchanging goods. Online catalogues of mail-order companies were created and metaphors of shopping baskets and virtual cash desks were introduced.

While these metaphors aim at easing the process of shopping by emulating real world experiences, current virtual market places often lack in the emulation of the social factor. The customers are mainly kept separated and everyone is shopping as if he was in an empty shop.

1.1 Voices for Social Market Places

A growing number of authors has recently argued for establishing communities in virtual shops. Marathe [13] states that "people don't like to shop in an empty store." To substantiate this thesis, he cites a survey which shows that 90% of shoppers prefer to communicate while shopping. Preece [14] argues for a community centered development of online communities and proposes an integration within E-commerce web sites. She states that online communities can help shop sites to establish trust and to draw people to their web site. Participate.com [20] argues for shopping communities because they "increase stickiness (customer loyalty), [and] viral marketing (word of mouth), reduce [the] cost of customer acquisition, and drive higher transaction levels."

L. Fiege, G. Mühl, and U. Wilhelm (Eds.): WELCOM 2001, LNCS 2232, pp. 51-62, 2001.
© Springer-Verlag Berlin Heidelberg 2001

Levine, Locke, Searls, and Weinberger express the importance of social factors in virtual market in a more provocative way. In "the cluetrain manifesto" [11], they state in 95 theses how life and cooperation will take place in virtual markets. Some of these theses help to enlarge our definition of a social virtual market:
"1. Markets are Conversations. [...]

11. People in networked markets have figured out that they get far better information and support from one another than from vendors. [...]

12. There are no secrets. The networked market knows more than companies do about their own products."

1.2 Historic Observations

The history of market places reveals that they have always been places for social contacts, communication, recreation, or exchange of news, even if in current implementations of the virtual market places these factors are often omitted.

Herodotus [7] reports on the importance of market places for consulting. He wrote that ill people were carried to the central place in the city of Babylon. Every person who passed a patient had to stop and ask him about his disease. Then the passer-by had to give advice, if he had comparable diseases before. It was strictly forbidden to pass by without talking to the patient. This example shows how different social needs were satisfied at one locale.

The Greek agoras and the Roman forum were initially political gathering places. But very soon they became market places as well. They were the central points in a city, where people not only discussed and traded, but also spent their spare time. In many cases, the trading crowd grew so large that political discussions could not take place anymore. In Athens, they therefore separated the political place from the market place. Aristotle [1] argued for this separation, to keep the politics free from commercial influences. On the other hand, it is proven that Socrates found his partners in discussions at the agora.

1.3 The Goal

Virtual market places reduce stores mainly to the presentation of goods. Other customers and salesmen are no more co-located in one store. They don't feel the presence of others and social contacts are often not established in the store.

We therefore argue to combine the virtual market with a social place again. Customers who participate in the virtual market should change their role: from consumers to people, who want to satisfy their wide range of needs. The purchase of goods is one of them, social interaction, learning, or excitement are others, which can be satisfied in a community. The role of markets that bring together people, who did not know each other, could create new social communities. If the members of the community are encouraged to exchange their ideas and their knowledge, this could have a large impact on all brands of live, as the discussions at the agora had large implications on ancient philosophy. The more interesting the community is, the more attractive will the market place be.

In the remaining part of this paper, we will first take a short look at current technologies for community support in shopping sites. After that, we will present an architecture for a social market place and discuss different possibilities for the implementation of this approach.

2   Online Communities at E-commerce Sites

Current implementations of virtual shops differ widely in their support for communities. For the focus of community support, the solutions can be distinguished by the following factors:

- the activities can be *synchronous* (same time) or *asynchronous* (longer periods of time between two statements);
- communication flow can be possible between business and customer (B→C), customer and business (C→B), and customers and other customers (C→C);
- results can be captured (*persistent*) or non-lasting (*transient*);
- communication can be initiated by business or customer;
- the formation of the involved (sub-)group of the community can be based on the website, buddy lists, or personal (current) interests;
- the tools can provide awareness or not;
- and the tools can provide means for shared experiences (performing a group task together).

Table 1 provides a classification according to the above criteria. In the following paragraphs, we will compare the different solutions according to table 1.

The most common support for social interaction is provided by e-mail. Customers can request information by e-mailing a sales representative and hopefully receive the desired information afterwards.

Newsletters allow to broadcast information from vendors to customers. This technology is widely used to advertise new products or special offers. In some cases, the customers can express their interests by configuring agents that look for specific topics. If the agent finds a product of interest it notifies the customer (see for instance the German book seller www.mediantis.com for an implementation of personalized agents).

Bulletin boards or newsgroups add the communication channel between customers. Since all customers can read all messages, knowledge can evolve within the community. This is why newsgroups can provide a basic impression of shared experiences. Vendors normally participate in the newsgroup and answer questions or guide the discussion in a desirable direction. Many newsgroups on e-commerce sites are moderated, which means that the vendor filters the messages and publishes only those messages that are desirable.

Mail, newsletters, and newsgroups all base on asynchronous technology. Vivid interaction is thus very complicated. Many systems are nowadays integrated within and accessed through the website.

Synchronous technology is dominated by chat systems. These systems allow fluid conversations by the exchange of short messages in a chat room. The content of the chat is visible to all participating users and all users can send contributions. Some chat rooms organize special events, where many users meet with experts (e.g. chats with authors on virtual bookstores). These events help the community to gain shared experiences. The chat communication is initiated by the customer when he enters a chat room web page. The page is normally a designated page at the vendor's site.

Table 1. Current technology used to support online communities at web sites. A "•" means that the feature is supported by the technology. If the "•" appears in parentheses, then the feature is only available for the customer or the business, or the feature is not possible, but not intended with the technology.

	e-mail	Newsletters	Newsgroups	Chat	IM	Odigo	Human-Click	GAMA-Mall
Communication								
Asynchronous	•	•	•			(•)		(•)
Synchronous				•	•	•	•	•
B→C	•	•	(•)				•	(•)
C→B	•		(•)	•			•	(•)
C→C			•	•	•	•		•
Persistence	•	(•)	•			(•)		(•)
Initiator								
Vendor		•					•	
Customer	•		•	•	•	•		•
Group building								
Web Site	•	•	•	•		•	•	•
Buddies				•	•	•		
Interests			•				•	•
Awareness				(•)	•	•	(•)	•
Shared experience			(•)	(•)		(•)	•	•

Instant messaging (IM) systems (such as ICQ or AIM) allow the users to keep a buddy list. Whenever a buddy comes online, this is indicated by a sound or a flashing icon. Thus, these systems provide awareness on the other members of the community. Most IM implementations are stand-alone applications. An integration within web pages is found rarely (an example is given at the end of this section).

Both, Chat and IM, do not support persistence for the community (users can save chat logs, but there is no integrated mechanism to bring these logs back into the community). They provide basic awareness information but only poor shared experiences, because the conversations held in the chat take place within subgroups of the community. The experiences of the subgroup are not transformed into experiences of the community.

Several research prototypes have addressed the activity of co-operative browsing. One of them is the proxy based approach, which was presented by Cabri et al. ([4]). In this approach, users can see what pages other members of their community are currently viewing and they can join browsing in a master slave manner: One user navigates and the content of all other browsers follows this user.

Odigo (www.odigo.com) combines the IM systems with the presence awareness of other users, who view the same website. Users can detect and contact other users, who are currently at the same web server (pages are not distinguished). When two users found one another, they can chat or browse the web together. Anyhow, the granularity of the awareness information is quite coarse: knowing for instance that another user is currently at amazon.com can imply anything. Thus it will not necessarily create communities with common purposes or interests.

An integration of co-operative web browsing in a shop system can be found in the HumanClick system [8]. This system allows site owners to see who is currently visiting specific pages and they can contact this user using a chat tool. If a contact is established, the sales person can initiate a cooperative browsing session, where she is steering the local user's browser.

We propose that for a social market place the system provides awareness between users who share the same section of a shop. The definition of sections should be topic centered. For instance, if two users currently browse crime stories by Agatha Christie, they share this current interest. They should then be able to start a synchronous communication and discuss their current interest or exchange their experiences of crime stories. At this point, they form a community of purpose (they go through the same process of browsing crime stories), but this community may soon mutate to a community of interest. That means that there is a new group, which shares a common interest and passion – in the example the passion for crime stories. These communities have shown to be sticky, which means that the members will return frequently to be aware of any activities in the community (cf. [13]). Besides discussion, the group should be able to perform other tasks together and thus gain shared experiences (which also leverages the identification with the community). These activities may include cooperative web browsing or the cooperative writing of a review. The following section will show how such an environment can be built.

3 The GAMA-Mall Approach

We propose an architecture that eases partner finding and collaboration in virtual shopping sites. The architecture is called GAMA-Mall. The basic idea for contact facilitation of our approach is the one of focus and nimbus, as it was suggested by Dourish and Bellotti [5] and generalized by Rodden [15]. They interpret the collaborative virtual environment in a spatial way. Each artifact, which is used by the group, is placed at a specific position. If a group member is currently working on the artifact, he focuses it. The nimbus forms an area around the focused artifact. It "represents an observed object's interests to be seen in a given medium" [6]. Rodden transfers the ideas of focus and nimbus to general graph structures. Nearness is, according to Rodden, defined as the set of adjacent artifacts in the graph.

With GAMA-Mall, we propose to apply this generalized model to shopping web sites. Whenever other users enter the local user's nimbus, this is visualized to him. For visualization, the designers of the collaborative web shop have to carefully create metaphors of space and presence. The metaphors have to be intelligible, so that they do not add additional cognitive load to the user. They have to be more intrusive, when the other user reaches the center of the local user's nimbus (the focus).

Awareness information serves as a means for locating potential partners. When the partners have found one another, they might start tighter collaboration. This should be supported by the system by offering tools for negotiating the upcoming collaborative activity, as well as tools for actually performing the collaborative activities.

We identified seven steps of how to introduce awareness information and collaborative tools to shopping web sites. The steps are as follows:

1. Analyze the artifacts and the relation between them.
2. Build spatial metaphors and define computable mappings between the physical representation and the metaphoric representation.
3. Find (or build) metaphors of activities that describe the users' actions.
4. Add a user representation to the application.
5. Identify the parts of the application, where the attachment and detachment of metaphors is best performed.
6. Insert additional layers at the identified parts of the application for detaching and applying the metaphors.
7. Identify and add additional tightly coupled collaborative tools.

After this overview of the required steps, we will discuss each step in a separate subsection and show how to perform this step in the example of a virtual bookstore. Note that we do not intend to provide exactly one solution. The goal of the following discussion is rather to highlight different alternative ways of how to implement a social virtual shop.

3.1 Artifacts and Relations

When considering web shops, there are several artifacts that may be of interest to the user. The selection of artifacts for the GAMA-Mall is driven by the constraint that each artifact has to be a possible focus of a user. Therefore, the goods are the most obvious artifacts. In most virtual stores each good has a virtual representation in forms of a HTML page. Other artifacts serve as groupings for goods. In real stores, goods are presented using shelves. Categories fulfill the same purpose in virtual stores.

Taking the pages of the amazon.com bookstore as an example, GAMA-Mall first identifies the currently displayed book, author, or category. These three classes are the artifact classes. An author is related to the books he wrote and books are classified in categories. The pages at amazon.com provide additional information that shows which books are alike.

3.2 Spatial Metaphors and Computable Mappings

The mapping between the identified artifact's representation in GAMA-Mall and their real representation in the store is quite straightforward: Each artifact is represented by its URL. Parsing the artifacts representation in the shop site creates relations. For each link, the GAMA-Mall removes personalized information (such as session indicators) and then calculates the internal representation based on this generalized URL.

For the pages at amazon.com, the system performs a mapping to artifacts and relations in the GAMA-Mall representation by parsing the address of the current HTML page, which includes the book's unique ISBN or the author's name. The next step is to parse the page's content and find other artifacts. This is done by analyzing targets of hyperlinks and interpreting the hyperlink's destination based on the link's structure.

The spatial arrangement, which is needed to apply the Focus-Nimbus model, is calculated from the graph of artifacts. Distances have to be applied to the relations as a prerequisite. Each link's distance has to conform to the semantic nearness of the artifacts, which the link is connecting.

The GAMA-Mall uses a very pragmatic approach to calculate distances: When analyzing the artifact, the system counts all links on the page and all pages that link to the target. The artifact's link's distances is then proportional to both values. Thus, two pages that have only links to one another are connected by very short distances.

The analysis could benefit from some more sophisticated algorithms (e.g. the algorithms provided by [9]), but on the other hand, this calculation forms a bottleneck in the whole system since it is done in real-time.

Another way for enhancing the structure of the spatial representation is to modify it according to the user's actions. We refer to this process as learning by browsing and have already applied and tested it in an earlier prototype in a different problem domain [18]. Whenever a user moves from one page to a related page, the two pages are moved closer together. All other pages are moved apart.

3.3 Metaphors of Activities

When browsing virtual shops, there are not many different kinds of activities. Either, users are navigating through the shop by selecting different links, or they are looking for something specific by entering a search query. Both activities can be abstracted to *moving through the virtual store*, whereas the first kind is not as targeted as the latter. When considering possible spontaneous collaboration, the first kind of movement is of greater importance, since people who are browsing are more likely accepting an interruption for collaboration.

Within the GAMA-Mall, all movements are recorded and they produce a trail comparable to Bush's trails in MEMEX [3]. The only difference between GAMA-Mall and MEMEX trails is that the trails in the GAMA-Mall fade away. Fading follows the analogy of footsteps at the beach. If a user has walked there recently, one can still recognize his trails. But as time goes by, the sand drifts away and the trails get very cloudy until a point in time is reached, when one can not distinguish the trails from the surrounding area anymore. If two users can sense each other's trails, they are possible partners for social contacts.

Another activity in shops is the *purchase of goods*, but this should be performed privately and not shared (e.g. for security reasons of payments). As a third activity, users can *co-operate*. The results of co-operation could again be of interest for other user's and awareness on other user's co-operation could attract additional user's to join the co-operation. Unlike single user's browsing activities, co-operative activities should not fade away. The results (e.g. comments on a specific good) are kept and surrounding users are aware of them (by means of the focus-nimbus model).

3.4 User Representation

Each activity has to be associated with a user. Therefore, the GAMA-Mall needs a way to uniquely identify each user and retain information about the user's current state. Using a shared object for the user representation solves the problem of associating the user's activity with the user.

The identification requires some traditional mechanisms: The most common way to identify users is by means of cookies. Another possibility is user identification by means of a login procedure.

3.5 Points for Attachment and Detachment of Metaphors

Up to this point, GAMA-Mall can represent users and their activities.

We argue for a proxy architecture to integrate users, activities and the spatial representation with the web pages of the shop. Loutonen and Altis [12] defined a WWW proxy server as a computer, which "provides access to the Web for people on closed subnets who can only access the internet through a firewall machine.". Another frequent application of proxies is caching of web pages to shorten response time. But, as described e.g. by Thomson [19], proxies can also modify the page's content. Modifications range from automatic outlines for better readability in the Zipper system [2] over the removal of unwanted information (such as banner advertisements in WebWasher [21]) up to automatic translation of web pages (e.g. [10]).

For the purpose of awareness on web pages, the proxy adds some awareness clues in to the retrieved page. Therefore, the GAMA-Mall proxy monitors the accesses, generates a spatial representation, and calculates and adds awareness information. The user has to configure his web browser in a way that all requests are made to the GAMA-Mall proxy. For cases where the user requests pages that are not a part of the shop, the proxy can behave like a HTTP gateway.

3.6 Layers for Detaching and Applying the Metaphors

Within the proxy, the awareness information can be calculated according to the focus-nimbus awareness model as it was described at the beginning of this chapter.

Whenever a user performs an activity on an artifact, this activity has an impact on the artifact and on all surrounding artifacts. The original activity is called source activity, whereas all calculated activities on surrounding artifacts are called dependent activities. If the access was for instance a view access, the proxy adds this access to the artifact. Then it searches for all surrounding artifacts and adds the dependent view access to these artifacts as well (with a lower intensity to signal a larger distance to the source activity).

One possible way for visualizing nearby activities is by adding awareness indicators in front of the artifacts. We have gained some experience with presence indicators that show how far away other users are working in the nimbus [18]. In the GAMA-Mall prototype, we use little colored figures, which are placed in front of the artifact's representation. The more red paint is used to draw the figure, the closer another user is. Colors range from dark red to green, which can be expressed as a mapping of the activity's intensity to the figure's hue.

A concrete example of the calculation of figures is shown in figure 1. It shows three different books, which are all in the same category. The books are written by two different authors and one of the books is written by both authors. One user is currently viewing the book *b3*. This implies that figures are shown in front of all the other artifacts according to the distance between *b3* and the other artifact.

The figures are combined with context information by using the capability of naming figures in HTML. The name of the figure reveals who is working nearby and where he is working on. Thus, the user can decide if it is worth following the link to the other user. Besides the context information the figures also provide access to detailed collaboration information and synchronous collaborative tools. These tools will be explained in depth in the next section.

Figure 2 provides a design study of the visualization. In front of each link that leads to an artifact GAMA-Mall added presence indicators. If a user has left a page the GAMA-Mall will still show the awareness indicator for his viewing activity, but the intensity will vanish over time. We model this ageing presence indicators by reducing the source activity's intensity, after a user has left the page.

3.7 Tightly Coupled Collaborative Tools

Without additional means for co-operative activities the awareness indicators would be quite useless. Therefore, users should be able to do something together, when they meet. Taking into account the real world setting, the most obvious activity would be to *chat*. Chats can be without any goal or they can be goal centered. Especially the second kind of chats is important for communities, since it produces reasonable events. Besides chatting, visitors can join and *browse through the shop together*. If they have noticed that they are looking for goods within the same topic they could find the desired good faster. Different strategies can be useful: co-operative and concurrent browsing.

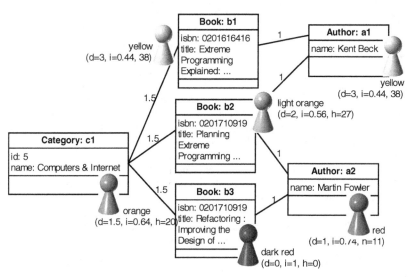

Fig. 1. Calculation of awareness indicators. The tuple below the color names includes the distance to the source activity, the resulting intensity, and the figure's hue.

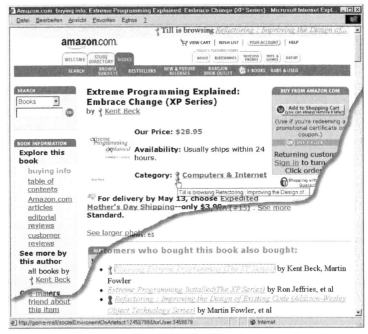

Fig. 2. Design study of awareness indicators in a the virtual bookstore (for space reasons, two screenshots were combined to show two different parts of the document).

Co-operative browsing would mean that they look at the same information in the shop. They can then discuss about the information and come to a mutual agreement, what related goods or shelves are the most promising ones for further inspection.

Concurrent browsing means that the group members browse the shop on their own. The GAMA-Mall can assist them by indicating which pages have already been visited. Thus, they will not visit pages that have already been visited by another member of the current browsing group. The group can capture findings in a cooperative chat, as it was described in the section above. They could also generate a report on their browsing experience using a synchronous cooperative text editor (the same editor that we used in the programming environment TUKAN [17]). Within this editor, each user can type and each user has a personal text cursor.

All synchronous cooperative tools can be launched using the social environment inspector. The inspector opens whenever a user follows the link of an awareness indicators and displays a web page with additional information about the other user and links that launch the synchronous tools.

All synchronous tools go beyond the technical capabilities of current web browser technology. Thus, the synchronous tools are implemented using the COAST framework for the creation of synchronous groupware [16].

4   Conclusions

Within this paper, we presented an architecture that introduces social presence and eases group formation based on the user's current interests. Community support exceeded traditional solutions primarily in the area of awareness, where we applied a focus-nimbus model. The awareness information was complemented by synchronous tools for spontaneous co-operation.

The system is currently under development and we gained first results concerning the behavior of the proposed proxy. It was possible to parse pages and monitor accesses as described in the sections above. The visualization is working fine. The synchronous tools have been used before in a synchronous programming environment and worked well.

The calculation of the nimbus and the parsing of the HTML pages revealed to be the most time critical parts in the architecture. Anyhow, we have already solutions in mind to balance the load on different servers. Since all information that is needed by the proxy for its calculations is modeled using shared objects, the distribution on different proxy servers is straight forward.

All these experiences encourage us to carry on with the development and create a scalable version soon. Then it will be tested in the field and we hope to get a critical mass of testers to test and proof our hypotheses that communities of purpose and interest gain real support using the tools.

Acknowledgements. I wrote this paper in plural voice. This was done on purpose to thank the valuable discussions in the CONCERT division. Especially Torsten Holmer and Alejandro Fernández participated in the generation of the presented ideas. Many thanks are due to my brother Jan Schümmer and Christian Schuckmann from the COAST team for technical discussions on the implementation. I would also like to thank Gero Mühl and Ludger Fiege for their impact and their REBECA architecture for using events to synchronize web pages.

This work was supported by the Deutsche Forschungsgemeinschaft (DFG) as part of the PhD program „Enabling Technologies for Electronic Commerce" at Darmstadt University of Technology.

References

1.   Aristotle, "Politics", 350 BC.
2.   *Brown, M. H.; Weihl, W. E.*: "Zippers: A Focus + Context Display of Web Pages", *Digital SRC Research Report*, 1996, ftp://ftp.digital.com/pub/DEC/SRC/research-reports/SRC-140.pdf.
3.   *Bush, V.*: "As We May Think", in: *The Atlantic Monthly*, 1945, 101-108 (online at: http://www.isg.sfu.ca/~duchier/misc/vbush/vbush-all.shtml).
4.   *Cabri, G.; Leonardi, L.; Zambonelli, F.*: "Supporting Cooperative WWW Browsing: a Proxy-based Approach", *7th Euromicro Workshop on Parallel and Distributed Processing*, Madeira, Portugal, 1999, 138-145.
5.   *Dourish, P.; Bellotti, V.*: "Awareness and coordination in shared workspaces", *Conference proceedings on Computer-supported cooperative work*, 1992, 107-114.

6. *Greenhalgh, C.; Benford, S.*: "Boundaries, Awareness and Interaction in Collaborative Virtual Environments", *Proceedings of the 6th Int. Workshop on Enabling Technologies: Infrastructure for Coll. Enterprises (WET-ICE)*, Cambridge, MA, USA, 1997.
7. *Herodotus*: "The History of the Persian Wars", New York, 1862: Dutton & Co, 430 BC (excerpt available online at: http://www.fordham.edu/halsall/ancient/greek-babylon.html).
8. *HumanClick Ltd.*: "HumanClick Pro Guide", http://www.humanclick.com/products/userguide.htm: 2001.
9. *Kruschwitz, U.*: "Exploiting Structure for Intelligent Web Search", *Proceedings HICSS'34*, Maui, HI, 2001, electronic proceedings.
10. *Language Partners International*: "New Multilingual Website Solutions Now Possible", in: *LPI Press Release*, 1996, http://www.languagepartners.com/news/pressre5.htm.
11. *Levine, R.; Locke, C.; Searls, D.; Weinberger, D.*: "The cluetrain manifesto", Cambridge, Massachusetts: Perseus Publishing, 2000.
12. *Luotonen, A.; Altis, K.*: "World-Wide Web Proxies", in: *Proceedings of the First International Conference on the World-Wide Web, WWW '94*, 1994, available online at: http://www1.cern.ch/PapersWWW94/luotonen.ps, accessed 2001.
13. *Marathe, J.*: "Creating Community Online", Durlacher Research Ltd, 1999.
14. *Preece, J.*: "Online Communities", Chichester, UK: Wiley, 2000.
15. *Rodden, T.*: "Populating the Application: A Model of Awareness for Cooperative Applications", *Proceedings of the ACM 1996 conference on Computer supported cooperative work*, 1996, 87-96.
16. *Schuckmann, C.; Schümmer, J.; Schümmer, T.*: "COAST - Ein Anwendungsframework für synchrone Groupware", *Proceedings of the net.objectDays*, Erfurt, 2000.
17. *Schümmer, T.; Schümmer, J.*: "Support for Distributed Teams in eXtreme Programming", *Proceedings of eXtreme Programming and Flexible Processes Software Engineering - XP2000*, Addison Wesley: 2000.
18. *Schümmer, T.*: "Lost and Found in Software Space", *Proceedings of HICSS-34*, IEEE-Press: Maui, HI, 2001.
19. *Thomson, J. R.*: "Proxy Servers and Databases for Managing Web-based Information", University of Alberta: 1997.
20. *Warms, A.; Cothrel, J.; Underberg, T.*: "Return on Community: Proving the Value of Online Communities in Business", Participate.com, April 12, 2000.
21. *Webwasher AG*: "WebWasher product homepage", accessed 2001, http://www.webwasher.com/en/products/wwash/index.htm.

Markets without Makers - A Framework for Decentralized Economic Coordination in Multiagent Systems

Torsten Eymann

Albert-Ludwigs-Universität Freiburg
IIG Telematik
79085 Freiburg, Germany
+49-761-203-4928
eymann@iig.uni-freiburg.de

Abstract. Most electronic marketplaces are derived from a client/server model, with a central coordinator institution in the middle and a closed group of market participants submitting bids and asks to that institution. In contrast, technical views on electronic commerce often envision ad-hoc cooperation between market participants in open and decentralized IT environments, where software agents negotiate for their human principals. Such environments will naturally form unregulated market-coordinated multi-agent systems with selfish agents negotiating for utility maximization, and they need concepts for decentralized economic coordination - a mechanism for distributed resource allocation that works without a market maker, with maximum privacy, security and coherent coordination as result. This article describes a framework used for the realization of a multiagent system which coordinates a supply chain using a decentralized economic approach.

1 Markets Are Needed, Market Makers Are Not

The short history of electronic marketplaces has already seen different business models appearing and vanishing again. The recent paradigm connected with all these business models seems to be the ubiquity of market makers, central institutions in the center of a electronic marketplace whose sole purpose is to bring supply and demand together. These are either catalogs, arbitrators, matchmakers, or auctioneers, and they gain money by either access fees or transaction fees. But are they necessary? Are centralized institutions mandatory to *control* economic coordination? Or is that view just another occurrence of the "centralized mindset" [27], which says that where is coordination, there has to be someone who controls?

We should note that our physical world does not have „the" market for steel, beverages, paper, not even for commodities like stocks. The multitude of marketplaces available creates a dynamic network of economic opportunities, interconnected supply and demand bids which create the dynamic pattern of constantly changing market situations. This emergent network is what we regard as „the market" for one good, and

L. Fiege, G. Mühl, and U. Wilhelm (Eds.): WELCOM 2001, LNCS 2232, pp. 63-74, 2001.
© Springer-Verlag Berlin Heidelberg 2001

the dependencies between the different goods and markets lead to our understanding of „the economy".

But what is a market, anyway? From an economic perspective, it is "paradoxical how variously and vaguely defined the concept of market is" [18]. The mechanism of price generation in a market is mostly connected to Adam SMITH's "invisible hand" [33], but until today there exists no commonly agreed-upon description of this market mechanism. The dominant neo-classical equilibrium theory, for example, has been criticized that "to answer the question, which mechanisms effectuate an equilibrium state, it has contributed only little and unsatisfyingly" [4].

Generally spoken, "markets describe the exchange and production of commodities in the private property regime" [20]. In other words, the purpose of the market is the realization of a dynamic, distributed resource allocation mechanism. Economics is thus essentially all about the coordination of systems consisting of utility-maximizing agents, who satisfy their needs using some *mechanism* for solving a distributed resource allocation problem. The effect of this mechanism is a *state* where prices are set so that supply and demand is perfectly balanced: the general equilibrium.

The proverbial *invisible hand* of Adam SMITH was a first concept of how a decentralised mechanism, without a central (thus visible) co-ordinator, leads to that desired effect, but SMITH gave no implementation of that mechanism. A century later, Leon WALRAS proposed the *tâtonnement* process therefore [37]. WALRAS made the *invisible hand* visible by introducing a central auctioneer, who iteratively solved the allocation problem out of his total knowledge of supply and demand. Most of today's economic research now investigates into the equilibrium state, and relies on WALRAS' tatônnement process as a valid picture of the mechanism. Starting with KEYNES, neo-classical economics even went one step further: the *homo oeconomicus* market participant is completely rational, has total knowledge of the market situation and processes this information in infinitesimal speed. A transition from one market state to another virtually takes no time – a dynamic picture of the mechanism is not needed at all..

In contrast, economic research on decentralized self-organization still aims at explaining the mechanism of the invisible hand. Not being satisfied with either the *homo oeconomicus* or the *tâtonnement process*, the research fields of evolutionary economics [21], econophysics [19] and neo-austrian economics (HAYEK's *spontaneous order*) [12] uses a bottom-up approach to explain economic coordination.

Multiagent system implementations of the coordination mechanism can be distinguished according to the types mentioned above. Computable general equilibrium models [31] apply no dynamic mechanism at all, but calculate results out of total, global knowledge. The WALRASIAN auctioneer is directly implemented in market-oriented programming [38]. In this article, we show how the third possibility, the decentralized self-organization, can be implemented and leads to coherent economic coordination with predictable results.

In the remainder of this article, we will first clarify some definitions and introduce a framework for building agent-based electronic marketplaces. Section 3 describes the software architecture of a prototypical multiagent system that coordinates by decentralized automated negotiation and price signals, and shows the results of some experimental runs. The article closes with an outlook to possible application areas and further research.

2   A Framework for Economic Coordination in Multiagent Systems

To distinguish between the different possible types of agent-supported electronic marketplaces, we modify the coordination framework described by MALONE [17] and KLEIN [15] to describe coordination in multiagent systems. To characterize different coordination processes more precisely, they are described here in terms of successively deeper levels of underlying processes, each of which depends on the levels below it. These layers are analogous to abstraction levels similar to the protocol layers for network communications. The advantages of layered frameworks are reduced complexity, hierarchical ordering of terms and functions, and the identification of dependencies [34].

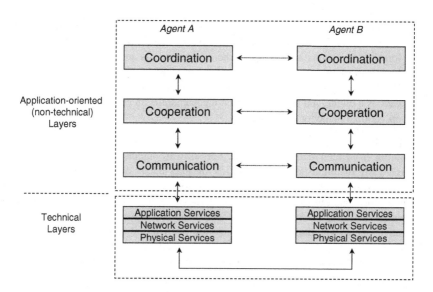

Fig. 1. Coordination Framework for Multiagent Systems

Fig. 1 shows how two agents on a marketplace may collaborate on a common task. To give an example, Agent A might want to buy a good from Agent B.

Coordination in this context can be described as „the act of managing interdependencies between activities" [17], given either a resource to be shared or a timing interdependency. A population of software agents in an electronic marketplace is required to coordinate itself with regard to sharing resources – to exchange money vs. goods, services or access rights, until every participant is satisfied with regard to his own utility maximization goal – some institution [22] has to coordinate how much Agent A will have to pay to Agent B to satisfy the utility goals of both. This institution might be either of the agents, a trusted third party, or the "invisible hand". Organizational and economic theory offers the use of either more centralized or decentralized coordination concepts – arbitrators, auctioneers, or decentralized direct search markets.

- *Arbitration* models [35] are the most rigid implementation – the participating clients give their bids to the central server, who computes the pareto-optimal resource allocation and gives the results back to the clients. Here, the clients have to decide nothing but to rely on the faultless and concise computation of the arbitrator. However, the computation time increases exponentially with the number of clients.
- An *auction mechanism* employs the visible hand of a central coordinator, resulting from the individual and decentralized decision-making by the participants, who raise and lower their bids accordingly to the market situation. The auctioneer collects information from the participants and makes it publicly available. Auctions are the dominant paradigm of agent-based marketplaces today, despite known problems [29].
- *Direct search markets* finally rely on catalog and directory services for the coordination of supply and demand. No mandatory market maker exists, but the agents form a "civil agent society" [5], where price signals and bilateral negotiation efforts lead to coherent coordination of the participants. In such coordination models, the client/server paradigm is no longer found – every participant is a server as well as a client, and the coordination mechanism is an emergent feature of the cooperational behavior of the agents.

Cooperation is viewed as the bilateral dissolution of conflicts between discrete agents stemming from their defined behavior. For software agents in electronic commerce, KRAUS [16] distinguishes two scenarios of inter-agent cooperational behavior. If agents have the same principal, it is possible to use cooperative or even benevolent agents, coordinated by a trusted authority. Benevolent agents are those who help other agents to maximize utility even if their own utility decreases through this action. Cooperative agents are those which collaborate even if the utility of the other agent knowingly increases more than their own. This behavior can be assumed in closed multiagent systems with a single designer, but not in open marketplaces.

Because agents in open marketplaces will act competitively on similar utility scales, benevolent and cooperative behavior can not be assumed. Human principals will probably define their agent's strategy and goals according to their own. RASMUSSON and JANSON [26] argue, that (1) if human market participants are allowed to create their own software agents, they will define selfish interests and goals according to their own. If they (2) can choose between selfish agents and cooperative agents, who may increase other agent's utility at their own expense, they will always choose selfish agents. But (3) if human users are only allowed to use cooperative agents, they will use them only if not using agents is worse. In effect, open electronic marketplaces will bustle with selfish agents aiming at antagonistic goals. These agents will cooperate only if their own utility increases through a transaction, and they will communicate with other agents to make their goals and desires clear.

Communication is thus considered a means to transport a message of cooperation between agents. The structure of economic environments makes this task easier, since the semantics of an "offer", a "bid", or an acceptance is rooted deep in the purpose of what the market is about – exchanging property. It is not surprising that communication standards for marketplaces already exist, e.g. RosettaNet [1]. Here, communication and data representation specifications are already given for the context of orders, contract nets and different types of auctions. From an architectural viewpoint, the question of whether communication occurs mediated or unmediated remains. Mediated communication uses a central institution which collects and forwards information – in this case the multiagent system can recur on central knowledge. In the case of unmediated communication, every agent is able to keep his communication links secret – on the other hand, it is not possible to create a consistent picture of the system as a whole.

Finally, agents, be they human beings or software agents, communicate using the communication media provided by information technology through the information technology interface. This interface includes all possibilities for transmitting messages or information from one individual to another. An example of using the technical layers is implementing RMI [6]in a multi agent system as means of transportation for communicated messages.

To sum up the results from this section according to the coordination layer framework shown in Fig. 1, the three topics of coordination, cooperation and communication may be instantiated in electronic marketplaces as shown in Table 1.

Table 1. Realization Alternatives for the Coordination Framework

Layer	Selected Realization Alternatives			
Coordination	Arbitration	Matchmaking	Auction	Decentralized / Direct Search
Cooperation	Benevolent	Cooperative	Selfish	
Communication	Unmediated	Mediated		

The combination of selfish cooperation and unmediated communication is regarded as the most realistic for future open multiagent environments [5; 26]. An example are systems where each agent's strategy is designed by a different principal to follow proprietary goals. The next section describes the construction of software agents for such an environment.

3   Decentralized Coordination in a Multiagent System

In order to evaluate the future impact and functionality of agent-driven coordination issues, a prototypical market-controlled MAS called AVALANCHE has been implemented. The key difference of AVALANCHE compared to many other agent-based marketplace projects is the absence of a central arbitrator or auctioneer. The research goal is to exhibit self-organizing, emergent coordination, achieved through the implementation of a strictly decentralized automated negotiation (bargaining) protocol.

Technically, software agents represent human users intending to buy, produce and sell different goods or services as "miniature automated businesses" [14]. A simple and arbitrary supply chain is modeled in which three different types of software agents produce a consumer good: "lumberjacks", that buy trees to produce and sell boards; "carpenters", that buy the boards and fix them together to sell as a panel; and "cabinetmakers", that buy the panels, build tables out of them and sell them. Two additional types, producers and consumers, which only define a seller or buyer strategy, respectively, provide the tight ends of the supply chain.

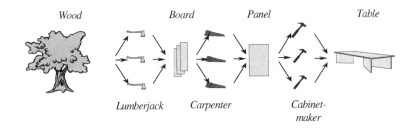

Fig. 2. A simple supply chain scenario

3.1 The Technical Setup and the Communication Layer

AVALANCHE is realized in JAVA 1.3 and uses the ORB class library VOYAGER 3.0 [23]. All agents are independent JAVA threads. The system architecture consists of three basic classes, the marketplaces, trader agents, and one experiment control object. Detailed information about AVALANCHE can be found in [7].

The agent class defines communication abilities and negotiation protocols. Each agent communicates with every other object on the marketplace in direct, bilateral and unmediated fashion via an event-driven messaging mechanism [2]. The message format and syntax is taken from the FIPA iterated-contract-net protocol [9].

The electronic marketplaces are based on Java Virtual Machines (JVM), which run as a server process in a TCP/IP-based network and are identifiable by a unique IP port address. The marketplace neither actively influences the software agents' strategies nor the communication – in particular, it does not explicitly synchronize or schedule the agents' activities. It only offers a single "white pages" directory service for any software agent to register as seller or buyer, and to inquire about other registered agents. Price bids are never publicly posted (as in catalogs). It is possible to create an environment of connected marketplaces, where mobile agents can choose where to trade, but this is not exploited in the context described here.

The experiment control object contains technical functions for logging the transaction data, which is not expected to have any effect on the market coordination.

3.2 The Cooperation Layer and the Agent's Negotiation Strategy

The exchange goods are defined as commodities, so the only negotiation variable is the price. All agents in AVALANCHE follow the economic goal of profit maximization. They try to buy input goods for less and to sell output goods for more. Depending on the actual market situation, its equity, and stock, the agent decides autonomously which action to take next - whether to buy, sell, produce, move or self-terminate.

The agent lifecycle "follows the money": if the agent has finished goods in stock, it tries to sell. If the agent has no goods, but input factors in stock, it simulates the production of output goods (by waiting an appropriate length of time). If the agent has no input factors in stock, it tries to buy some. If the market situation is not satisfying at all, e.g. if there are no offers or demands within a certain time span, the agent tries to move to another marketplace. If the agent has spent its entire budget or all marketplaces are shut down, it has to terminate – every few milliseconds the agent has to pay utilization fees to the market anyway, so doing nothing is never a rewarding strategy.

In the case of buying or selling, the software agent goes through the three stages of a market transaction: information, agreement, and settlement [30]. In the information phase of any transaction, a buyer or seller has to identify its potential trading partners. If a seller agent wants to sell its output, it currently enters his ID in the directory, and waits until a prospective buyer agent demands a negotiation. Simultaneously, the agent will actively search in the directory for potential transaction partners. Buyer agents apply a mirror procedure.

The buyer agent then initiates the agreement phase by communicating with any supplier from the list. Both software agents negotiate using a monotonic concession protocol [28], where propose and counter-propose messages with subsequent price concessions are exchanged. If the negotiation process is successful, both agents will reach a compromise price agreement; otherwise, someone will sooner or later drop out of the negotiation. In this event, the agents will restart with other partners obtained from the directory.

In the final settlement phase, the transaction is carried out and monitored. Sellers and buyers exchange goods and money, respectively. If any party misbehaves in this phase, the resulting reputation information might be used to modify strategies and behavior to be used in future encounters with that agent as in [24].

To maximize the spread between input and output prices, and thus its utility, the agent follows a certain negotiation strategy. Comparable automated negotiation efforts in multiagent systems can be found in the research context of agent-mediated electronic commerce [10; 32] and market-oriented programming [38]. Human negotiation uses parameters such as *demand level*, *concession*, and *concession rate*:

"A bargainer's *demand level* can be thought of as the level of benefit to the self associated with the current offer or demand. A *concession* is a change of offer in the supposed direction of the other party's interests that reduces the level of benefit sought. *Concession rate* is the speed at which demand level declines over time. [...] These definitions [...are] unproblematic, when only one issue or underlying value is being considered, as in a simple wage or price negotiation" [25].

The human principal chooses the initial values of these parameters as part of the strategy definition during the initialization of the software agent. In the real world, the values are influenced by determinants such as expectations about the other's ultimate demand, position and image loss, limit and level of aspiration and time pressure [25].

In this implementation, the AVALANCHE agents use an adaptive strategy based on a stochastic finite state automaton, in which action paths are taken depending on stochastic probes against certain internal parameters. It is of course possible to use different strategies in the cooperation layer of the framework presented. In AVALANCHE, a combination of six variables, collectively called the *Genotype*, describes the strategy:

- *Acquisitiveness (p_acq)* defines the probability of maintaining the agent's own last offer. The lower the acquisitiveness value, the higher the average concession rate. Whether an agent concedes in an actual situation is subject to a stochastic probe against this parameter.

- If the agent concedes, the *In-negotiation delta price change (del_change)* parameter calculates the amount of the price concession between two negotiation steps. Both partners calculate a percentage from the price difference of their original offers. If the buyer has *del_change* = 50% and the supplier *del_change* = 0%, the agents will reach agreement after two negotiation steps at the initial price of the supplier, if no agent drops out.

- To maximize their income, the agents will try to raise their initial demand level between different negotiations by the value of *Pre-negotiation delta price change (del_jump)*.

- The *Satisfaction* parameter *(p_sat)* determines if an agent will drop out from an ongoing negotiation. The more steps the negotiation takes, or the more excessive the partner's offers are, the sooner the negotiation will be discontinued. Effectively, this parameter creates time pressure.

- Information from past performance in earlier successful and unsuccessful negotiations computes into a subjective market price for each agent, which modifies the parameter *Memory* using a weighted exponential average with weight *w_memory (w_mem)*.

- *Reputation (p_rep)* affects the cooperative behavior of the software agents. In this article, all agents are assumed to cooperate; for other cases, see [24].

3.3 The Coordination Layer - Experimental Results

To test the behavior of the AVALANCHE system we conduct several test series. Every series consists of several experiment runs, which under similar conditions lead to comparable outcome patterns. In the current implementation we run a generator program, an experimental control object, a single marketplace and 50 trading agents of each type (for a total of 250 agents) in parallel on a Pentium PC under Windows NT for about 10 minutes. The following presentations all show similar patterns when repeatedly starting with the same initial values. However, absolute price levels or points in time have no meaning since they change in every run.

In this article we show only one experiment to understand the design outcome. The experiment shown here has homogenous strategies, which means that all agents are equipped with an identical *Genotype* and there is no variation of parameter values in the population: *p_acquisitiveness* = 0.50, *del_change* = 0.25, *del_jump* = 0.15, *p_satisfaction* = 0.75, *w_memory* = 0.2, and *p_reputation* = 1. The agents hold no stock, but some initial equity money. Every 10 milliseconds a new "wood" is produced by any producer agent. The consumer agents never run out of money. Initial goods valuations are preprogrammed equally for every agent type (e.g. 25 money units for boards).

In Fig. 3, the horizontal axis measures the time in milliseconds, and the vertical axis shows the price level. Every dot in the chart points out time and agreement price of a transaction, e.g. the x-value of a triangle marks the time when some carpenter software agent has sold a table to a cabinetmaker software agent for y-value price. The type of goods is represented by different symbols as indicated by the legend, which shows the supply chain from top to bottom. In the chart, the lowest price curve is wood and the highest are tables. The time lag at the beginning is caused by software initialization and initial negotiation until the first goods are moved up the supply chain. The rise in the price levels over time is an artifact caused by an increase in the money supply in the chain, by the buying consumer agents – this has to be dealt with in future development of the experimentation environment.

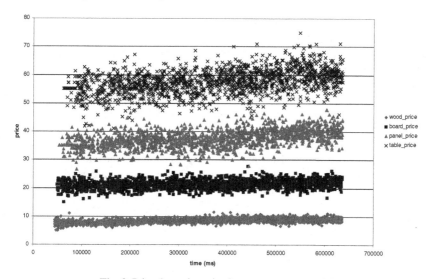

Fig. 3. Price dynamics using homogeneous strategies

In Fig. 3 it is not possible for a single agent to gain an advantage, since all agents possess an identical static negotiation strategy. The price levels do not substantially change during the course of the experiment.

The negotiation profit gained from a specific *Genotype* is correlated to the relative setting of other agent's strategies, not the absolute values. By varying the setting of the *Genotype* parameters in subsequent experimental runs, it can be shown how dominant parameter combinations either succeed or are counterbalanced. "Learning" the right values relative to the other agents is thus essential to gain a higher profit in the future. This aspect is covered in [8] and not elaborated here.

4   Market Coordination between Economic Concepts and Technical Realization

In this article, we introduced a coordination mechanism framework for agent-based process management and applied it to the design of a multiagent system for economic environments, where the coordination mechanism is based on automated negotiation and price signaling.

But decentralized, economic systems have some clear caveats. It is desired to design mechanisms for self-interested agents such that if agents maximize their local utility, the overall system behavior will at least be acceptable [3]. Among the problems which such a complex system faces are the over-usage of a shared resource known as "tragedy of the commons" [11], chaotic behavior [13; 36], and the appearance of malevolent agents, which may be countered by the embodiment of centralized and decentralized reputation mechanisms in the system [24]. These problems have to be watched closely, because they will determine appearance and acceptance of decentralized systems consisting of autonomous devices.

However, a successful implementation of the distributed resource allocation mechanism introduced here has the advantage of a flexible structure and inherent parallel processing. From an application viewpoint, an appealing aspect lies in the inherently distributed structure, which mirrors the division of work in companies and the network of businesses and markets. It could be used for the coordination of virtual enterprises, management of factory resources, creation of electronic marketplaces, intelligent energy consumption, control of workflow processes, collaborative product design and more. By using the same coordination rules that govern the real world, decentralized market mechanisms may allow the creation of innovative fast, flexible, parallel working, and self-regulating IT systems, in cases where a centralized coordinator is not efficient or not applicable.

References

1. RosettaNet Implementation Framework. *RosettaNet Consortium.* http://www.rosettanet.org, 2001. Access date: 2001-3-1.
2. Bigus, J.P. and Bigus, J. *Constructing intelligent agents with Java: a programmer's guide to smarter applications.* New York: Wiley & Sons, 1997.
3. Binmore, K. *Fun and games - a text on game theory.* Lexington, Mass: D.C. Heath, 1992.
4. Böventer, E.v. and Illing, G. *Einführung in die Mikroökonomie.* München: Oldenbourg Verlag, 1995.

5. Dellarocas, C. and Klein, M. Civil Agent Societies: Tools for Inventing Open Agent-Mediated Electronic Marketplaces. *Proceedings of the Workshop on Agent-Mediated Electronic Commerce*. Stockholm, Sweden: ACM Press, 1999. http://citeseer.nj.nec.com/dellarocas99civil.html.

6. Downing, T. *Java RMI remote method invocation*. Foster City, CA: IDG Books Worldwide, 1998.

7. Eymann, T.: Avalanche - ein agentenbasierter dezentraler Koordinationsmechanismus für elektronische Märkte. *Ph.D. Thesis*. Albert-Ludwigs-Universität Freiburg, 2000. http://www.freidok.uni-freiburg.de/volltexte/147 .

8. Eymann, T. Co-Evolution of Bargaining Strategies in a Decentralized Multi-Agent System. *AAAI Fall 2001 Symposium on Negotiation Methods for Autonomous Cooperative Systems*. Forthcoming.

9. FIPA - Foundation for Intelligent Physical Agents: Agent Communication Language. 1999. http://www.fipa.org

10. Guttman, R. and Maes, P. Agent-mediated Integrative Negotiation for Retail Electronic Commerce. *Proceedings of the Workshop on Agent Mediated Electronic Trading (AMET'98)*. Minneapolis, Minnesota: 1998. http://ecommerce.media.mit.edu/papers/ amet98.pdf.

11. Hardin, G.: The Tragedy of the Commons. In: Science 162 (1968) 1243-1248.

12. Hayek, F.A., Bartley, W.W., Klein, P.G., and Caldwell, B. *The collected works of F.A. Hayek*. Chicago: University of Chicago Press, 1989.

13. Huberman, B.A. and Hogg, T.: The behavior of computational ecologies. Huberman, B.A. (ed.). *The Ecology of Computation*, 77-115. Amsterdam: Elsevier (North Holland), 1988.

14. Kephart, J.O., Hanson, J.E., and Greenwald, A.R. Dynamic Pricing by Software Agents. *IBM Research*. http://www.research.ibm.com/infoecon/paps/html/rudin/rudin.html, 2001.

15. Klein, M.: Coordination Science: Challenges and Directions. Conen, W. and Neumann, G. (eds.). *Coordination Technology for Collaborative Applications*, 161-176. Heidelberg: Springer, 1997.

16. Kraus, S. Negotiation and cooperation in multi-agent environments. *Artificial Intelligence*, 94, (1997), 79-97. http://www.cs.biu.ac.il:8080/~sarit/Articles/ct.ps.

17. Malone, T.W. and Crowston, K. The Interdisciplinary Study of Coordination. *ACM Computing Surveys*, 26, 1 (1994), 87-119.

18. Menard, C. Markets as institutions versus organisations as markets? Disentangling some fundamental concepts. *Journal of Economic Behavior and Organization*, 28, (1995), 161-182.

19. Mirowski, P.J. *More heat than light*. Cambridge University Press, 1992.

20. Moulin, H. *Cooperative microeconomics - a game-theoretic introduction*. London: Prentice Hall, 1995.

21. Nelson, R.R. and Winter, S.G. *Evolutionary Theory of Economic Change*. Harvard University Press, 1985.

22. North, D.C. *Institutionen, institutioneller Wandel und Wirtschaftsleistung*. Tübingen: Mohr, 1998.

23. ObjectSpace. Voyager Documentation. *Objectspace Website*. http:// www.objectspace.com/ products/voyager/, 1999. Access date: 2000-3-1.

24. Padovan, B., Sackmann, S., Eymann, T., and Pippow, I. A Prototype for an Agent-based Secure Electronic Marketplace including Reputation Tracking Mechanisms. *Proceedings of the 34th Hawaiian International Conference on Systems Sciences*. Outrigger Wailea Resort, Maui: IEEE Computer Society, 2001. http://www.hicss.hawaii.edu/ HICSS_34/ PDFs/INBTB06.pdf.

25. Pruitt, D.G. *Negotiation behavior*. New York: Academic Press, 1981.
26. Rasmusson, L. and Janson, S. Agents, self-interest and electronic markets. *Knowledge Engineering Review*, 14, 2 (1999), 143-150.
27. Resnick, M. *Turtles, termites, and traffic jams - explorations in massively parallel microworlds*. Cambridge, Mass: MIT Press, 1994.
28. Rosenschein, J.S. and Zlotkin, G. *Rules of encounter - designing conventions for automated negotiation among computers*. Cambridge, Mass: MIT Press, 1994.
29. Sandholm, T.W. Issues in Computational Vickrey Auctions. *International Journal of Electronic Commerce*, 4, 3 (2000), 107-129.
30. Schmid, B. and Lindemann, M. Elements of a Reference Model for Electronic Markets. *Proceedings of the 31st Hawaiian International Conference on Systems Sciences*. Los Alamitos, CA: IEEE Press, 1998.
31. Shoven, J. and Walley, J. Applied General-Equilibrium Models of Taxation and International Trade: An Introduction and Survey. *Journal of Economic Literature*, 22, September 1984 (1984), 1007-1051.
32. Sierra, C.: A roadmap for Agent-Mediated Electronic Commerce. Sierra, C. and Dignum, F. (eds.). *Agent Mediated Electronic Commerce - The European AgentLink Perspective*. Heidelberg: Springer, 2001.
33. Smith, A. *An inquiry into the nature and causes of the wealth of nations*. London: Printed for W. Strahan; and T. Cadell, 1776.
34. Tanenbaum, A.S. *Computer networks*. Upper Saddle River, N.J: Prentice Hall PTR, 1996.
35. Tesch, T. and Fankhauser, P.: Arbitration and Matchmaking for Agents with Conflicting Interests. Klusch, M. (ed.). *Proceedings of Third International Workshop on Cooperative Information Agents (CIA '99)*, 323-334. Heidelberg: Springer, 1999.
36. Thomas, J. and Sycara, K. Stability and heterogeneity in multi agent systems. *Proceedings of the Third International Conference on Multi-Agent Systems (ICMAS-98)*. Paris, France: 1998.
37. Walras, L. *Elements of pure economics*. London: Allen and Unwin, 1954.
38. Wellman, M.P.: Market-Oriented Programming: Some Early Lessons. Clearwater, S.H. (ed.). *Market-Based Control: A Paradigm for Distributed Resource Allocation*, 74-95. Singapore: World Scientific, 1996.

Incentives for Sharing in Peer-to-Peer Networks

Philippe Golle[1*], Kevin Leyton-Brown[1*], Ilya Mironov[1**], and
Mark Lillibridge[2]

[1] Computer Science Department, Stanford University
{pgolle,kevinlb,mironov}@cs.stanford.edu
[2] Systems Research Center, Compaq Computer Corporation
mark.lillibridge@compaq.com

Abstract. We consider the *free-rider* problem in peer-to-peer file sharing networks such as Napster: that individual users are provided with
no incentive for adding value to the network. We examine the design
implications of the assumption that users will selfishly act to maximize
their own rewards, by constructing a formal game theoretic model of the
system and analyzing equilibria of user strategies under several novel
payment mechanisms. We support and extend this work with results
from experiments with a multi-agent reinforcement learning model.

1 Introduction

Peer-to-peer (P2P) file-sharing systems combine sophisticated searching techniques with decentralized file storage to allow users to download files directly
from one another. The first mainstream P2P system, Napster, attracted public
attention for the P2P paradigm as well as tens of millions of users for itself. Napster specialized in helping its users to trade music, as do most of its competitors;
P2P networks also allow users to exchange other digital content.

The work of serving files in virtually all current P2P systems is performed for
free by the systems' users. Since users do not benefit from serving files to others,
many users decline to perform this altruistic act. In fact, two recent studies of the
Gnutella network have found that a very large proportion of its users contribute
nothing to the system [2,11]. The phenomenon of selfish individuals who opt
out of a voluntary contribution to a group's common welfare has been widely
studied, and is known as the *free-rider* problem [8,12]. The communal sharing
of information goods in "discretionary databases" and the resulting free-rider
problem has also been studied before the advent of P2P systems [13].

This problem is not simply theoretical. Some P2P systems plan to charge
users for access in the near future, both in order to make money for their investors
and to pay any needed royalties. However, a system run for profit may not receive
the level of altruistic 'donations' that power a free community. There is therefore
both a need and an opportunity to improve such P2P file-sharing systems by

---

* Supported by Stanford Graduate Fellowship
** Supported by NSF contract #CCR-9732754

L. Fiege, G. Mühl, and U. Wilhelm (Eds.): WELCOM 2001, LNCS 2232, pp. 75–87, 2001.
© Springer-Verlag Berlin Heidelberg 2001

using an incentive scheme to increase the proportion of users that share files, making a greater variety of files available. This would increase the system's value to its users and so make it more competitive with other commercial P2P systems.

In the following section, we introduce our formal game theoretic model. Section 3 describes the Napster system, which we use as a motivating example throughout this paper. In sections 4 and 5, we propose two classes of novel payment mechanisms, analyzing user strategies and the resulting equilibria. Finally in section 6, we use a multi-agent reinforcement learning model to validate our analytical results and to explore further properties of our mechanisms.

2   Problem Definition

We turn to a more formal, game theoretic characterization of the problem. (Readers unfamiliar with game theoretic analysis may consult [5,10].) First, we describe the game that we use to model the file sharing scenario during one time period (e.g., one month). n agents participate in the system; we denote them $a_1, \ldots, a_n$. Each agent a_i's strategy, denoted $S_i = (\sigma, \delta)$, consists of two independent actions:

1. **Sharing:** Agents select what proportion of files to share. In our model, sharing takes three levels: σ_0 (none), σ_1 (moderate) or σ_2 (heavy).
2. **Downloading:** Each agent must also determine how much to download from the network in each period. We model downloads with agents choosing between three levels: δ_0 (none), δ_1 (moderate) or δ_2 (heavy).

2.1   Agent Utility

Agents' utility functions describe their preferences for different outcomes. The following factors concern agents:

- **Amount Downloaded (AD):** Agents get happier the more they download.
- **Network Variety (NV):** Agents prefer to have more options from which to select their downloads.
- **Disk Space Used (DS):** There is a cost to agents associated with allocating disk space to files to be shared.
- **Bandwidth Used (BW):** Similarly, there is a cost to agents associated with uploading files to the network.
- **Altruism (AL):** Some agents derive utility from the satisfaction of contributing to the network.
- **Financial Transfer (FT):** Agents may end up paying money for their usage of the network, or conversely they may end up getting paid.

We assume that agents have quasilinear utility functions; that is, each agent's utility functions is a sum of arbitrary functions, each of which maps one of the above variables to a dollar value. Furthermore, we assume that agents are risk-neutral, and so agents' utility for money is linear. We can thus write the equation for agent a_i's utility function as:

$$U_i = \left[f_i^{AD}(AD) + f_i^{NV}(NV) + f_i^{AL}(AL)\right] - \left[f_i^{DS}(DS) + f_i^{BW}(BW)\right] - FT.$$

Each f function is concerned with a particular variable (e.g., bandwidth used) and an agent; it describes that agent's preference for different values of the variable, in money. There is no f function for the variable FT because this variable represents an amount of money that is transferred to or from the agent. Without restricting ourselves to particular f functions, we can make several observations that justify the signs of the terms above. First, f^{AD}, f^{NV} and f^{AL} must be monotonically increasing, with minimum value 0, as these variables only ever contribute positive utility. Likewise, DS and BW only contribute negative utility, explaining the subtraction of f^{DS} and f^{BW} above. Finally, we make two assumptions about agents' relative preferences for different outcomes:

$$f^{AD}(k) > k\beta \tag{1}$$
$$f^{DS}(k) + f^{BW}(k) < k\beta \tag{2}$$

First, in inequality (1) we assume that the monetary equivalent of the utility agents gain from downloading files at level k is more than $k\beta$, for some constant β. Second, in inequality (2) we assume that the monetary cost to agents of sharing files at level k and uploading them at level k is less than $k\beta$.

We say that two agents a_i and a_j have the same *type* if they have the same utility function; i.e., if $f_i = f_j$ for all five f functions. To simplify our game theoretic analysis in the first part of this paper we often make the assumption that all agents have the same type. In section 6 we approach the file sharing problem experimentally; this approach allows us to discuss the convergence of agent strategies under a wide variety of different agent types.

2.2   Equilibria

As is central to any game theoretic model, we assume that agents are economically rational: they act to maximize their expected utility, given their beliefs about the actions that other agents will take and their knowledge about the way that their payoffs are calculated. We denote the joint strategies of all agents as $\Sigma = \{S_1 \ldots S_n\}$. Following the usual definition, we say that Σ is a *weak Nash equilibrium* when no agent can gain by changing his strategy, given that all other agents' strategies are fixed. Similarly, Σ is a *strict Nash equilibrium* when every agent would be strictly worse off if he were to change his strategy, given that all other agents' strategies are fixed. Finally, an agent has a *dominant strategy* if his best action does not depend on the action of any other agent.

2.3   Assumptions and Observations

In our analysis, we restrict ourselves to file sharing systems that make use of centralized servers. These servers maintain a database of the files currently available on the network and connect download requests with available clients.

We assume that the servers are able to determine the identities of files provided by users, which may be needed both to pay royalties to the appropriate copyright holders and to detect users who make false claims about the files they share. File identification may be achieved by a cryptographic watermarking scheme [1,7]; alternately, users who spoof files could be penalized.

One likely payment model for peer-to-peer systems is a flat rate membership fee. We do not explicitly consider this option anywhere in the discussion that follows, as it has no impact on the equilibria that arise from any mechanism (although it can affect agents' decisions about participation). All the mechanisms discussed here are *compatible* with the addition of flat rate pricing; note especially that the fact that flat fees are unrelated to agents' behavior implies that such pricing does not help avoid a free-rider problem.

3   The Napster System

We analyze the Napster system that operated from May 1999 through July 2001, since it is probably the best-known peer-to-peer application. This is one of the simplest system that can be represented by our model: regardless of the actions of agents, Napster imposes no financial transfers. Using the model described in section 2, we start with an equilibrium analysis that disregards the 'altruism' component of agents' utility functions; we then go on to consider altruism.

Unsurprisingly, $\Sigma = \{(\sigma_0, \delta_2), \dots, (\sigma_0, \delta_2)\}$ is an equilibrium. As all agents have the same type, it is enough to analyze the choice made by a single agent. Assume that agents other that a_i follow the strategy $S = (\sigma_0, \delta_2)$, and consider agent a_i's best response. Since a_i is not altruistic, his utility is strictly decreased by sharing files; he will thus choose the action σ_0 which leaves his utility unchanged. Downloading will usually increase a_i's utility; when no other agent shares his utility is zero regardless of how much he intends to download. We can therefore see that the strategy $S = (\sigma_0, \delta_2)$ is dominant. If all other agents choose σ_0 then S yields the same (maximal) payoff as (σ_0, δ_0) and (σ_0, δ_1); if any other agent does share then S yields strictly higher revenue than any other strategy. Because Σ is an equilibrium in dominant strategies, it is unique.

We have identified a unique equilibrium in which nothing is shared and there is nothing to download. Yet songs were plentiful and actively traded on Napster. We identify two reasons that users might have contributed. First, Napster offered its service free of charge and went to great lengths to foster a sense of community among its users, notably through such features as chat-rooms, a newsletter, and messaging between users. This may have been sufficient to encourage users to altruistically contribute resources that cost them very little. Second, Napster offered a (modest) disincentive for non-contribution: by default, the Napster client shared all songs that an agent downloaded. This could be circumvented, but only by manually moving songs to another directory after download or explicitly shutting down the Napster service. Again, because the donation of resources cost users very little, many users may not have bothered to "opt out". We represent both of these incentives through the variable (AL).

In the analysis of this situation, we consider two types of agents. First, altruistic agents are those whose reward for altruistic behavior (AL) exceeds its cost in terms of disk space (DS) and expected bandwidth usage (BW). We assume that f functions for these agents are such that they would prefer the action σ_2 to either the action σ_1 or σ_0 regardless of the value of BW. These agents still gain utility from downloads: following an argument similar to the one given above, (σ_2, δ_2) is a dominant strategy for altruistic agents. The second type of agents are those for whom the cost of altruistic behavior exceeds its benefit.[1] These agents are essentially the same as those described in the previous section: although they may receive some payment for altruistic behavior, it will be insufficient to alter their behavior. They thus have the dominant strategy given above: (σ_0, δ_2).

This analysis is arguably a description of the way users behaved on the Napster system. Some proportion of agents were sufficiently altruistic to share files and did so; other agents were not altruistic and shared nothing. Regardless of their level of altruism, agents were unrestrained in their downloads. This conclusion coheres with the empirical research cited in the introduction claiming that only a small proportion of Gnutella users share any files. Likewise, it supports our claim that Napster experienced a free-rider problem: regardless of the contributions of others, selfish agents had no incentive to share. As with all such problems, the situation in this case appears somewhat paradoxical, because all agents would be better off if they all shared (due to the resulting increase in NV, the variety of files available on the network) than they are under the unique equilibrium.

We now turn to an examination of several alternative mechanisms that overcome the free-rider problem through the imposition of financial transfers. In order to avoid relying on altruism we assume that agents have no altruistic motivation, and so drop the term $f^{AL}(AL)$ from agents' utility functions from here until section 6, in which we present our experimental results. (Of course, all of our results also hold for agents motivated by altruism.)

4   Micro-Payment Mechanisms

We wish to encourage users to balance what they take from the system with what they contribute. A natural approach is to charge users for every download and to reward then for every upload. In this section, we propose and analyze

---

[1] More realistically, we could have assumed three types of agents: those whose level of altruism led them to take each of the three levels of sharing. We analyzed the simpler case to simplify the exposition; the analysis of the case with three agent types proceeds in the obvious way.

a micro-payment mechanism designed according to this principle, as well as a variant of the basic mechanism.

We begin with a detailed description of our micro-payment mechanism. For each user the server tracks the number δ of files downloaded, and the number υ of files uploaded during the time period. The server is aware of all such transfers since it processes all download requests. Note also that there exist standard cryptographic protocols (fair exchange, [3]) to ensure that both parties agree on whether their exchange was aborted or ended successfully. At the end of each period, each user is charged an amount $C = g(\delta - \upsilon)$. We assume that g is linear with a coefficient β representing the cost/reward per file (e.g., \$0.05), and that the value of this coefficient is such that inequalities (1) and (2) hold. Note that the global sum of all micro-payments is 0; individual users, however, may make a profit by uploading more than they download.

Before considering the equilibria that arise under this mechanism, we must simplify it so that it can be represented in our model.[2] Let σ^{-i} be the total number of units shared by agents other than a_i, and δ^{-i} be the total number of units downloaded by agents other than a_i. If agent a_i chooses the action[3] (σ_s, δ_d) then we express the expected value of FT (a_i's expected payment to the system) as

$$E[FT] = \beta \left(d - \delta^{-i} \frac{s}{\frac{n-2}{n-1}\sigma^{-i} + s} \right). \tag{3}$$

This reflects the assumption that the central server matches downloaders uniformly at random with shared units, with the constraint that no agent will download from himself. Note that β is the coefficient representing the cost per net unit downloaded.

Proposition 1. $\Sigma = \{(\sigma_2, \delta_2), \ldots, (\sigma_2, \delta_2)\}$ *is a unique, strict equilibrium.*

Sketch of proof. Inequality (1) states that $f^{AD}(k) > k\beta$. Therefore, agents have an incentive to download as much as possible—their marginal profit per file is reduced, as compared to the case discussed in section 3, but it remains positive. Thus δ_2 dominates δ_1 and δ_0. If all agents other than a_i follow the strategy $S = (\sigma_2, \delta_2)$, and a_i follows the strategy $S_i = (\sigma_s, \delta_2)$, a_i can calculate his expected utility for the different values of s: he will have $E[FT] = \beta \left(2 - 2(n-1) \frac{s}{2n-4+s} \right)$. Given our assumption about the cost of uploading a file, a_i will strictly prefer the strategy $S_i = (\sigma_2, \delta_2)$; thus Σ is a strict equilibrium. Now we show uniqueness of the equilibrium. Note that it is dominant for all agents to choose δ_2, as described above. Thus δ^{-i} is $2n - 2$ in all

---

[2] Although the following analysis makes explicit use of the fact that there are only three levels of sharing and of downloading possible, this restriction has been made only for ease of exposition; a similar (albeit more complicated) proof exists for any number of levels of sharing and downloading.

[3] To simplify the exposition we assume that σ_s denotes sharing s units, and likewise δ_d denotes downloading d units. This assumption is not needed for our results.

equilibria for all i. Inequality (2) states that $f^{DS}(k) + f^{BW}(k) < k\beta$: sharing is worthwhile for an agent if every unit of sharing yields at least one unit of uploading on expectation. Substituting $s = 2$ into the expression for expected uploading from equation (3), we find that it is thus worthwhile for an agent to choose the action σ_2 when $2(n - 1)\frac{2}{\frac{n-2}{n-1}\sigma^{-i}+2} \geq 2$. Rearranging, we find that σ_2 is the most profitable strategy as long as $\sigma^{-i} \leq 2(n - 1)$. This condition always holds since there are $n - 1$ agents other than i and each agent can only share up to 2 units; hence Σ is unique. $\qquad\square$

Note that the same analysis does not suffice for the case of risk-averse agents. The problem is that agents directly control their number of downloads, but only indirectly control their number of uploads through the number of files shared. Depending on the nature and degree of agents' risk aversion and their particular utility functions, they may prefer to reduce their downloads to reduce their worst-case payments to the network. Since the behavior of risk-averse agents depends so heavily on the particular assumptions we make about them we do not give a formal analysis here; however, we return to this issue in section 6.

4.1 Quantized Micro-Payment Mechanisms

Empirical evidence suggests that users strongly dislike micro-payments: having to decide before each download if a file is worth a few cents imposes mental decision costs [9]. Users often prefer flat pricing plans, even when such mechanisms may increase their expected costs. To address this problem we introduce a quantized micro-payment mechanism where users pay for downloads in blocks of b files, where b is a fixed parameter. At the end of a time period, the number of files downloaded by a user is rounded up to the next multiple of b, and the user is charged for the number of blocks used. The pricing mechanism for serving files is unchanged. Note that when $b = 1$ we return to the original micro-payment mechanism, while we approach a purely flat-rate pricing plan as b grows. In practice, we consider values of b on the order of the number of files that an average user would download per time period.

We do not present an analysis of this class of mechanisms, for two reasons. First, in the abstract these quantized mechanisms are the same as general micropayment schemes, except that it is irrational for agents to download a number of files that is not an even multiple of b (unless of course an agent has reached the maximum number of files that he desires). The key advantage of this class of mechanisms is that agents are spared the mental decision costs associated with per-download pricing; since we do not explicitly include this cost in agents' utility functions, the elimination of this cost does not affect the analysis. Second, this class of mechanisms does not fit easily into our simplistic model for user actions: as we allow only three levels of downloading, it is unclear what to quantize. From the analysis in section 4 it is easy to see that if we charge agents the same for δ_1 as for δ_2 the original equilibrium is preserved: agents will simply be provided with additional incentive for taking the actions that they would take anyway.

There are, however, some interesting practical issues arising from this class of micro-payment mechanisms. First we expose a way in which agents could gain through collusion, and present two possible remedies. We also consider problems arising from the trading of rare files and suggest one solution.

First we examine an important way in which this mechanism could be attacked. Quantized micro-payment mechanisms have the property that after one file has been downloaded, the marginal cost of downloading the remaining $b - 1$ files belonging to the same block is zero. Towards the end of a payment period, users may take advantage of zero-marginal-cost downloads left in their account to download files from friends, in order to cause these friends to receive the payment for serving these files. A coalition of users could agree to download excess files from each other and share the profit. The cost to the server is proportional to the difference between the number of files in a block and the average number of files actually desired by agents. However, this collusion can only reduce profits back to the case of simple micro-payments discussed above, where every download corresponds to an upload credited to another agent.

We can modify the quantized payment mechanism so that it is harder for users to direct their zero-marginal-cost downloads to other specific users. This makes it harder for a coalition to generate money for itself: if a user has no control over who is making a profit out of his downloads, this attack becomes less profitable. We could modify our mechanism in one of two ways. First, the server can reply to each download request with a list of users serving files that match the request, but hide the identities of all the users. A user can choose to download from any of the locations listed, but cannot specifically single out his friends. Second, the server can reply to each download request with a random subset of all the users serving files that match the request. In this case user identities do not need to be hidden.

Observe that these solutions only make it less efficient to direct zero-marginal-cost downloads to friends, but by no means make it impossible. Furthermore, these solutions are less and less effective as the number of users sharing a given file decreases, because a user who stores files that are sufficiently rare will receive a large fraction of all the download requests for these files. Thus we propose that rare files (file for which the number of copies available falls below a threshold) be treated differently from files that are more frequent. We cannot simply refuse to credit users who serve rare files, because this would create a strong disincentive for introducing new files into the system. Instead, the central server can give users no credit for serving rare files, but keep track of all the exchanges of rare files. If a file exceeds the threshold of frequency and becomes sufficiently popular, the users who shared it while it was still rare can be credited retroactively.

5   Rewards for Sharing

Previously, we focused on influencing users' consumption by penalizing downloads and rewarding uploads. We take a different approach here: we continue to penalize downloads, but we now consider rewarding agents in proportion to the amount of material they share rather than the number of uploads they provide.

The mechanism we consider makes use of an internal currency, "points."[4] Agents are allowed to buy points either with money or with contributions to the network, but they are not allowed to convert points back into money. Since agents cannot "cash out" their points, they might be allowed to maintain a balance from one time period to the next. We do not consider such a rolling balance since we model a single time period; furthermore, in a repeated equilibrium agents would have no incentive for accumulating more points than they spend.[5] Agents' payment for sharing is $\int M(t)\, dt$, where $M(t)$ is a measure of the amount of data made available for download at time t and the integral is taken over the whole time period. Downloading a file costs cm points, where m is a measure of the file's size and c is a constant. Intuitively, c represents the number of hours one file must be shared in order for the cost of one download to be waived.

As above, we must simplify this mechanism in order to analyze it according to our game theoretic model. One point costs β, where β is set to a value such that inequalities (1) and (2) hold. Furthermore, assume that all files have the same size and that agents always share files for the same amount of time (one time period). Each level of sharing in one time period earns one point (e.g., σ_2 is worth two points). We take $c = 1$, so each level of downloading costs one point. Downloaded files are not shared in the same time period as they were downloaded. As above, we assume that downloaders are matched uniformly at random with shared units, and that no agent may download from himself. Thus, if a_i shares at level s then his expected number of uploads, v_i, is:

$$E[v_i] = \delta^{-i}\frac{s}{\frac{n-2}{n-1}\sigma^{-i} + s}.\qquad(4)$$

Proposition 2. $\Sigma = \{(\sigma_2, \delta_2),\ \ldots\ ,(\sigma_2, \delta_2)\}$ *is a strict equilibrium.*

Sketch of proof. Consider $n-1$ agents playing the strategy $S = (\sigma_2, \delta_2)$, and an agent a_i who must determine his best response. From inequality (1), $f^{AD}(k) > k\beta$, δ_2 dominates δ_1 and δ_0. Thus a_i will play $S = (\sigma_s, \delta_2)$ and must choose a value for s. If a_i plays σ_0, σ_1 or σ_2 his expected number of uploads (given the other agents' strategies) will be 0, just under 1 or 2 respectively, and thus his expected financial transfer to the system will be 2β, slightly more than β or 0. Inequality (2), $f^{BW}(k) + f^{DS}(k) < k\beta$, tells us that agents prefer to share at level k and upload at level k than to pay the system for k points. Since sharing at level 2 leads to uploading at level 2 on expectation, given the other agents' strategies, a_i's expected utility is maximized by the action σ_2. Therefore Σ is a strict equilibrium. $\qquad\square$

However, Σ is not a unique equilibrium. Indeed, point-based schemes have the drawback that they can give rise to a degenerate equilibrium in which all

---

[4] Similar ideas have been used by a variety of web services, e.g. *www.mojonation.net*.

[5] Agents might be encouraged to accumulate points if high balances were rewarded with faster downloads, early access to popular files or other privileges. However, as this intriguing possibility depends heavily on agents' particular utility functions as well as on details about the file sharing system, we do not pursue it further here.

agents download at the highest level and share nothing at all. This can be proven in several ways; we present the simplest proof, which requires the assumption that points have no value if not redeemed to pay for downloads.

Proposition 3. $\Sigma = \{(\sigma_0, \delta_2), \ldots, (\sigma_0, \delta_2)\}$ *is a strict equilibrium.*

Sketch of proof. Consider $n - 1$ agents playing the strategy $S = (\sigma_0, \delta_2)$, and an agent a_i who must determine his best response. As above, δ_2 is dominant by the first assumption. Thus a_i who will play $S = (\sigma_s, \delta_2)$ and must choose a value for s. Since all other agents play σ_0, there exist no files to download. Thus gaining points will yield no utility for a_i, by the assumption in the preamble. Furthermore, since all other agents play δ_2, a_i will be made to serve files for all other agents' download requests, bringing him negative utility. He is therefore best off following strategy S, and so Σ is a strict equilibrium.   □

This analysis leaves it unclear what equilibrium will be reached in play. We attempt to provide some answers in our experimental section.

We now consider more practical issues arising from this mechanism. First we consider agents' opportunities for collusion and for other undesirable exploitation of the system, and discuss remedies.

Unlike quantized micro-payments, this mechanism does not interfere with download patterns. Instead it always gives the right incentives for consumption, since there is no way for colluding users to make money by downloading from each other. However, this mechanism alters agents' incentives for sharing files. The key problem is that agents have negative utility for the consumption of bandwidth, which only occurs when shared files are actually downloaded. In order to conserve bandwidth, agents may make their collections available at low-usage times, or alternately offer unpopular files. This may reduce the overall value of the network. A possible remedy is to offer distributors different rewards based on expected download demand. The formula to reward distributors thus becomes $\int M(t)\lambda(t)\ dt$, where $\lambda(t)$ is a scaling factor proportional to expected demand. This ensures that the files are available at the right times. The problem of users preferring to share unpopular files can also be addressed through the introduction of a similar coefficient.

Another challenge is that agents cannot be expected to make (and honor) a commitment to share a file for hours into the future. It is much more likely that agents will start and stop sharing unpredictably, sharing only when their computer is idle. A mechanism that accommodates such behavior is likely to be more useful; however, this accommodation must be balanced by ensuring that agents are not able to cheat by suddenly claiming to lose their idle status as soon as they receive an upload request.

6   Experiments

The previous sections analyzed the existence of equilibria for all our mechanisms under simplifying assumptions. Here we test our mechanisms in simulations that more accurately reflect the real world. We enrich our theoretical model by introducing different types of files and agents, and by considering risk-averse agents.

6.1 Experimental Setup

We extend upon our theoretical model in two ways. First, we consider action spaces for agents more fine-grained than the three levels of downloading and sharing discussed so far. Second, we consider files of several kinds and agents of several types. Recall that agents with different types have different utility functions; in our experiments agents differ according to their (fixed) preferences for different kinds of files. Agent utility functions differ as follows:

- **Altruism:** $f(AL) = \rho AL$ where ρ is drawn uniformly from $[\rho_{min}, \rho_{max}]$.
- **Disk space:** the function $f(DS)$ is set to emulate an agent with maximal storage space d, where d is chosen uniformly from $[d_{min}, d_{max}]$.
- **File type preferences:** the term $f(AD)$ is decomposed into $\mu \sum_i f_i(AD_i)$, where each i represents a different kind of file. Agents' preferences for each kind of file are reflected by different f_i functions. The factor μ is chosen uniformly at random in $[\mu_{min}, \mu_{max}]$ for each agent.

In the simulation of micro-payment mechanisms, our agents are stateless (they do not keep track of the amount of money they spend or make). In the simulation of point-based mechanisms, we define states according to the number of points accumulated by an agent. Points have no intrinsic value to agents, but an agent who runs out of points must purchase more with money.

All the other parameters of our mechanisms are fixed and equal for all agents. We model agents' utility for money as $U(x) = A\ln(1 + \frac{x}{A})$. As A tends to infinity, U becomes linear; this allows us to observe changes as agents go from risk-aversion to risk-neutrality. This model of risk aversion is supported by experimental evidence; see, e.g., [6].

6.2 Learning Algorithm

We take an approach similar to that of fictitious play [4] to model the behavior of agents. Agents behave as if other agents' strategies were fixed (i.e., as though other agents do not act strategically), and make a best response based on their observations of other agents' actions. Although agent behavior is not strategic in this model, strategy convergence corresponds to a Nash equilibrium. This is because convergence corresponds to the situation where each agent's best response is to maintain his strategy, given the assumption that all other agents are fixed in their strategies. An agent could attempt to learn either the joint distribution of other agents' strategies, as in a fictitious play model, or the expected payoffs associated with its own strategies. In a sufficiently symmetric and regular world populated by sufficiently many agents, the joint distribution can safely be neglected. As P2P systems typically involve very large numbers of agents, agents in our model attempt to learn the payoffs associated with their own strategy, without modelling other agents.

Agents use the temporal difference (TD) Q-learning algorithm to learn these best responses. This algorithm learns the expected utilities of (state,action)-pairs (called Q-values). The best response is the action that gives the highest expected payoff. The Q-learning algorithm assumes that the environment does not evolve over time, but decay enables agents to also do well in a slowly changing environment. We use the standard update equation for TD Q-learning, $Q(a, s) \leftarrow (1 - \alpha)Q(a, s) + \alpha(P(a, s) + c \cdot \max_{a'} Q(a', s'))$, where a is the action that the agent took, s is the current state, s' is the new state and $P(a, s)$ is the payoff of the current round (both are chosen probabilistically by the model as a function of other agents' behavior). The decay $0 < \alpha < 1$ and the future income discount $0 < c < 1$ are fixed.

6.3   Experimental Results

First, our simulations confirm the existence of equilibria for the micro-payment and point-based mechanisms in the richer setting described above. These equilibria generalize those described in our analysis, giving evidence that our experimental assumptions are reasonable. Fig. 1 shows strategy convergence:

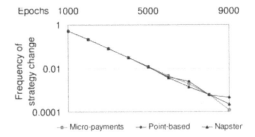

Fig. 1. Strategy convergence (logarithmic scale).

Second, we demonstrate that our model is complex enough to exhibit non-trivial effects. Fig. 2 shows the behavior of non-altruistic agents in the presence of altruistic agents under the point-based mechanism. As the proportion of altruistic agents increases from 0 to 1, non-altruistic agents discover that they can download more and therefore have to share more to compensate for the point cost of their downloads. Third, we tested the robustness of our simulations. Overall, we found the simulations to be quite robust: we observed qualitatively similar results under very different sets of parameters for the number and types of files and for the size of the action space for agents. Agents with a wider choice of actions (more options for downloads and sharing) achieve higher payoffs, but the results remain quantitatively the same. As an example, two runs of the experiment described above, with agents given 9 and 35 actions in their strategy spaces, produced essentially the same result (Fig. 2). Finally, we studied the influence of risk aversion on agent's behavior in the micro-payment scheme (Fig. 3). We plot the number of files shared in the system as a function of A, agents' value for money. As A decreases, agents become more risk-averse. We observed that risk-averse agents tend to cut their spending and scale down their contributions to the system because of their uncertainty about how many other agents will download their shared files.

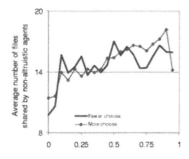

Fig. 2. Files shared as a function of the proportion of altruistic agents.

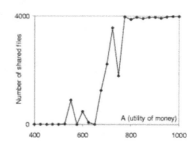

Fig. 3. Risk-aversion in micropayment mechanism.

7 Conclusion

The free-rider problem is a real issue for P2P systems, and is likely to become even more important in commercial systems. We have proposed a simple game theoretic model of agent behavior in centralized P2P systems and shown that our model predicts free riding in the original Napster mechanism. We analyzed several different payment mechanisms designed to encourage file sharing in P2P systems. Finally, we have presented experimental results supporting our theoretical analysis.

References

1. Secure digital music initiative. http://www.sdmi.org.
2. E. Adar and B. Huberman. Free riding on Gnutella. *First Monday*, 5(10), 2000.
3. N. Asokan. *Fairness in Electronic Commerce*. PhD thesis, University of Waterloo, Ontario, Canada, 1998.
4. D. Fudenberg and D. Levine. *The Theory of Learning in Games*. MIT Press, 1998.
5. D. Fudenberg and J. Tirole. *Game Theory*. MIT Press, 1991.
6. C. Grayson. *Decisions Under Uncertainty: Drilling Decisions by Oil & Gas Operators*. Ayer Company, 1979.
7. B. Macq, editor. *Special Issue on Identification and Protection of Multimedia Information*, volume 87(7), July 1999.
8. G. Marwell and R. Ames. Experiments in the provision of public goods: I. resources, interest, group size, and the free-rider problem. *American J. of Sociology*, 84, 1979.
9. A. M. Odlyzko. The history of communications and its implications for the Internet, 2000. Available online at http://www.research.att.com/~amo.
10. M.J. Osborne and A. Rubinstein. *A Course in Game Theory*. MIT Press, 1994.
11. S. Saroiu, P. Gummadi, and S. Gribble. Measurement study of peer-to-peer file sharing systems. Tech Report UW-CSE-01-06-02, University of Washington, 2001.
12. J. Sweeny. An experimental investigation of the free-rider problem. *Social Science Research*, 2, 1973.
13. B. Thorn and T. Connolly. Discretionary data bases. *Comm. Research*, 14(5), October 1987.

Mobile Payments –
State of the Art and Open Problems

Konrad Wrona[1], Marko Schuba[1], and Guido Zavagli[2]

[1] Ericsson Research, Ericsson Allee 1,
D-52134 Herzogenrath, Germany
{Marko.Schuba, Konrad.Wrona}@eed.ericsson.se
[2] Ericsson, Koraku Mori Building, 1-4-14 Koraku
Tokyo 112-0004, Japan,
Guido.Zavagli@nrj.ericsson.se

Abstract. We describe electronic payment solutions and the technical problems, which have to be solved in order to make these payments mobile. Mobile payments should be both secure and convenient for the consumer. The problems of implementing mobile payment systems are manifold. The technical capabilities of mobile devices are – at least today – too limited to allow a simple re-use of existing Internet payment protocols. Moreover, a number of different mobile application environments exist today, which differ from a technical perspective as well as from geographical spread. This makes it extremely difficult to define mobile payment protocols, which can be used on a global basis. Therefore, compromise solutions have to be found and standardized, which offer a reasonable level of security based on the existing functions offered in mobile devices and networks.

1 Introduction

Mobile commerce is seen as one of the enablers for the 3rd generation of mobile communication networks. A huge number of applications can be imagined for mobile commerce, including banking, shopping, betting, trading, ticketing, entertainment, gaming, and logistics. A lot of these applications will have one thing in common: in the end the consumer has to pay for services she has used or goods she has purchased. Thus, mobile payment will be one of the key services, which has to be deployed in mobile communication networks during the next years.

However, mobile payments face a number of problems, both from a technological and business point of view. First of all, the mobile devices are constrained with respect to cryptographic functionality, which is one of the main requirements for payment systems. There is also a difference in performance when mobile devices using a wireless link are compared to desktop computers connected over a fixed line to the Internet. Thus, it is not possible to access the existing payment infrastructure from a mobile device in the same way as from a PC. This makes it difficult to design a mobile pay-

L. Fiege, G. Mühl, and U. Wilhelm (Eds.): WELCOM 2001, LNCS 2232, pp. 88-100, 2001.

ment solution and furthermore requires a know-how exchange and co-operation between different stakeholders in the mobile network and electronic payment area.

This paper describes the current status of mobile payment systems and the problems, which are still open. Section 2 of the paper gives a general classification and some examples of electronic payment systems in the market today. In section 3 different forms of mobile networks and their limitations with regard to security and performance are described. Mobile payment systems in the market or under discussion today are explained in section 4. Section 5 gives a conclusion and a forecast for the market of mobile payment systems in the next years.

2 Electronic Payment Systems

2.1 Electronic Payment Models

Existing electronic payment systems used in data and telecommunication networks typically follow either a three party or a four party model. One party is the payer, i.e. the consumer who has an account agreement with a financial institution, for example with a bank. Another party is the payee, typically a retailer, who is paid for services or goods delivered to the payer. Whether the model consists of three or four parties depends on the payment provider, which could be either a single financial institution or a network of them. A very good example for this difference can be observed in the credit card market today:

- The three party model, i.e. the single financial institution, is what we observe at for instance American Express or Discover. Both of them handle card payments within single organizations, i.e. these companies are issuer to the cardholders and acquirer to the merchant at the same time.
- The four party model, i.e. the network of financial institutions, is what we observe e.g. at Visa or MasterCard. Both have a number of member banks, some of them issuing cards, others authorize and acquire the payments for merchants. Typically, there are in addition central operators, who co-ordinate authorizations, captures and clearings.

Although a number of different electronic payment systems exist today (e.g. several forms of account-transfer systems, check systems, token systems, see for instance [1] for an overview), the credit card is the preferred method of payment for most consumers. Therefore, the rest of this paper will concentrate mainly on this type of electronic payment method. There are two main protocols, which are used to secure online purchases with credit cards: the Secure Socket Layer (SSL) protocol, and the Secure Electronic Transaction (SET™) protocol. However, both protocols have some disadvantages, and therefore other payment systems for credit cards have been developed as well. The following section describes some of the most important protocols used for credit card payments.

2.2 Examples of Existing Payment Systems

Secure Socket Layer (SSL).

SSL [2] is actually no payment system in itself but has been developed for securing transport layer connections in the Internet. The protocol comprises among others data confidentiality, server authentication, and client authentication. The protocol is widely used to encrypt credit card or other payment information transmitted from a payer to a payee. The authentication part, especially the client authentication, is often omitted in order to make the payment process simpler for the consumer. The problem of using SSL for securing payments is the potential fraud, which might be caused through

- the misuse of credit card information sent to merchants (or servers pretending to be a merchant),
- or users, who pretend to be a cardholder by presenting valid credit card and other user information.

Secure Electronic Transaction (SET™).

SET has been developed mainly by the credit card industry to secure payment card transactions over open networks. SET has been published as open specification for the industry [3]. The current version of SET was designed for common desktop PCs as the typical user terminal, and with the Internet as the transport network. SET provides an electronic commerce infrastructure with a very robust security model that delivers confidentiality of information, integrity of data, interoperability, and certificate based authentication. Nevertheless, the success of SET has not yet fulfilled the high expectations. Two of the main reasons for this are

- complicated wallet installation and certificate download for consumers,
- and expensive software and hardware for merchants.

Both led to an increased acceptance problem of SET, often compared to the "chicken and egg problem". If there are no consumers using SET, merchants are not interested in installing SET. At the same time the consumer interest in SET will not increase, if there are no merchants offering SET as payment method.

In order to overcome the fraud problems of SSL and the acceptance problems of SET a number of alternative electronic payment systems for credit cards have been proposed recently: Three Domain (3D) Secure and EMV-based Chip Electronic Commerce.

Three Domain Secure.

Three Domain Secure actually consists of two different payment methods, namely Three Domain SSL (3D SSL) and Three Domain SET (3D SET) [4]. As the name suggests the system consists of three domains:

- an issuer domain,
- an acquirer domain,
- and an interoperability domain.

Issuer and acquirer are responsible for defining and managing the relationship with their customers, respectively. The interface between issuer and acquirer domain is supplied by the interoperability domain, which is operated by the credit card industry.

In 3D SSL the security between the communicating parties is achieved mainly by using SSL connections. The issuer digitally signs payment requests on the behalf of the cardholder, thereby providing the merchant with a guarantee of payment. Before signing the payment request, the issuer must ensure that it is talking to the correct customer through an authentication mechanism of its choice, which makes this approach rather flexible. The message flow of a 3D SSL transaction is depicted in Fig. 1.

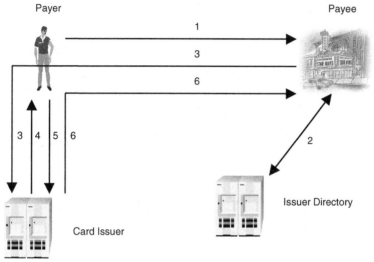

Fig. 1. Three Domain SSL transaction flow.

The basic steps of a 3D SSL transaction are as follows:
1. The user submits a checkout page using an SSL connection.
2. The merchant checks an issuer directory to obtain a URL for the specific card.
3. The merchant redirects the cardholder to the issuer and provides a payment request message.
4. The issuer displays a window to the cardholder, which contains the payment details and requests entry of a secret authentication code.
5. The cardholder enters the secret code. If successful, the issuer will sign the payment message.
6. The issuer redirects the cardholder to the merchant and provides a signed response message

The merchant validates and stores the issuer's signature and processes the transaction.

The 3D SET approach adapts the standard SET protocol to the Three Domain concept by implementing a so-called SET Wallet Server solution. The idea in this concept is to let the issuing bank perform the SET transactions on behalf of the cardholder, i.e. the issuer hosts the SET Wallet. The following steps describe the basic SET Wallet Server concept, which is quite similar to 3D SSL except the usage of SET as payment method (see also Figure 2):

1. The user selects SET as payment mechanism on the merchant's web page.
2. The merchant sends a SET Wake-up message to the cardholder.
3. The cardholder's browser redirects this message to the issuer's SET Wallet Server.
4. The issuer displays a window to the cardholder that displays the payment details and requests entry of a secret authentication code.
5. The cardholder enters the secret code. If successful, the issuer will perform the respective SET transaction on the user's behalf.
6. After the transaction the issuer redirects the cardholder back to the merchant.

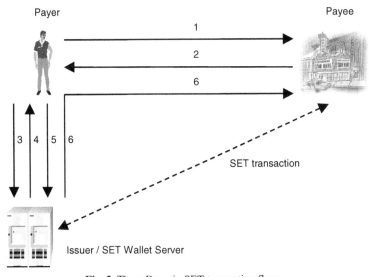

Fig. 2. Three Domain SET transaction flow.

To assure the security of user information, the SET Wallet Server keeps the user's information in a highly secured tamper-resistant hardware system.

EMV.
Europay, MasterCard, and Visa (EMV) jointly developed specifications, which define a set of requirements to ensure interoperability between integrated circuit cards (smart cards) and terminals on a global basis, regardless of manufacturer, financial institution, or location of card usage [5]. The combination of the card's tamper-resistance with asymmetric (public key) and symmetric (shared key) cryptographic operations allow for a high level of security in EMV card transactions:

- asymmetric security mechanisms authenticate the smart card as a valid card to the terminal,
- symmetric security mechanisms generate and verify transaction cryptograms (essentially Message Authentication Codes, MACs) based on a key shared between card and issuer.

Chip Electronic Commerce.

Chip Electronic Commerce is a part of the EMV 2000 specification [5]. It defines the use of a smart card application to conduct a credit or debit transaction in an electronic commerce environment using SET compliant software. Chip Electronic Commerce combines the EMV functions with the Secure Electronic Transaction specification to provide a protocol for secure smart card based transactions over the Internet. It takes advantage of two enhancements to the SET protocol:

- SET Common Chip Extension: extends the SET protocol to support the transport of smart card related data.
- Online PIN extension: extends the SET protocol to support the online transport of a cardholder's PIN.

In addition, Chip Electronic Commerce extends the SET specification by supporting two key features of EMV smart card applications:

- Online card authentication, through the use of a cryptogram.
- Cardholder verification, through the use of an optional cardholder PIN.

Chip Electronic Commerce does not require any modification to EMV-compliant smart cards.

3 Mobile Technology and Its Limitations

During the last couple of years, a number of mobile application environments have emerged in different geographic areas of the world. Europe for instance focuses on the Wireless Application Protocol (WAP), Japan is very successful with the i-mode system, and North America offers a number of systems as well. Besides a lot of technical differences, there are some common, mobile specific characteristics, which cause some problems to the implementation of mobile payment systems. The provided security, especially with respect to the functions offered at application layer, is weaker than in fixed networks. Additionally, the performance of the devices is naturally limited because the systems have to operate wirelessly.

3.1 Mobile Payments - Security Limitations

All the mobile application environments mentioned above rely on a two-tier transport layer security model, where the secure connection between a mobile terminal and a service provider consists actually of two independent secure connections: one between service provider and mobile operator and one between mobile operator and mobile user. This model, involving two separate security domains, has important consequences for the implementation of secure mobile applications. The most important implication is that every secure transaction involves three separate entities (i.e. provider, operator and user) and thus requires both provider and user to trust the additional middleman (i.e. operator). This trust is required for the following reasons:

- None of the end parties (i.e. provider and user) can be sure that its connection is really continued in the secure way behind the operator proxy.

- The content of the connection is being decrypted and encrypted in the operator's proxy, making it vulnerable to possible attacks by both "trusted" operator or third parties (i.e. hackers). The end parties have to trust the operator to ensure and enforce an adequate security policy concerning both remote and physical access to the proxy server and its premises.
- No end-to-end authentication is possible.

The predominant technology used on the provider-operator link is the SSL protocol. The way in which messages, if at all, are secured on the link between mobile operator and mobile user depends on the mobile application environment and class of device being involved. For WAP, the Wireless Transport Layer Security (WTLS) protocol is being used. HDML uses a form of an encrypted Handheld Device Transport Protocol. I-mode offers no data encryption between the mobile terminal and the operator's proxy at all, though SSL can be used between the operator's and the service provider's domain. With i-appli it is possible to have an SSL connection to the mobile device, but this is restricted to Java phones. GoAmerica, Palm and others implement proprietary transport layer security protocols, mostly based on elliptic curve cryptosystems.

At least some level of end-to-end security can be provided in WAP by using WMLScript with cryptographic API. Currently, there is only one WMLScript cryptographic API function defined, signText(), which provides users with an ability of signing text messages. This can be used for simple user authentication and contract signing. Unfortunately, the WMLScript programs are sent through the operator's gateway, so there is no guarantee that it will not be skipped or modified on its way to the user. Even if the operator is a trustworthy entity, there are several ways of impersonating e.g. a merchant server. Because WAP lacks higher layer server authentication a user has no way of authenticating the source of a signing request, which makes him vulnerable to classical man-in-the-middle attacks. An attacker can masquerade as a legitimate server and request the user to sign contracts/challenges, which then can be used to authenticate some bogus transactions on behalf of the user. In case of a simple password-based authentication, an attacker can generate a WML-interface identical to the legitimate server pages and elude in this way the user to disclose her password or authentication information, which can be used for authentication in subsequent transactions.

Some application developers rely on building custom applications in order to provide security through additional authentication handshakes etc., but this would require support by the phone which cannot be expected – at least in the mass market – for the next couple of years. A simpler approach, which would offer application layer security with existing WAP devices, is to implement basic cryptographic functionality with WMLScript arithmetic operations. This is important - especially in the short-term - since most of the WAP terminals available today belong to the so-called WTLS class 0 terminals, which literally means that they do not implement WTLS at all and thus provide no transport layer security. However, a drawback of this approach is the possibility of man-in-the-middle attacks like in the signText() case, because neither server nor content authentication exists with this kind of terminals.

3.2 Mobile Payments - Performance Limitations

Apart from the security limitations mobile payment systems also have to consider the inherent performance problems of the mobile environment. Firstly, the bearer service in wireless networks is rather limited when compared to fixed networks, i.e. less bandwidth, longer latencies and more errors. Secondly, cheap mobile devices produced for the mass market have several restrictions, e.g. concerning the input and output of data (small keyboard and display), processing power, and memory. Thus, payment protocols suitable for desktop computers in fixed networks cannot be deployed in wireless systems without modification. To illustrate this problem let us take a closer look at the time, which would be required to perform a SET transaction with a mobile device.

Measurements of example messages exchanged by the SET protocol led to an overall of 18608 bytes, which are transmitted between the cardholder and the merchant. On a 9600 bps link the transmission of this amount of data would require about 15 s. Note that 9600 bps is what is typically used for WAP and i-mode today. This time neither includes the processing time of messages at cardholder or merchant, nor does it consider the payment initiation messages, which have to be exchanged just before the SET transaction starts.

According to the SET specification the processing of a SET transaction at the client requires the following cryptographic operations:
- four random numbers have to be generated,
- eight SHA-1 hash operations,
- one signature with an 1024 bit RSA private key,
- three to eight decrypt operations with 1024 bit RSA public keys,
- and one padding operation according to Optimal Asymmetric Encryption Padding (OAEP).

Although it is possible to implement such cryptographic functions in mobile devices, not all of them are supported or available to applications today. Moreover, the processing is rather time consuming if no cryptographic hardware is available. Additional delays will result from the processing at the merchant and bank systems, and from the communication between those.

All in all it can be expected that the sum of transmission time and processing time will exceed the time consumers are willing to accept for mobile transactions.

3.3 Functional Model of a Mobile Commerce Terminal

The ultimate goal of a mobile commerce system is to provide mobile users with an ability to perform every possible electronic commerce transaction in a simple, fast and secure way, anytime and anywhere. In order to fulfill these expectations, sophisticated mechanisms and protocols have to be employed by all involved parties. From the user's point of view the most important and visible is the structure of a mobile terminal. Fig. 3 presents a functional model of a terminal designed with mobile commerce application in mind.

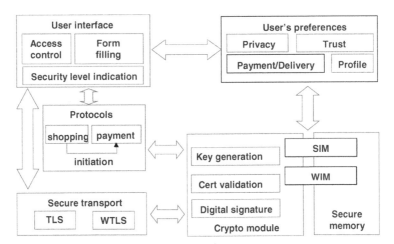

Fig. 3. Functional model of a mobile terminal designed for mobile commerce applications.

In addition to transport layer security protocols, i.e. TLS and WTLS, it is important to provide an access to basic cryptographic primitives from the application layer. Commonly used cryptographic algorithms, e.g. SHA-1, 3DES or, in future, AES, can be implemented in the terminal. More complicated functions, required by a particular mobile commerce application, can be downloaded to the terminal in a form of an authenticated script.

Almost every electronic commerce application requires user to perform some operations using a secret data, e.g. digital signature or cryptogram generation, or to disclose some confidential information, e.g. credit card information. Thus, the terminal must be equipped with tamper resistant memory and access control mechanisms.

A public-key infrastructure used for mobile commerce must support efficient mechanisms for certificate management, i.e. issuing, distribution and revocation, as well as certificate validation.

Last but not least, the user interface should provide easy access to the security mechanisms and intuitive information about the security level of the current transaction. Very important is providing protection against attackers imitating services belonging to legitimate providers. The very limited user interface in mobile devices makes such masquerading attacks even simpler than in case of fixed Internet, where they have already been employed successfully.

4   Mobile Payment Systems

As a result of the previous section two types of payment solutions are feasible for implementation in the mobile environment:

- *proxy solutions*, which allow access of existing payment protocol through the use of a proxy server in the fixed network,

- and *non-proxy solutions*, i.e. payment protocols designed specifically for the capabilities of mobile devices.

The decision for a proxy or a non-proxy solution for mobile systems often originates from a business model.

4.1 Mobile Payment Systems with Proxy

The business model of a proxy solution is typically driven by the fact that there is already an expensive payment infrastructure in place, which cannot be changed cheaply. Usually this infrastructure is already in use for fixed network customers. Changing the payment protocol in the infrastructure in order to support mobile payments would require not only changes to the protocol itself, but also to all the software installations at fixed network clients. For a widely used system this is unacceptable.

A simple solution to support mobile payments without the change of the existing infrastructure is the use of a proxy between the mobile device and the payment infrastructure. The task of the proxy is to behave like a usual payment client towards the infrastructure while using mobile technology for authentication of the mobile customer and authorization of the payment.

Several proxy-based payment systems have been developed in the last couple of years and especially the standardization bodies in the mobile and financial industry seem to go for this type of solution. The following sections describe some proposals of proxy architectures for mobile credit card payments.

3D SET for Mobiles.

In order to allow a 3D SET transaction with a mobile device, the mobile user has to authenticate herself towards the SET Wallet Server hosting her credit card information. Assuming that the trust relation between the user and the SET Wallet Server is already established, this concept has several advantages, when used in the mobile environment:

- The mobile station does not need to process the SET transaction itself. It triggers the transaction at the SET Wallet Server, which then performs the SET processes. Finally, the SET Wallet Server sends back the result of the SET transaction to the mobile station.
- There are only a few and small messages exchanged over the air interface between the mobile station and the SET Wallet Server.
- A better performance can be reached by extending the equipment of the SET Wallet Server, e.g. special hardware for cryptographic purposes can be installed.
- The solution provides high portability by introducing a unique trigger protocol between the mobile station and SET Wallet Server.
- If there is a new release of SET software, this update must be done only centrally at the SET Wallet Server.

Besides the benefits listed above, some disadvantages must be accepted:

- The users must grant full trust to the SET Wallet Server.

- The private key, public key, certificates, and other information of the cardholders will be lost at once by successful attacks to the SET Wallet Server.
- The SET Wallet Server can trace the user's buying customs and build a detailed user profile.

Mobile Chip Electronic Commerce.
Mobile Chip Electronic Commerce is a mobile adaptation of the Chip Electronic Commerce specification and is based also on a proxy architecture [8]. The cardholder part of the original architecture is divided into a Mobile Chip Electronic Commerce Client and a Mobile Chip Electronic Commerce Server (the proxy). The server performs the main part of the protocol. It checks certificates of the involved parties, compiles the transaction messages and exchanges these messages with the merchant. The task of the client is to provide the security operations required in the transaction like authentication of the user or authorization of the payment transaction (achieved by an EMV cryptogram calculated on a smart card). As in other proxy architectures the splitting of functionality between client and server not only substantially limits the processing load on the mobile device, but also reduces the traffic on the wireless link.

4.2 Mobile Payment Systems without Proxy

Apart from the well-established financial industry, mobile payments also offer the opportunity for new or formerly non-financial companies to grab a share of the mobile commerce business. These companies do not have an expensive payment infrastructure in place, so they can afford to build new protocols, which take the specific constraints of mobile payments into account, and therefore require no proxy. Most often, the systems implement a three party model, with the payment provider being issuer and acquirer at the same time.

Paybox.
Paybox is an example of a class of mobile payment systems, which have emerged in different countries in the last time. The Paybox system is currently only available in Germany, but the rollout for several other European countries is planned. The system allows payments from a mobile phone to Internet shops, to mobile retailers (e.g. taxi drivers), and to other mobile phone users. It is a three party system and the mobile user needs a bank or credit card account to which the transaction amount is debited/credited. A Paybox transaction basically consists of the following steps:
1. The payee contacts the Paybox system via telephone or data network.
2. The payee says/transmits the amount and the mobile telephone number of the payer.
3. The payer is called back immediately and has to authorize the payment with a PIN.
4. The amount is transferred from the account of the payer to the account of the payee.
   The security of the system corresponds to the security of the telephone system. No additional data security is introduced.

Mobile Operator Payment Systems.

A number of mobile operators try to get into the payment market as well. On the first sight, it looks very easy for them, because mobile network operators have

- a large customer basis,
- a billing infrastructure, which could be used for invoicing payments to customers,
- control over the SIM card (at least in GSM systems) and thus the possibility to implement necessary security functions,
- and they already provide portal services to customers, which can be easily extended to support the operator specific payment system.

The actual installation of a payment system is thus rather simple for operators. On the other hand, such a payment system has all the drawbacks of a three party system. The user is bound to a single operator although most users want to have access to online services and shops worldwide. In order to have an open solution, co-operation between different providers including an interoperability protocol is required.

5 Conclusions

This paper described the technology and problems of mobile payment systems. The mobile specific problems can be overcome either by proxy or non-proxy solutions, depending on whether these systems rely on an existing payment infrastructure or define a new payment protocol specifically designed for mobiles.

Right now the focus of standardization bodies seems to be on proxy systems. The relevant technological requirements are currently under discussion, for example the redirection to a wallet server. In this context 3D SET is a promising candidate for mobile credit card transactions, because this approach is considered in all major initiatives.

There is also a chance for operators to be successful with their own payment solutions. These should, however, concentrate on mobile specific payments in the first place, e.g. phone-to-phone payments, and should also include an interoperability protocol between different operators. The existing roaming and billing systems might offer a good platform for such payment systems.

References

1. R. Weber, "Chablis – Market Analysis of Digital Payment Systems", Technical Report TUM-I9819, Technical University of Munich, August 1999.
2. A. O. Freier, P. Karlton, P. C. Kocher, "The SSL Protocol - Version 3.0", Internet Draft, March 1996, http://home.netscape.com/eng/ssl3/ssl-toc.html
3. "SET Secure Electronic Transaction Specification, Book One: Business Description. Version 1.0", SETCo, http://www.setco.org/
4. T. Trench, K. Wrona, "Card Payment Transactions in an m-Commerce Environment Feasibility Study", August 2000.
   http://www1.wapforum.org/member/wg/ecomeg/p200009_Card_Payment_Study.doc.
5. "EMV2000 Integrated Circuit Card Specification for Payment Systems, Book 3: Application Specification. Draft Version 4.0", EMVCo, http://www.emvco.com/

6. "Wireless Application Protocol Architecture Specification. Version 30. April 2000, http://www.wapforum.org.
7. K. Wrona, G. Zavagli, "Adaptation of the Secure Electronic Transaction Protocol to Mobile Networks and WAP", Proceedings of European Wireless '99, pp. 193-198, Berlin: VDE Verlag, 1999, http://www1.wapforum.org/member/wg/ecomeg/d001_SET_for_WAP.pdf
8. M. Schuba, K. Wrona, "Mobile Chip Electronic Commerce: Enabling Credit Card Payment for Mobile Devices", Proceedings of eBiz-2000 Specialist Conference, June 2000, Singapore, http://www1.wapforum.org/member/wg/ecomeg/d002_Credit_Card_for_Mobile.doc.

Using Smart Cards for Fair Exchange

Holger Vogt*, Henning Pagnia, and Felix C. Gärtner

Department of Computer Science
Darmstadt University of Technology
D-64283 Darmstadt, Germany
{holgervo|pagnia|felix}@informatik.tu-darmstadt.de

Abstract. Fair exchange protocols ensure that the participating parties, customer and vendor, can engage in electronic commerce transactions without the risk of suffering a disadvantage. This means that neither of them delivers his digital item without receiving the other party's item. In general, fair exchange cannot be solved without the help of a *trusted third party* (TTP), a dedicated computer which is trusted by both participants. Trust can be established by carefully securing the TTP or even better by introducing tamper-proof hardware. However, if the communication to the TTP is unreliable or disrupted, then the exchange cannot be performed in a timely fashion or not at all. Up to now, this has been a problem especially for the exchange of time-sensitive items, i.e., items which lose value over time. We present a novel approach to perform fair exchange using tamper-poof hardware on the customer's side. More specifically, co-located to the customer's machine we use a smart card which partially takes over the role of the TTP. The challenge of designing protocols in this environment lies in the fact that the communication between the smart card and the vendor is under control of the customer. Our approach has the following benefits: It supports the exchange in mobile environments where customers frequently experience a disconnection from the network. Furthermore, our approach is the first to handle time-sensitive items properly.

1 Introduction

The central vision of electronic commerce is to advertise, sell, and deliver goods via electronic networks like the Internet. While many of these goods, like clothing, books or CDs, still have to be shipped to the customer by using traditional postal services, an increasing amount of business transactions today cover intangible goods, i.e., digital items like software, music files, or electronic documents. In these cases, the exchange can be performed *entirely* over the electronic network. Not only does this service usually offer near to instantaneous delivery of the desired item to the customer, it is often also more cost effective for the

---

* This author's work was supported by the Deutsche Forschungsgemeinschaft (DFG) as part of the PhD program (Graduiertenkolleg) "Enabling Technologies for Electronic Commerce" at Darmstadt University of Technology.

L. Fiege, G. Mühl, and U. Wilhelm (Eds.): WELCOM 2001, LNCS 2232, pp. 101–113, 2001.

vendor. The customer and vendor normally begin their business relationship in a state of mutual distrust, often even without knowing each other's identity. Therefore it is important that the exchange is performed *fairly*, i.e., in such a way that neither party is in danger of suffering a disadvantage. This led to the development of network protocols that allow the *fair exchange* of digital items over electronic networks [3,7,10,2,1,8].

Fair exchange protocols are not easy to design in environments like the Internet where the quality of service of the network is rather unpredictable. If a vendor sends a music file to a customer, there is no guarantee that it will reach its destination within a certain time. Consequently, fair exchange protocols operating in these types of environments can merely guarantee *eventual delivery* of an item. Eventual delivery though is too weak for *time-sensitive items*, i.e., items that lose value over time. Examples are location dependant information in mobile environments. For instance, consider the case where Alice is walking through New York and through her mobile device requests information about restaurants in the area of 5th Avenue and 42th Street. While waiting for the reply Alice continues to walk around town, but as the information appears on her display, she has already reached the far end of Central Park. Alice is reluctant to walk all the way back and so the information is of little value to her now. However, the service provider has already billed her the full price of the service. Such items which lose their value over time are called *time-sensitive* [1]. In general, location based services in mobile environments offer time-sensitive information. Stock exchange data is another example for this type of information. The handling of this class of items is considered to be difficult [1, p. 33].

Another aspect which makes fair exchange such a difficult problem is *security*. Because of mutual distrust in distributed business environments, protocols must rely on *trusted intermediary* to enable the fair exchange. Such an intermediary is a dedicated computer which is usually called *trusted third party* (TTP) or *trustee*. The machine either actively participates in the exchange or is used to resolve a dispute in case something went wrong. In any cases it is important that both parties which engage in a fair exchange *trust* this machine, i.e., they have reason to believe that it will correctly follow its protocol. This is however difficult to achieve if the computer is, for example, located at the vendor's office since there is no guarantee that the hard- and software has not been tampered with. This has given rise to the use of *trusted tamper-proof hardware* in fair exchange protocols such as the *trusted processing environment* (TPE) [9] to solve fair exchange with mobile agents [6].

Today, tamper-proof hardware to implement a TPE (like the IBM 4758 PCI card [4]) is available but, unfortunately, it is also quite expensive. On the other hand, smart cards, a different form of tamper-proof hardware, are rather cheap but their limited memory and processing power makes them unsuitable for implementing a full-blown TPE. Karjoth [5] has shown that in some cases a fully featured TPE is not required to perform certain business transactions. The idea here is that only *critical operations* (like encrypting or signing messages) need to be performed on trusted hardware while a lot of processing work can be performed through untrusted hardware handling solely encrypted items. The question which we pursue in this paper is the following: How can fair exchange be implemented with smart cards in a mobile computing environment?

Designing protocols under the above design goals is difficult due to the restricted processing power of smart cards. Another problem to consider is the potential mobility of the users which can lead to temporary disconnection from the network. Throughout this paper, we consider the case where a vendor sells a digital item to a mobile customer who pays for it electronically. We develop solutions for fair exchange under the assumption that the customer has access to a tamper-proof smart card.

Our contributions are manyfold. We are the first to investigate the use of smart cards for exchanging arbitrary items. Especially, we show that the use of smart cards results in efficient protocols which can properly handle the exchange of time-sensitive information, whereas in previous protocols, a customer has no guarantees when a desired time-sensitive item is received. Our protocols for time-sensitive items can be decomposed into two phases. During the first phase the item and the payment are uploaded onto the smart card, checked and the payment is transmitted to the vendor. During the second phase the smart card hands out the item to the customer only if the customer is still interested in it. Note that the second phase can be executed without being connected to the network as only local communication is required. This explains why our protocols are very suitable in mobile environments and for exchanging time-sensitive items. If the customer rejects the item in the second phase, it is essential to roll back the exchange.

The paper is structured as follows: We first recall the basic terminology of fair exchange in Section 2 and then present the system assumptions, smart card properties as well as a basic solution for hardware-supported fair exchange in Section 3. In Section 4 we present extended exchange protocols which ensure fairness even for time-sensitive items. Section 5 concludes the paper.

2   Fair Exchange Concepts

We follow the definitions and presentation of Asokan [1] with modifications made by Vogt, Pagnia, and Gärtner [8] to present the problem of fair exchange. In a fair exchange there are two participating parties and each party starts with an electronic item and a formal description of what that party would like to receive in exchange for its own item. In our case the first party is a vendor V offering an arbitrary electronic item (e.g., a text or music file) and the second party is the customer C who is willing to pay for the item with electronic money. A *fair exchange protocol* is a protocol which implements the following three requirements between V and C:

1. **Effectiveness:** If both parties behave according to the protocol and both items match the description then, when the protocol has completed, C has received V's item and V has received the payment from C.

2. **Termination:** The protocol will terminate for any party which behaves correctly (i.e., according to the protocol).
3. **Fairness:**[1] If one party does not behave according to the protocol or if one item does not match the description, no participant will win or lose anything valuable.

As noted in the introduction, fair exchange protocols rely on the services of a TTP, which is trusted by both participants. One way to implement fair exchange is to use an active TTP which receives the two items, checks them, and forwards them to the respective parties. Since this makes the TTP a bottleneck of an e-commerce system, protocols have been devised in which the two parties try to complete the exchange on their own and where the TTP only comes into play if something went wrong. Such *optimistic* protocols [2] are quite efficient, as no TTP is used in the faultless case. All fair exchange protocols presented in the following sections belong to this efficient class of protocols.

3   Fair Exchange Using Smart Cards

In this section, we describe an approach to perform fair exchange using smart cards. We first describe general assumptions we make about the system and its communication. Then we sketch some necessary requirements of the used smart card. Next we present the basic protocol for fair exchange. Finally, we show how such a protocol can be implemented efficiently.

3.1   System Assumptions

The system in which we consider fair exchange is sketched in Figure 1. We assume that both customer and vendor are connected through a communication network (e.g., the Internet) and that the customer's machine is equipped with some form of trusted hardware device (a smart card in the figure). The customer's machine can be a mobile phone, a personal digital assistant (PDA), a laptop computer

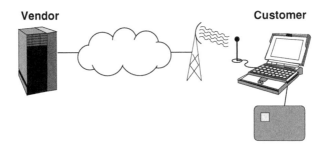

Vendor   **Customer**

Fig. 1. Smart card support for the exchange of money and goods.

---

[1] Our definition of fairness corresponds to the definition of *strong fairness* in [2].

or specialized hardware like a car navigation system. The trusted hardware device can be embedded into the above items but it can also be attached through an interface mechanism (like a card reader). However, throughout the paper we restrict our attention to smart cards. Smart cards are widely used for authentication, issuing digital signatures, or making payments. The main reason for implementing exchange protocols on a smart card is that it is usually assumed to be tamper-resistant, which means that it protects secret keys even from the owner of the smart card. The card possesses a distinguished interface, meaning that only predefined operations can be invoked with carefully chosen input and output parameters. Invoking the interface operations is usually only possible, while a smart card is placed within a card reader which is connected to a regular computer. For the smart card this also is the only way to communicate with the vendor.

The communication between all participants and the smart card is expected to be secure, i.e., cryptographic mechanisms are used to protect the integrity and confidentiality of messages. We assume that an attacker and especially the owner of the smart card is limited to the following attacks: The attacker can disrupt the communication with the smart card at any point of time. Data stored by the participants may be deleted or modified. The smart card may permanently be disconnected or even be damaged by the owner, which destroys the smart card's state information. In contrast, eavesdropping, replay, and forging of messages are assumed to be impossible.

A crucial part of fair exchange protocols is the ability to check whether the received item really is the expected item. The effort for this verification strongly depends on the exchanged item. Consider for example a software package for which its hash value is publicly known. The received item is correct, if it hashes to the known value. Other examples are items like digital concert tickets or electronic cheques that consist of a digital signature on a certain message. Such a signature can be checked by a smart card, if it knows the public key for verifying the signature. A thorough discussion about the verification of items can be found in [6].

3.2 Smart Card Requirements

If a smart card shall support the fair exchange of digital items, we have to presume that it fulfills the following requirements:

Tamper-resistance: The smart card must be protected so that it is impossible to read out secret data or to change the behavior of the card. This must even be true, if an attacker has physical access to the smart card.

Trust and authenticity of messages: Customer and vendor must be sure that the card correctly executes the algorithms, e.g., processes all requests correctly. As most people will not be able to verify the functionality of such a card, they will have to trust the issuer of the device that it always works as it is supposed to. To this end, anybody connecting to this card must be able to check the authenticity of all messages generated by it. This can be achieved, if the smart card contains a private key to generate digital signatures. The corresponding public key for the card's signature must be certified by some trusted authority, probably the issuer of the smart card. Any party communicating with the smart card can then verify whether a message is unaltered and has been created by the smart card itself.

Furthermore, a smart card should be able to identify the sender of messages by using digital signatures. Therefore the card must possess some built-in authentication information, e.g., the public key of a trusted certification authority. It can then validate whether the customer's or the vendor's public key certificate was issued by this authority. This prevents the smart card from being fooled by somebody who claims to be somebody else.

Reliable state information: The smart card must be able to send signed messages describing its current state. A party communicating with the card thus has a simple and reliable method to verify the state of the card which is especially useful after communication has been disrupted and must be re-established. The smart card will provide trustworthy state information supporting the correct execution of the protocol.

Additionally, we assume that the state together with the currently processed data is stored persistently on the card and that shutting down the power supply will not cause any loss of information.

3.3   The Basic Protocol

Our basic fair exchange protocol is given in Table 1. It is an optimistic protocol in the sense that it does not require an *external* TTP in the faultless case. It enables the exchange of arbitrary items with any kind of electronic payment without any assumption about the item or the payment. In contrast, the best known optimistic protocols *without* trusted hardware cannot exchange *arbitrary* items, as they need additional assumptions to ensure fairness [1, p. 25].

Table 1. Fair exchange between the customer C and the vendor V using the customer's smart card S.

1a. V → S	: item, description
1b. C → S	: payment, description
2. S	: check item, check payment
3. S → V	: payment
4. V	: check payment
5. V → S	: acknowledge payment
6. S → C	: item

The protocol starts with the vendor V sending the item and the customer C delivering the payment to the smart card S. The card will abort the exchange in step 2, if the item or the payment does not match the description of what both parties expect. The verified payment is transferred to the vendor, who also checks its validity. If an on-line payment system is used, the vendor additionally has to deposit the payment at the bank to verify it. The vendor then sends a notification to the smart card, whether he accepted the payment. Finally, the smart card delivers the item in step 6, if the vendor accepted the payment.

If the smart card does not receive an acknowledgment from the vendor or if the vendor falsely claims the payment to be invalid, the customer can instruct the smart card to resolve the exchange to ensure fairness. There are three alternatives how the smart card will react on such a request of the customer. If the smart card has not yet sent the payment to the vendor in step 3, the smart card simply deletes the item and the payment. If the item has been delivered to the customer in step 6, a resolve request will be ignored, as the exchange has already been finished successfully. In all other cases the help of an external TTP is needed. For simplicity we assume that the bank B offers the trusted third party services so that no additional communication between the bank and another party is needed.

The protocol for resolving such a conflict utilizes the fact that the smart card stores the vendor's item after it passed the test in step 2. To ensure fairness the customer must not be able himself to instruct the smart card to release this item. Instead the bank has the power to do so.

Table 2. The customer starts this conflict resolution protocol, if he does not receive an acknowledgment from the vendor.

5'. $C \rightarrow S$: tell to resolve the exchange
6'. $S \rightarrow B$: payment
7'. B : check and deposit payment
8'. $B \rightarrow S$: acknowledge payment
9'. $S \rightarrow C$: item

The protocol for resolving an exchange is displayed in Table 2. The smart card connects to the bank and sends it the payment. The bank deposits the money on the vendor's account (if it has not already been deposited by the vendor himself) and notifies the smart card about this. After receiving the bank's acknowledgment the smart card releases the item, which guarantees that both parties get the expected items and that the fair exchange is finished successfully.

3.4   Efficiency Considerations

Compared to other computing devices like a PC, smart cards have only limited storage and computing power. Therefore, items which allocate a huge amount of storage or which require an extensive computation for checking their correctness might cause problems. To overcome these limitations, we suggest the following measures, which can in principle be applied to any fair exchange protocol that relies on trusted hardware.

External storage of items. The persistent storage of a smart card is limited to a few kilobytes today, which prevents it from saving larger items on the card. This can be circumvented if the smart card stores an item as in the following example: The smart card receives and processes the item. Subsequently it outputs the item encrypted to the customer's computer that simply saves it to its hard disk. If needed again later, the smart card can request the item from the computer.

The smart card must remember the decryption key for this item, and additionally it should store a hash value of the item, which can be compared to the hash value of the data received from the customer's computer at a later point of time. Then the smart card can be sure that it will get the same encrypted item back.

Using the described mechanism the storage requirements can be reduced significantly. However, we have to take care that we do not create another bottleneck: The communication speed of the smart card is not very high so that we should avoid sending the same data back and forth. E.g. if in step 1a of Table 1 the vendor sends the item, it would be inefficient to first read it by the smart card and then output it to the customer's computer. Instead, such a protocol step, where the smart card only receives an item without immediately processing it, should be implemented as follows: The vendor encrypts the item and transmits it to the customer's computer, where it is stored for later use. The decryption key is sent to the smart card, which stores this key. In contrast to the first solution the smart card is not able to compute a hash value. We can compensate this, if both the customer and the vendor compute the hash value of the encrypted item and send it to the smart card, which only accepts if both parties sent the same hash value. Then neither the vendor nor the customer can cheat by sending a hash value that does not match the delivered encrypted item.

Deferred Verification. Another limitation of a smart card is its computing power. It can happen that the verification of item or payment exceeds the computing power of a smart card and that it would take unacceptably long to finish this computation. Thus, it is important to minimize the amount of computation, which the smart card spends for verifying the items.

The main idea is to *defer* verification and proceed with the protocol as if the verification had been successful. If this assumption is right (in most cases it should be this way), the outcome of the exchange will satisfy both parties. Otherwise, one party will detect a failure during the exchange and start a special protocol for resolving this problem. Then there are two possibilities of how to solve the conflict: First, we can provide the smart card with the item, which is then verified inside the card. Now it might be acceptable to wait a longer time till the verification finishes, as we assume that such problems do not occur often. However, if the smart card cannot execute the verification, we can also transfer this task to a trusted third party. We simply send the item to an external TTP, which checks its validity. For the external TTP the verification will be much easier, as it is usually implemented using a high-speed server, which has several orders of magnitude more processing power and main memory. The result of the verification is sent back to the smart card, which now acts on behalf of this result, because it can always trust the TTP's computations.

As an example we can apply this technique to the exchange protocol of Table 1: We can skip the checking of the payment in step 2, as the vendor will always detect an invalid payment in step 4. If the vendor claims the payment to be invalid in step 5, the customer can send the payment either to the smart card, which resumes the exchange in step 2 with checking the payment, or to an external TTP. This latter case leads in principle to the same solution as shown in Table 2, where the bank B acting as the TTP checks the payment and forwards the result to the smart card, which either aborts the exchange due to an invalid payment or otherwise reveals the item.

3.5   Discussion

Our approach demonstrates that a smart card is able to partly provide services of a trusted third party. If the smart card performs the checks of the item, the resulting decision can be trusted by both, the customer and the vendor. But besides trust, we also have to consider availability: In a mobile scenario the communication link is not always very stable and the customer might be disconnected after he has sent the payment. Although it is ensured that he will get the item as soon as he can build up a connection to the vendor or the bank, such a time delay is unacceptable, if the item is time-sensitive. Thus, we additionally propose fair exchange protocols, which guarantee the timely delivery of such items.

4   Fair Exchange of Time-Sensitive Data

Fair exchange of time-sensitive data is a difficult problem via unreliable networks. The main drawback of previously published solutions without secure hardware is that it is impossible to provably record the time at which messages are received. A party can therefore always claim that it has received the item after it has lost its value.

In our solution the owner of the smart card decides locally at a certain point of time whether he wants to finish the exchange right now or whether he is not interested anymore. As the decision is made locally, the customer is independent from the time delay that messages from and to other parties have.

In this section we focus on the purchase of time-sensitive items and propose a modification of the basic protocol from Section 3. In particular we require *revocable payments* to resolve an interrupted exchange. Subsequently we refine our exchange protocol so that it minimizes the time delay between the vendor sending the item and the customer deciding whether he wants it or not.

4.1   A Protocol Extension for Time-Sensitive Items

In our extended protocol (see Table 3) we require revocability of payments. The solution works with any payment system that supports revocation by a trustee, particularly we are not restricted to payment systems based on secure hardware.

Table 3. The extended protocol for fair exchange of time-sensitive items.

1a. V → S : item, description
1b. C → S : payment, description
2.   S   : check item, check payment
3. S → V : payment
4.   V   : check payment
5. V → S : acknowledge payment
6. S → C : ask, if the item is still valuable
7. C → S : tell to proceed the exchange
8. S → C : item

Before revealing the item to the customer, the smart card asks the customer, if he is still interested in the item. If the customer wants to proceed, the smart card will release the item. There will only be a negligible delay for the customer between his decision in step 7 and the time he receives the item in step 8. Thus he can be sure that the time-sensitive item will still be valuable.

If the customer does not want to receive the item anymore, he has to start the abort protocol given in Table 4 to get his payment back with the help of the bank. This protocol must also be used, if the customer does not receive a message in step 5 or if the merchant falsely claims a correct payment to be invalid.

Table 4. The abort protocol for time-sensitive items.

5'. C → S : tell to abort the exchange
6'. S → B : state information
7'.   B   : verify state, cancel payment
8'. B → S : payment canceled
9'.   S   : reset the state for this exchange

There are again three possibilities how the smart card may react on such an abort request from the customer in step 5'. If the smart card has not yet sent the payment to the vendor in step 3, the smart card simply deletes the item and the payment. If the item has been delivered to the customer in step 8, an abort request will be ignored, as the exchange has been finished successfully. In all other cases the smart card contacts the bank and asks it to cancel the payment. The smart card informs the bank that it has not revealed the item of the vendor so that the exchange is guaranteed to be fair, after the payment has been canceled. The bank notifies the smart card about the canceled payment and the smart card resets itself for this exchange, i.e. it deletes the stored item and depending on the used payment system it provides the customer with the necessary information about the payment revocation.

The exchange protocol guarantees fairness to the customer, as he will not loose his money, if he has not received the item or if he rejected the time-sensitive item. The protocol also ensures fairness to the vendor, as the smart card will only cancel the payment, if and only if the customer did not obtain the item.

4.2   A Minimal Delay Fair Exchange Protocol

In the exchange protocol shown in Table 3 the item is sent in step 1a, while the customer has to wait with his purchase decision till step 7. However, for highly time-sensitive items like "real-time" stock market informations the customer needs to minimize the time delay, or he will often have to refuse buying these items. Therefore, we suggest a modified fair exchange protocol in Table 5, which is especially designed for the exchange of highly time-sensitive items. This protocol has a minimal message complexity, as it only needs one message to and one back from the vendor. Furthermore, it requires only the minimal number of steps between the vendor transmitting the item in step 4 and the customer deciding to take it or not in step 6.

Table 5. A minimal delay protocol for fair exchange of highly time-sensitive items.

1. C → S : payment, description
2. S → V : payment
3.   V   : check payment
4. V → S : item, description
5. S → C : ask, if the item is still valuable
6. C → S : tell to proceed the exchange
7. S → C : item
8.   C   : check item

Again we assume the payment to be revocable by the bank in order to resolve any failures. First the customer sends the payment to the smart card, which forwards it to the vendor for checking the payment. The vendor responds on receiving a valid payment by sending the desired item in step 4. On receipt of the item the smart card asks the customer *immediately* in step 5, whether he still wants the time-sensitive item to be delivered. Obviously the time delay between sending the item in step 4 and asking the customer in step 5 is minimal, and thus the item will probably still be valuable.

If the customer wants the item to be delivered in step 6, he obtains it without further network communication in step 7, as this transfer can be performed locally from the smart card to the customer's computer. Otherwise the customer starts the abort protocol described in Table 4.

In this protocol we extensively apply the technique of deferred verification (see Section 3.4). The smart card checks neither the payment nor the item. Therefore the customer has to check the validity of the item himself in step 8. If the item is not valid, the customer will complain and demand a verification from either the smart card or the external TTP. If the complaint is considered to be justified, the bank will cancel the payment which the vendor has received during this exchange. This finally reestablishes fairness for the customer. Also for the vendor fairness is enforced, as the item will only be delivered after payment and as revocation of a payment is only possible, if the item has not been delivered to the customer or if the item was not valid.

5   Conclusion

We have presented fair exchange protocols in which the trusted third party is partly implemented using a smart card co-located with the customer's machine. Although we have used a smart card as a trusted device, other ones like mobile phones or PDAs might also be used instead. The basic protocol presented in Section 3 ensures fairness and hence can be used to exchange arbitrary (even high priced) digital items. We have shown how the basic protocol should be modified for obtaining a protocol which is very well-suited for exchanging time-sensitive items, a property which existing fair exchange protocols lacked. Additionally, we designed an exchange protocol for the class of highly time-sensitive items that hardly tolerates a time-delay during the exchange. The presented protocols are well-suited for the exchange in mobile scenarios, since even if the network connection is disrupted during the final protocol phase, the smart card will still be able to deliver the item in a timely fashion.

References

1. N. Asokan. *Fairness in electronic commerce*. PhD thesis, University of Waterloo, May 1998.
2. N. Asokan, M. Schunter, and M. Waidner. Optimistic protocols for fair exchange. In Tsutomu Matsumoto, editor, *4th ACM Conference on Computer and Communications Security*, pages 6–17, Zürich, Switzerland, April 1997. ACM Press.
3. Holger Bürk and Andreas Pfitzmann. Value exchange systems enabling security and unobservability. *Computers & Security*, 9(8):715–721, 1990.
4. IBM. The IBM 4758 PCI Cryptographic Coprocessor, 2001. Homepage: http://www.ibm.com/security/cryptocards/.
5. Günter Karjoth. Secure mobile agent-based merchant brokering in distributed marketplaces. In *Proceedings of the Second International Symposium on Agent Systems and Applications and Fourth International Symposium on Mobile Agents (ASA/MA2000)*, volume 1882 of *Lecture Notes in Computer Science*, pages 44–56, Zürich, Switzerland, September 2000. Springer-Verlag.

6. Henning Pagnia, Holger Vogt, Felix C. Gärtner, and Uwe G. Wilhelm. Solving fair exchange with mobile agents. In *ASA/MA 2000*, volume 1882 of *Lecture Notes in Computer Science*, pages 57–72. Springer-Verlag, 2000.

7. J. D. Tygar. Atomicity in electronic commerce. In *Proceedings of the 15th Annual ACM Symposium on Principles of Distributed Computing (PODC'96)*, pages 8–26, New York, May 1996. ACM.

8. Holger Vogt, Henning Pagnia, and Felix C. Gärtner. Modular fair exchange protocols for electronic commerce. In *Proceedings of the 15th Annual Computer Security Applications Conference*, pages 3–11, Phoenix, Arizona, December 1999. IEEE Computer Society Press.

9. U. G. Wilhelm. *A Technical Approach to Privacy based on Mobile Agents protected by Tamper-resistant Hardware*. PhD thesis, École Polytechnique Fédérale de Lausanne, Switzerland, May 1999.

10. Jianying Zhou and Dieter Gollmann. An efficient non-repudiation protocol. In *Proceedings of the 10th IEEE Computer Security Foundations Workshop*, pages 126–132. IEEE Computer Society Press, 1997.

Rational Exchange – A Formal Model Based on Game Theory

Levente Buttyán and Jean-Pierre Hubaux

Institute for Computer Communications and Applications
Swiss Federal Institute of Technology – Lausanne
EPFL-DSC-ICA, CH-1015 Lausanne, Switzerland

Abstract. We introduce game theory as a formal framework in which exchange protocols can be modeled and their properties can be studied. We use this framework to give a formal definition for rational exchange relating it to the concept of Nash equilibrium in games. In addition, we study the relationship between rational exchange and fair exchange. We prove that fair exchange implies rational exchange, but the reverse is not true. The practical consequence of this is that rational exchange protocols may provide interesting solutions to the exchange problem by representing a trade-off between complexity and what they achieve. They could be particularly useful in mobile e-commerce applications.

1 Introduction

There are many applications where two parties have to exchange their digital items via communication networks. Examples include electronic contract signing, certified e-mail, and purchase of network delivered services. An inherent problem in these applications is that a misbehaving party may bring the other party in a disadvantageous situation. For instance, a service provider may deny service provision after receiving payment from a user. This may discourage the parties and hinder otherwise desired transactions.

There are two different approaches proposed in the literature to solve this problem that we can characterize as follows:

- **Fair exchange.** A fair exchange protocol guarantees for a correctly behaving party (i.e., a party that follows the protocol) that it cannot suffer any disadvantages – no matter whether the other party behaves correctly or tries to cheat. Thus, executing the protocol faithfully is safe for both parties.
- **Rational exchange.** A rational exchange protocol provides incentives so that rational (self-interested) parties have more reason to follow the protocol faithfully than to deviate from it. In other words, if one of the parties deviates from the protocol, then she may bring the other, correctly behaving party in a disadvantageous situation, but she cannot gain any advantages by the misbehavior. Therefore, cheating is uninteresting, and should happen only rarely.

L. Fiege, G. Mühl, and U. Wilhelm (Eds.): WELCOM 2001, LNCS 2232, pp. 114–126, 2001.
© Springer-Verlag Berlin Heidelberg 2001

Fair exchange has been extensively studied by the research community (see e.g., [8] for a comprehensive overview). On the other hand, rational exchange has received less attention. We are aware of a few protocols [4,10,2] that seem to be rational; however, it is difficult to tell what exactly these protocols achieve, because no formal definition of rational exchange exists. In addition, there seems to be some confusion regarding the relationship between fair exchange and rational exchange. The authors of [4] and [10], for instance, refer to fair exchange in the title of their papers, although the protocols that they describe are rational exchange protocols.

In order to better understand what rational exchange is, in this paper, we give a formal definition for it. Our approach is based on game theory. First, we introduce a framework to model an exchange protocol as a game. Then, we define the concept of rational exchange in terms of a Nash equilibrium in this game. Finally, we study the relationship between rational exchange and fair exchange, and show that fair exchange implies rational exchange, but the reverse is not true in general.

Our theoretical results, thus, justify the intuition that a fair exchange protocol achieves stronger guarantees than a rational exchange protocol. However, the "price" of this is that a fair exchange protocol is usually more complex than a rational exchange protocol. Fair exchange protocols proposed in the literature require either a lot of computation or communication, or a trusted third party that assists the exchange. Rational exchange protocols, on the other hand, may not use any trusted third party, while still keeping computational and communication complexity at a low level [10], or they may take advantage of an already existing trusted party in the system, without requiring additional functions from it [4,2].

An interesting application area of rational exchange could be mobile e-commerce. In mobile systems, devices are often battery powered and bandwidth is a scarce resource. Therefore, protocols that require a lot of computation or communication are not desirable. In addition, connectivity is sporadic, which means that a trusted third party that resides in the fixed infrastructure may often be unavailable. Thus, fair exchange protocols may not be practical for certain mobile e-commerce applications. On the other hand, rational exchange protocols may provide interesting solutions in these applications by representing a trade-off between complexity and what they achieve.

1.1 An Example for Rational Exchange

As an example, let us consider the following payment protocol:

$$U \rightarrow V : \; m_1 = (U, V, tid, val, h(rnd), \sigma_U(U, V, tid, val, h(rnd)))$$
$$V \rightarrow U : \; m_2 = srv$$
$$U \rightarrow V : \; m_3 = rnd$$
if V received m_1 and m_3:
$$V \rightarrow B : \; m_4 = (m_1, rnd, \sigma_V(m_1, rnd))$$
if V received only m_1:
$$V \rightarrow B : \; m_4' = (m_1, \sigma_V(m_1))$$

The above protocol can be used for transferring payment from a user U to a vendor V in exchange for some service provided by V to U. Besides the main parties U and V, the protocol uses a trusted third party, the bank B. We assume that before starting the protocol, U and V have already agreed on the details of the transaction. In particular, we assume that U and V agreed on the value val of the payment that U is supposed to pay to V, and the description of the service srv that V is supposed to provide to U. In addition, we assume that U and V also agreed on a fresh transaction identifier tid.

U starts the protocol by generating a random number rnd and computing its hash value $h(rnd)$. Then, she generates the digital signature $\sigma_U(U, V, tid, val, h(rnd))$, and sends m_1 to V. When V receives m_1, it provides the service to U (represented by sending $m_2 = srv$). If U is satisfied, then she reveals the random number rnd to V. If V received m_1 and m_3, then it generates the digital signature $\sigma_V(m_1, rnd)$, and sends m_4 to B. If V received only m_1, then it generates the digital signature $\sigma_V(m_1)$, and sends m_4' to B.

Upon reception of m_4, B verifies that it has never processed a transaction between U and V with the transaction identifier tid before by looking up its internal database, where it logs all processed transactions. Then, it verifies that the hash value of rnd equals the hash value in m_1, and the digital signatures of U and V in the message are valid. If these verifications are successful, then it logs the transaction, and transfers the value val from the account of U to the account of V. Upon reception of m_4', B performs similar verifications, and if these are successful, then B logs the transaction, and it debits U's account with the value val, but it does *not* credit V's account.

What does this protocol achieve? It is clear that it does not provide fairness, since any of the parties can bring the other, correctly behaving party in a disadvantageous situation. For instance, U can refuse to reveal rnd to V. In this case, V can send only m_4' to B, which means that V does not get paid for the service that it provided. Similarly, V can refuse the provision of the service after having received m_1 from U. In this case, V can send m_4' to B, which means that U's account is debited, although she did not receive any service.

On the other hand, note that none of the parties gain any (financial) advantages by cheating. The reason is that V cannot obtain any money without providing the service to U (since U reveals rnd only if she received the service); and U cannot receive any service without being charged (since V provides the service only if it received m_1, in which case it can send at least m_4' to B). This means that none of the parties is interested in deviating from the protocol. In a word, the protocol seems to be a rational exchange protocol. Indeed, this can be proven formally within the model that we will introduce in this paper.

2   Preliminaries

In this section, we introduce some basic definitions from game theory [7] that we will use later.

2.1 Extensive Games

An *extensive game* is a tuple $\langle P, Q, p, (\mathcal{I}_i)_{i \in P}, (\leq_i)_{i \in P} \rangle$, where

- P is a set of *players*;
- Q is a set of *action sequences* that satisfies the following properties:
  - the empty sequence ϵ is a member of Q,
  - if $(a_k)_{k=1}^{w} \in Q$ and $0 < v < w$, then $(a_k)_{k=1}^{v} \in Q$,
  - if an infinite action sequence $(a_k)_{k=1}^{\infty}$ satisfies $(a_k)_{k=1}^{v} \in Q$ for every positive integer v, then $(a_k)_{k=1}^{\infty} \in Q$;

  If q is a finite action sequence and a is an action, then $q.a$ denotes the finite action sequence that consists of q followed by a. An action sequence $q \in Q$ is *terminal* if it is infinite or if there is no a such that $q.a \in Q$. The set of terminal action sequences is denoted by Z. For every non-terminal action sequence $q \in Q \setminus Z$, $A(q)$ denotes the set $\{a : q.a \in Q\}$ of *available actions* after q.
- p is a *player function* that assigns a player in P to every action sequence in $Q \setminus Z$;
- $\mathcal{I}_i$ is an *information partition* of player $i \in P$, which is a partition of the set $\{q \in Q \setminus Z : p(q) = i\}$ with the property that $A(q) = A(q')$ whenever q and q' are in the same *information set* $I_i \in \mathcal{I}_i$;
- $\leq_i$ is a preference relation of player $i \in P$ on Z.

The interpretation of an extensive game is the following: Each action sequence in Q represents a possible history of the game. The action sequences that belong to the same information set $I_i \in \mathcal{I}_i$ are indistinguishable to player i. This means that i knows that the history of the game is an action sequence in I_i but she does not know which one. The empty sequence ϵ represents the starting point of the game. After any non-terminal action sequence $q \in Q \setminus Z$, player $p(q)$ chooses an action a from the set $A(q)$. Then q is extended with a, and the history of the game becomes $q.a$. The action sequences in Z represent the possible outcomes of the game. If $q, q' \in Z$ and $q \leq_i q'$, then player i prefers the outcome q' to the outcome q.

The preference relations of the players are often represented in terms of *payoffs*: a vector $y(q) = (y_i(q))_{i \in P}$ of real numbers is assigned to every terminal action sequence $q \in Z$ in such a way that for any $q, q' \in Z$ and $i \in P$, $q \leq_i q'$ iff $y_i(q) \leq y_i(q')$.

Conceptually, an extensive game can be thought of as a tree. The edges and the vertices of the tree correspond to actions and action sequences, respectively. A distinguished vertex, called the root, represents the empty sequence ϵ. Every other vertex u represents the sequence of the actions that belong to the edges of the path between the root and u. Let us call a vertex u terminal if the path between the root and u cannot be extended beyond u. Terminal vertices represent the terminal action sequences in the game. Each non-terminal vertex u is labeled by $p(q)$ where $q \in Q \setminus Z$ is the action sequence that belongs to u. Finally, the terminal vertices may be labeled with payoff vectors to represent the preference relations of the players.

2.2   Strategy

A *strategy of player* $i \in P$ is a function s_i that assigns an action in $A(q)$ to every non-terminal action sequence $q \in Q \setminus Z$ such that $p(q) = i$ and q is *consistent* with the strategy, with the restriction that it assigns the same action to q and q' whenever q and q' are in the same information set of i. A non-terminal action sequence $(a_k)_{k=1}^{w} \in Q \setminus Z$ is consistent with the strategy s_i of player i iff $s_i((a_k)_{k=1}^{v}) = a_{v+1}$ for every $0 \leq v < w$ such that $p((a_k)_{k=1}^{v}) = i$. We denote the set of all strategies of player i by S_i.

A *strategy profile* is a vector $(s_i)_{i \in P}$ of strategies, where each s_i is a member of S_i. Sometimes, we will write $(s_j, (s_i)_{i \in P \setminus \{j\}})$ instead of $(s_i)_{i \in P}$ in order to emphasize that the strategy profile specifies strategy s_j for player j.

2.3   Nash Equilibrium

Let $o((s_i)_{i \in P})$ denote the resulting outcome when the players follow the strategies in the strategy profile $(s_i)_{i \in P}$. In other words, $o((s_i)_{i \in P})$ is the (possibly infinite) action sequence $(a_k)_{k=1}^{w} \in Z$ such that for every $0 \leq v < w$ we have that $s_{p((a_k)_{k=1}^{v})}((a_k)_{k=1}^{v}) = a_{v+1}$. A strategy profile $(s_i^*)_{i \in P}$ is a *Nash equilibrium* iff for every player $j \in P$ and every strategy $s_j \in S_j$ we have that

$$o(s_j, (s_i^*)_{i \in P \setminus \{j\}}) \leq_j o(s_j^*, (s_i^*)_{i \in P \setminus \{j\}})$$

This means that if every player i other than j follows s_i^*, then player j is also motivated to follow s_j^*, because she loses or at least does not gain anything by not doing so.

3   Protocol Games

Let us consider a set of principals that want to execute a given exchange protocol. Moreover, let us assume that the principals may misbehave, and may not follow the protocol faithfully. In such a situation,

- each principal has choices at various stages during the interaction with the others (e.g., to quit the protocol or to continue);
- the decisions that the principals make determine the outcome of their interaction;
- in order to achieve the most preferable outcome, a principal may follow a plan that does not coincide with the faithful execution of the exchange protocol.

Considering its striking similarity to games, it appears to be a natural idea to model this situation with a game. We refer to this game as the *protocol game*.

We want that the protocol game of an exchange protocol models all the possible ways in which the protocol participants can misbehave *within the context of the protocol*. The crucial point here is to make the difference between misbehavior within the context of the protocol and misbehavior in general. Letting the protocol participants misbehave in any way they can would lead to a game that would allow interactions that has nothing to do with the protocol being studied. Clearly, such a game would not be a good model of the protocol, because it would be far too rich, and we suspect that it would be difficult to analyze, and thus, to draw interesting conclusions about the protocol. Therefore, we want to limit the possible misbehavior of the protocol participants. However, we must do so in such a way that we do not lose generality. Essentially, the limitation that we will impose on protocol participants is that they can send only messages that are *compatible* with the protocol. We make this precise in the following paragraphs.

We consider an exchange protocol to be a description $\pi(L)$ of a distributed computation on a set L of parameters. $\pi(L)$ consists of a set $\{\pi_1(L_1), \pi_2(L_2), \ldots\}$ of descriptions of local computations, where each L_k is a subset of L. We call these descriptions of local computations shortly *programs*. Each program $\pi_k(L_k)$ is meant to be executed by a protocol participant. Typically, each $\pi_k(L_k)$ contains instructions to wait for messages that satisfy certain conditions. When such an instruction is reached, the local computation can proceed only if a message that satisfies the required condition is provided (or a timeout occurs). Let us call a message m *compatible* with $\pi_k(L_k)$ if the local computation described by $\pi_k(L_k)$ can reach a state in which a message is expected and m would be accepted. Let us denote the set of messages that are compatible with $\pi_k(L_k)$ by $M_{\pi_k}(L_k)$. Then, the set of messages that are compatible with the protocol is defined as $M_\pi(L) = \cup_k M_{\pi_k}(L_k)$.

Apart from requiring the protocol participants to send messages that are compatible with the protocol, we do not impose further limitations on their behavior. In particular, we allow the protocol participants to quit the protocol at any time, or to wait for some time without any activity. Furthermore, the protocol participants can send any messages (compatible with the protocol) that they are able to compute in a given state.

We assume that the network that is used by the protocol participants to communicate with each other is reliable, which means that it always delivers messages to their intended destinations within a constant time interval. Such a network allows the protocol participants to run the protocol in a synchronous fashion. We will model this by assuming that the protocol participants interact with each other in synchronous *rounds*, where each round consists of the following two phases:

1. each participant generates some messages based on her current state, and sends them to some other participants;
2. each participant receives the messages that were sent to her in the current round, and performs a state transition based on her current state and the received messages.

We adopted this approach from [6], where the same model is used to study the properties of distributed algorithms in a synchronous network system. In [3], we also introduce a more general asynchronous model, where we assume that the network is unreliable. Due to space limitation, we do not describe that model here.

3.1   Players

We model each protocol participant (i.e., the two main parties and the trusted third party if there is any) as a player. In addition, we model the communication network as a player too. Therefore, the player set P of the protocol game is defined as $P = \{p_1, p_2, p_3, net\}$, where p_1 and p_2 represent the two main parties of the protocol, p_3 stands for the trusted third party, and net denotes the network. If the protocol does not use a trusted third party, then p_3 is omitted. We denote the set $P \setminus \{net\}$ by P'.

It might seem that it is useless to model the trusted third party explicitly as a player, because it always behaves correctly, and thus, its actions are fully predictable. Nevertheless, we model the trusted third party in the same way as we model the main parties, which leads to a more uniform model. We will make the distinction between the trusted third party and the potentially misbehaving main parties in another way: We restrict the player that represents the trusted third party to follow a particular strategy, whereas we allow the players that represent the potentially misbehaving main parties to choose among several strategies.

3.2   Information Sets

Each player $i \in P$ has a local state $\Sigma_i(q)$ that represents all the information that i has obtained after the action sequence q. If for two action sequences q and q', $\Sigma_i(q) = \Sigma_i(q')$, then q and q' are indistinguishable to i. Therefore, two action sequences q and q' belong to the same information set of i iff it is i's turn to move after both q and q', and $\Sigma_i(q) = \Sigma_i(q')$.

We define two types of events: send and receive events. The send event $snd(m, j)$ is generated for player $i \in P'$ when she submits a message $m \in M_\pi(L)$ with intended destination $j \in P'$ to the network, and the receive event $rcv(m)$ is generated for player $i \in P'$ when the network delivers a message $m \in M_\pi(L)$ to i. We denote the set of all events by E.

The local state $\Sigma_i(q)$ of player $i \in P'$ after action sequence q is defined as a tuple $\langle \varrho_i(q), \alpha_i(q), H_i(q) \rangle$, where

- $\varrho_i(q) \in N$ is a positive integer that represents the round number for player i after action sequence q;
- $\alpha_i(q) \in \{\mathsf{true}, \mathsf{false}\}$ is a boolean, which is true iff player i is still active (i.e., she has not quitted the protocol) after action sequence q;
- $H_i(q) \subseteq E \times N$ is player i's local history after action sequence q, which contains the events that were generated for i together with the round number of their generation.

Initially, $\varrho_i(\epsilon) = 1$, $\alpha_i(\epsilon) = \mathsf{true}$, and $H_i(\epsilon) = \emptyset$ for every player $i \in P'$.

The local state $\Sigma_{net}(q)$ of the network consists of a set $M_{net}(q) \subseteq M_\pi(L) \times P'$, which contains those messages together with their intended destination that were submitted to the network in the current round and have not been delivered yet. We call the set $M_{net}(q)$ the network buffer. Initially, $M_{net}(\epsilon) = \emptyset$.

3.3   Available Actions

In order to determine the set of actions available for a player $i \in P'$ after an action sequence q, we first tag each message $m \in M_\pi(L)$ with a vector $(\phi_i^m(\Sigma_i(q)))_{i \in P'}$ of conditions. Each $\phi_i^m(\Sigma_i(q))$ is a logical formula that describes the condition that must be satisfied by the local state $\Sigma_i(q)$ of player i in order for i to be able to send message m after action sequence q. Our intention is to use these conditions to capture the assumptions about cryptographic primitives at an abstract level. For instance, it is often assumed that a valid digital signature $\sigma_i(m)$ of player i on message m can only be generated by i. This means that a message $m' \in M_\pi(L)$ that contains $\sigma_i(m)$ can be sent by a player $j \neq i$ iff j received a message that contained $\sigma_i(m)$ earlier. This condition can be expressed by an appropriate logical formula for every $j \neq i$.

Now, let us consider an action sequence q, after which player $i \in P'$ has to move. There is a special action, called quit_i, which is always available for i after q. Every other action available for i after q is a subset of the set $B_i(\Sigma_i(q))$ of *action atoms*, which is defined as

$$B_i(\Sigma_i(q)) = \{\mathsf{send}_i(m, j) : m \in M_\pi(L),\ \phi_i^m(\Sigma_i(q)) = \mathsf{true},\ j \in P' \setminus \{i\}\}$$

The set $A_i(\Sigma_i(q))$ of available actions of player $i \in P'$ after action sequence q is then defined as

$$A_i(\Sigma_i(q)) = \{\mathsf{quit}_i\} \cup \mathcal{B}_i(\Sigma_i(q))$$

where $\mathcal{B}_i(\Sigma_i(q))$ denotes the power set of $B_i(\Sigma_i(q))$.

The interpretation of the above formulae is the following: every player other than the network can quit the protocol at any time, or if she does not quit, then she can send any subset of the messages that she is able to send in her current local state to any other player in P'. Note that $\emptyset \in A_i(\Sigma_i(q))$. By convention, choosing the action $\emptyset$ means that the player does nothing.

Let us consider now an action sequence q, after which the network has to move. There is only one action, called $\mathsf{deliver}(M_{net}(q))$, that is available for the network after q. Thus, $A_{net}(\Sigma_{net}(q)) = \{\mathsf{deliver}(M_{net}(q))\}$. The interpretation of this is straightforward: the only available action of the network is to deliver all messages in the network buffer to their intended destinations.

The above defined actions change the local states of the players as follows:

- If a player $i \in P'$ performs the action quit_i, then the activity flag of i is set to false. The state of every other player $j \in P \setminus \{i\}$ remains the same as before.
- If a player $i \in P'$ performs the action $\emptyset$, then the state of every player $j \in P$ remains the same as before.
- If a player $i \in P'$ performs an action W such that $W \neq \mathsf{quit}_i$ and $W \neq \emptyset$, then the messages in W, together with their intended destination, are inserted in the network buffer, and the corresponding send events are generated for i. The state of every other player $j \in P \setminus \{i, net\}$ remains the same as before.

– If the network performs the action $\mathsf{deliver}(M_{net}(q))$, then for every message-destination pair $(m, j) \in M_{net}(q)$, a $rcv(m)$ event is generated for j if j is still active. Then, every message is removed from the network buffer, and the round number of every active player is increased by one.

3.4   Action Sequences and Player Function

The game is played in repeated rounds, where each round consists of the following two phases: (1) each active player in P' moves, one after the other, in order; (2) the network moves. The game is finished when every player in P' becomes inactive.

In order to make this precise, let us denote the set of players that are still active after action sequence q and have an index larger than v by $P'(q, v)$. Formally, $P'(q, v) = \{p_k \in P' : \alpha_{p_k}(q) = \mathsf{true}, \ k > v\}$. Furthermore, let $k_{min}(q, v)$ denote the smallest index in $P'(q, v)$, which is defined as $k_{min}(q, v) = \min_{k:p_k \in P'(q,v)} k$.

We define the set Q of action sequences and the player function p of the protocol game together in an inductive manner. By definition, $\epsilon \in Q$. Moreover, $p(\epsilon) = p_1$. In addition,

– if an action sequence q is in Q and $p(q) = p_v$, then
  - $q.a \in Q$ for every $a \in A_{p_v}(\Sigma_{p_v}(q))$;
  - if $P'(q.a, v) \neq \emptyset$, then $p(q.a) = p_{k_{min}(q.a,v)}$, otherwise $p(q.a) = net$;
– if an action sequence q is in Q and $p(q) = net$, then
  - $q.a \in Q$ for the single action $a = \mathsf{deliver}(M_{net}(q)) \in A_{net}(\Sigma_{net}(q))$;
  - if $P'(q.a, 0) \neq \emptyset$, then $p(q.a) = p_{k_{min}(q.a,0)}$, otherwise $q.a$ is a terminal action sequence.

3.5   Payoffs

Let us denote the items that the main parties of the protocol represented by p_1 and p_2 want to exchange in the protocol by γ_{p_1} and γ_{p_2}, respectively. Typically, γ_{p_1} and γ_{p_2} are members of the parameter set L of the protocol. Furthermore, let us denote the value that γ_j is worth to i ($i, j \in \{p_1, p_2\}$) by $u_i(\gamma_j)$. In practice, it may be difficult to quantify $u_i(\gamma_j)$. However, our approach does not depend on the exact value of $u_i(\gamma_j)$; we require only that $u_{p_1}(\gamma_{p_2}) > u_{p_1}(\gamma_{p_1}) > 0$ and $u_{p_2}(\gamma_{p_1}) > u_{p_2}(\gamma_{p_2}) > 0$ hold. We consider these to be necessary conditions for the exchange to take place at all.

The payoff $y_i(q)$ for player $i \in \{p_1, p_2\}$ assigned to the terminal action sequence q is defined as $y_i(q) = y_i^+(q) - y_i^-(q)$. We call $y_i^+(q)$ the *income* and $y_i^-(q)$ the *expenses* of i, and define them as follows:

$$y_i^+(q) = \begin{cases} u_i(\gamma_j) & \text{if } \phi_i^+(q) = \mathsf{true} \\ 0 & \text{otherwise} \end{cases}$$

$$y_i^-(q) = \begin{cases} u_i(\gamma_i) & \text{if } \phi_i^-(q) = \mathsf{true} \\ 0 & \text{otherwise} \end{cases}$$

where $j \in \{p_1, p_2\}$, $j \neq i$, and $\phi_i^+(q)$ and $\phi_i^-(q)$ are logical formulae. The exact form of $\phi_i^+(q)$ and $\phi_i^-(q)$ depends on the particular exchange protocol being modeled, but the idea is that $\phi_i^+(q) = \mathsf{true}$ iff i gains access to γ_j, and $\phi_i^-(q) = \mathsf{true}$ iff i loses control over γ_i in q. A typical example would be $\phi_i^+(q) = (\exists \varrho : (rcv(m), \varrho) \in H_i(q))$, where we assume that m is the only message in $M_\pi(L)$ that contains γ_j.

Note that according to the above definition, the payoff $y_i(q)$ of player i can take only four possible values: 0, $u_i(\gamma_j)$, $-u_i(\gamma_i)$, and $u_i(\gamma_j) - u_i(\gamma_i)$ for every terminal action sequence q of the protocol game.

Since we are only interested in the payoffs of p_1 and p_2 (i.e., the players that represent the main parties), we define the payoff of every other player in $P \setminus \{p_1, p_2\}$ to be 0 for every terminal action sequence of the protocol game.

Before leaving this section, we define a property of exchange protocols:

Definition 1. *Let us consider a two-party exchange protocol $\pi(L)$ and its protocol game $G_\pi(L)$. $\pi(L)$ is said to be* closed for incomes *iff for every terminal action sequence q of $G_\pi(L)$ we have that*

$$y_{p_1}^+(q) > 0 \Rightarrow y_{p_2}^-(q) > 0$$
$$y_{p_2}^+(q) > 0 \Rightarrow y_{p_1}^-(q) > 0$$

If a protocol is closed for incomes, then no income comes from outside of the system. This means that if a main party gains something, then the other main party must lose something. Exchange protocols usually satisfy this property. On the other hand, exchange protocols are not necessarily closed for expenses: a main party may lose something without the other main party gaining anything.

4   Formal Definition of Rational Exchange

Informally, a two-party rational exchange protocol is an exchange protocol in which both main parties are motivated to behave correctly and to follow the protocol faithfully. If one of the parties deviates from the protocol, then she may bring the other, correctly behaving party in a disadvantageous situation, but she cannot gain any advantages by the misbehavior. This is very similar to the concept of Nash equilibrium in games. This inspired us to give a formal definition of rational exchange in terms of a Nash equilibrium in the protocol game.

Let us consider an exchange protocol $\pi(L) = \{\pi_1(L_1), \pi_2(L_2), \ldots\}$ and its protocol game $G_\pi(L)$ constructed according to the framework described in the previous section. Recall that each $\pi_k(L_k)$ is a description of a local computation (i.e., a program). As such, each $\pi_k(L_k)$ must specify for the protocol participant that executes it what to do in any conceivable situation. Considering its similarity to a strategy, it seems to be reasonable to relate each $\pi_k(L_k)$ to a strategy in $G_\pi(L)$.

Before going further, we need to introduce the concept of *restricted games*. Let us consider an extensive game G, and let us divide the player set P into two disjoint subsets P_{free} and P_{fix}. Furthermore, let us fix a strategy $s_j \in S_j$ for each $j \in P_{fix}$, and let us denote the vector $(s_j)_{j \in P_{fix}}$ of fixed strategies by s. The restricted game $G_{|s}$ is the extensive game that is obtained from G by restricting each $j \in P_{fix}$ to follow the fixed strategy s_j.

Note that in $G_{|s}$, each player $j \in P_{fix}$ has a single strategy to follow, namely, the strategy that is induced by the fixed strategy s_j in $G_{|s}$. This means that the outcome of $G_{|s}$ solely depends on what strategies are followed by the players in P_{free}. For any player $i \in P_{free}$ and for any strategy $s_i \in S_i$, let $s_{i|s}$ denote the strategy that s_i induces in the restricted game $G_{|s}$. Let $o_{|s}((s_{i|s})_{i \in P_{free}})$ denote the resulting outcome in $G_{|s}$ when the players in P_{free} follow the strategies in the strategy profile $(s_{i|s})_{i \in P_{free}}$.

As we said before, we want to define the concept of rational exchange in terms of a Nash equilibrium in the protocol game. Indeed, we define it in terms of a Nash equilibrium in a restricted protocol game. To be more precise, we consider the restricted protocol game that we obtain from the protocol game by restricting the trusted third party (if there is any) to follow its program faithfully (i.e., to behave correctly), and we require that the strategies that correspond to the programs of the main parties form a Nash equilibrium in this restricted protocol game. In addition, we require that no other Nash equilibrium be strongly preferable for any of the main parties in the restricted game. This ensures that the main parties are indeed interested in behaving correctly and executing their programs faithfully.

Definition 2 (Rational Exchange). *Let us consider a two-party exchange protocol $\pi(L) = \{\pi_1(L_1), \pi_2(L_2), \pi_3(L_3)\}$, where $\pi_1(L_1)$ and $\pi_2(L_2)$ are the programs for the main parties, and $\pi_3(L_3)$ is the program for the trusted third party. Furthermore, let us consider the protocol game $G_\pi(L)$ of $\pi(L)$ constructed according to the framework described in Section 3. Let us denote the strategy of player p_k that represents $\pi_k(L_k)$ within $G_\pi(L)$ by $s_{p_k}^*$ ($k \in \{1, 2, 3\}$), and let us denote the single strategy of the network by s_{net}. $\pi(L)$ is said to be* rational *iff*

1. *$(s_{p_1|s}^*, s_{p_2|s}^*)$ is a Nash equilibrium in the restricted protocol game $G_{\pi|s}(L)$, where $s = (s_{p_3}^*, s_{net})$; and*
2. *for any other Nash equilibrium $(s_{p_1|s}, s_{p_2|s})$ in $G_{\pi|s}(L)$, we have that*

$$o_{|s}(s_{p_1|s}, s_{p_2|s}) \leq_{p_1} o_{|s}(s_{p_1|s}^*, s_{p_2|s}^*)$$

$$o_{|s}(s_{p_1|s}, s_{p_2|s}) \leq_{p_2} o_{|s}(s_{p_1|s}^*, s_{p_2|s}^*)$$

It can be proven formally that the payment protocol described in Subsection 1.1 satisfies the above definition of rational exchange, however, due to space limitation we must omit the details of the proof. The interested reader is referred to [3].

5   Relation to Fair Exchange

Informally, a fair exchange protocol ensures for each main party A that if A behaves correctly, then the other party B cannot get the item of A unless A

gets the item of B. In terms of our game theoretic model, this property can be expressed as follows, where $s = (s_{p_3}^*, s_{net})$:

- for every strategy s_{p_1} of p_1, $y_{p_1}^+(q) = u_{p_1}(\gamma_{p_2}) \Rightarrow y_{p_2}^+(q) = u_{p_2}(\gamma_{p_1})$, where $q = o_{|s}(s_{p_1|s}, s_{p_2|s}^*)$; and
- for every strategy s_{p_2} of p_2, $y_{p_2}^+(q) = u_{p_2}(\gamma_{p_1}) \Rightarrow y_{p_1}^+(q) = u_{p_1}(\gamma_{p_2})$, where $q = o_{|s}(s_{p_1|s}^*, s_{p_2|s})$.

Theorem 1. *If the protocol is closed for incomes, then fair exchange implies rational exchange.*

Proof. First, we have to prove that $(s_{p_1|s}^*, s_{p_2|s}^*)$ is a Nash equilibrium in $G_{\pi|s}(L)$. Let us suppose that it is not. This means that either $s_{p_1|s}^*$ is not the best response to $s_{p_2|s}^*$, or $s_{p_2|s}^*$ is not the best response to $s_{p_1|s}^*$. Without loss of generality, let us assume that the first is the case. This means that p_1 has a strategy $s_{p_1|s}'$ such that $y_{p_1}(q^*) < y_{p_1}(q')$, where $q^* = o_{|s}(s_{p_1|s}^*, s_{p_2|s}^*)$, and $q' = o_{|s}(s_{p_1|s}', s_{p_2|s}^*)$. Since q^* is the outcome when both parties behave correctly, $y_{p_1}^+(q^*) = u_{p_1}(\gamma_{p_2}) > 0$ and $y_{p_1}^-(q^*) = u_{p_1}(\gamma_{p_1}) > 0$. Therefore, $y_{p_1}(q^*) < y_{p_1}(q')$ is possible only if $y_{p_1}^+(q') = u_{p_1}(\gamma_{p_2}) > 0$ and $y_{p_1}^-(q') = 0$. However, this is impossible, because, from the properties of fair exchange, $y_{p_1}^+(q') > 0$ implies $y_{p_2}^+(q') > 0$, and from the income closed property, $y_{p_2}^+(q') > 0$ implies $y_{p_1}^-(q') > 0$.

Next, we have to prove that no other Nash equilibrium is strongly preferable for any of the players. Let us suppose the contrary, and assume that there exists a Nash equilibrium $(s_{p_1|s}', s_{p_2|s}')$ in $G_{\pi|s}(L)$ such that $y_{p_1}(q^*) < y_{p_1}(q')$, where $q^* = o_{|s}(s_{p_1|s}^*, s_{p_2|s}^*)$, and $q' = o_{|s}(s_{p_1|s}', s_{p_2|s}')$. This is possible only if $y_{p_1}^+(q') = u_{p_1}(\gamma_{p_2}) > 0$ and $y_{p_1}^-(q') = 0$. From the income closed property, we get that $y_{p_1}^+(q') > 0$ implies $y_{p_2}^-(q') > 0$, and $y_{p_1}^-(q') = 0$ implies $y_{p_2}^+(q') = 0$. Therefore, if p_1 follows $s_{p_1|s}'$ and p_2 follows $s_{p_2|s}'$, then p_2's payoff is negative. However, p_2 can always do better, and achieve a non-negative payoff, for instance, by quitting right at the beginning of the game. This means that $s_{p_2|s}'$ is not the best response to $s_{p_1|s}'$, and thus, $(s_{p_1|s}', s_{p_2|s}')$ cannot be a Nash equilibrium. □

It is easy to see that rational exchange does not imply fair exchange. The payment protocol of Subsection 1.1, for instance, does not guarantee fairness, nevertheless, it can be proven to be a rational exchange protocol [3].

6   Related Work

In [1], Asokan *et al.* model their exchange protocol as a game that is played by a misbehaving party against a correctly behaving party and a trustee according to some well defined rules. They define fairness to mean that the probability that the misbehaving party wins the game is negligible. In [5], Kremer and Raskin model non-repudiation protocols (which are strongly related to fair exchange protocols) as games in a similar way as we do. However, they use neither payoffs nor the concept of equilibrium to specify properties of the protocol. Instead, they introduce a game based alternating temporal logic for this purpose. In

[9], Sandholm introduces the notion of *unenforced exchange*, and relates it to the concept of Nash equilibrium. None of these papers attempt to formalize the concept of rational exchange in general and to investigate the relationship between rational exchange and fair exchange.

7   Conclusion

In this paper, we introduced game theory as a formal framework in which exchange protocols can be modeled and their properties can be studied. We used this framework to give a formal definition for rational exchange relating it to the concept of Nash equilibrium in games. In addition, we studied the relationship between rational exchange and fair exchange. We proved that fair exchange implies rational exchange if the protocol is closed for incomes (which is usually the case), but the reverse is not true.

Our theoretical results, thus, justify the intuition that a fair exchange protocol provides stronger guarantees than a rational exchange protocol. On the other hand, fair exchange protocols are usually more complex than rational exchange protocols. Therefore, rational exchange protocols may provide an interesting solution to the exchange problem by representing a trade-off between complexity and what they achieve. In certain applications, notably in mobile e-commerce, rational exchange protocols may provide more practical solutions than fair exchange protocols.

References

1. N. Asokan, V. Shoup, and M. Waidner. Optimistic fair exchange of digital signatures. *IEEE Journal on Selected Areas in Communications*, 18(4), April 2000.
2. L. Buttyán. Removing the financial incentive to cheat in micropayment schemes. *IEE Electronics Letters*, 36(2):132–133, January 2000.
3. L. Buttyán. Building Blocks for Secure e-Commerce Services: Authenticated Key Transport and Rational Exchange Protocols. Ph.D. Thesis, in preparation.
4. M. Jakobsson. Ripping coins for a fair exchange. In *Proceedings of EURO-CRYPT'95*, pages 220–230, 1995.
5. S. Kremer and J.-F. Raskin. Formal verification of non-repudiation protocols – a game approach. In *Formal Methods for Computer Security*, Chicago, USA, July 2000.
6. N. Lynch. *Distributed Algorithms*. Morgan Kaufmann, 1996.
7. M. Osborne and A. Rubinstein. *A Course in Game Theory*. MIT Press, 1994.
8. H. Pagnia, H. Vogt, and F. Gärtner. Fair exchange. manuscript, August 2001.
9. T. Sandholm. Unenforced e-commerce transactions. *IEEE Internet Computing*, pages 47–54, November-December 1997.
10. P. Syverson. Weakly secret bit commitment: applications to lotteries and fair exchange. In *Proceedings of the 11th IEEE Computer Security Foundations Workshop*, pages 2–13, June 1998.

Enabling Privacy Protection in E-commerce Applications

Dennis Kügler

Department of Computer Science*
Darmstadt University of Technology
D-64283 Darmstadt, Germany
kuegler@cdc.informatik.tu-darmstadt.de

Abstract. Blind signatures are a cryptographic tool that is well suited to enable privacy protecting e-commerce applications. In cryptographic frameworks however, only the major cryptographic tools like digital signatures and ciphers are provided as abstract tools. Cryptographic protocols, especially blind signatures, are not available in those frameworks. We strongly believe that a modular framework is necessary for all cryptographic tools to enable the immediate replacement of an algorithm in the case of its possible breakdown. In this paper, we show how to abstract blind signatures and how to integrate them into the framework of the Java Cryptography Architecture.

1   Introduction

With e-commerce services continously increasing, there also is an increasing demand for security and privacy. While security enhancing techniques like the Secure Socket Layer (SSL) [8] are available and commonly used, the efforts to protect the privacy of individuals are scarcely perceptible. As e-commerce services also enable the service provider to easily acquire personal data, e.g. the consummation habits of the customers, countermeasures must be taken to protect the privacy of customers, who are afraid that their personal data may be misused or sold. Privacy is important for customers and even governments become more and more concerned about privacy issues. To make e-commerce successful, we need to bring privacy protecting techniques into the applications to guarantee that no misuse can occur.

One basis for privacy are blind signatures, a cryptographic protocol invented by Chaum [5]. Blind signatures allow to receive a digital signature from an authority on any message or document so that the authority is neither able to recognize the signed document later nor can the authority determine the content of the document to be signed. Due to the publicly verifiable signature given by an authority, blind signatures provide authentication of messages, but

---

* This work was supported by the Deutsche Forschungsgemeinschaft (DFG) as part of the PhD program (Graduiertenkolleg) "Enabling Technologies for Electronic Commerce" at Darmstadt University of Technology.

L. Fiege, G. Mühl, and U. Wilhelm (Eds.): WELCOM 2001, LNCS 2232, pp. 127–138, 2001.

hide anything else. Therefore, blind signatures are an ideal tool for untraceable, cash-like payment systems, allow for anonymous tickets for electronic services, and can even be used for anonymous electronic voting.

Current privacy enabled e-commerce applications, mostly electronic payment systems, use a single blind signature algorithm in a hard coded way. If this algorithm turns out to be insecure, no immediate replacement is possible. In the case of a payment system, the breakdown of the used blind signature algorithm allows to forge electronic money, which is of course a major economical threat.

We call a cryptographic algorithm provably secure, if we can reduce its security to the solution of a hard mathematical problem. However, for many algorithms no such proof has been found yet. Furthermore, even for a provably secure algorithm, we have to consider that its security only relies on the assumption that the underlying mathematical problem is hard. This problem may as well turn out to be weaker than previously assumed, e.g. with the invention of the number field sieve the problem of factoring large integers became much easier.

Therefore, cryptographic algorithms should be made replaceable against other algorithms as far as possible. While this can be easily done with single party cryptographic primitives like signatures and ciphers, it is more complicated with cryptographic protocols like blind signatures that rely on communication and interaction between two parties to complete the task. In this paper we show how to abstract blind signatures so that any algorithm can easily be replaced by other algorithms.

The remainder is structured as follows: Section 2 focuses on the general construction of secure blind signatures. In section 3 an abstraction of blind signatures to a general model is given that can be used to implement blind signatures as abstract cryptographic service. Finally, section 4 presents a concrete implementation of blind signatures in the framework of the Java Cryptography Architecture.

2   Construction and Security of Blind Signatures

We will start this section with an introduction to blind signatures and we present the two major sources for blind signature algorithms, trapdoor one-way functions and three-move identification protocols. However, not every digital signature has a blind counterpart, especially the DSA signature [14] and the original ElGamal signature [7] are not efficiently blindable, but slight modifications of them can be blinded [6,11].

2.1   Security of Blind Signatures

Formal definitions for blind signatures can be found in [12,1]. Basically, a blind signature must be blind and unforgeable. We distinguish between perfect and computational blindness:

- A blind signature *perfect blind*, if it is impossible for any unrestricted attacker to revoke blindness.

- A blind signature is *computational blind*, if any attacker who is restricted to probabilistic polynomial time algorithms has only negligible chance to revoke blindness.

For many anonymity related applications, e.g. electronic voting, unconditional anonymity is necessary and perfect blindness is required, which gives strong guarantees that the anonymity will never be revokable. In contrast computational blindness is always perishable.

The security notions that are used for digital signatures, e.g. *no existential forgery under adaptive chosen message attacks* are not applicable for blind signatures, as blind signatures are somehow based on such attacks. But it is still important to guarantee that it is impossible to forge signatures. This definition of security has been formalized by Pointcheval and Stern [17] as *one-more-unforgability*. Informally, if a signer has issued ℓ signatures, the probability that any attacker who is restricted to probabilistic polynomial time algorithms can output $\ell + 1$ signatures must be negligible.

2.2   Building Blind Signatures from Trapdoor One-Way Functions

Security proofs can be given either in a complexity based model or in the random oracle model [4], where the hash function is assumed to behave like an ideal random function. While complexity based security proofs are superior, they are hard to construct. Juels et al. [12] showed that provably secure blind signatures exist in the complexity based model for arbitrary one-way trapdoor permutations. However, their construction is inefficient and only of theoretical interest as it is based on general computation protocols.

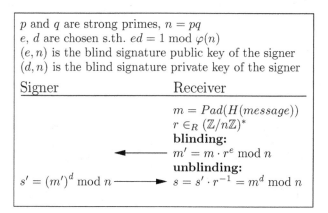

Fig. 1. The RSA blind signature.

A more practical approach is the blinded version of the RSA signature [18], which recently has been proven secure in the random oracle model for an ℓ

polynomially bounded in the security parameter, if either the RSA known-target inversion problem or the RSA chosen-target inversion problem is hard [3]. So far, this is the only known practical and provably secure blind signature that is based on a trapdoor one-way function.

The RSA blind signature: The signer has a standard RSA key pair, where (e, n) is the public key, and (d, n) is the private key. To have an already hashed and padded message m blindly signed, the message is blinded to $m' = mr^e \bmod n$ using a randomly chosen blinding parameter $r \in_R (\mathbb{Z}/n\mathbb{Z})^*$ and the public key of the signer. The blinded message is given to the signer, who creates the signature $s' = m'^d \bmod n$ with his private key. This results in a blinded signature $m^d r \bmod n$, which can only be unblinded with the knowledge of the random value r. The RSA blind signature is shown in figure 1.

2.3   Building Blind Signatures from Identification Protocols

Okamoto and Otha [15] have shown that all three-move identification protocols based on commutative random self reducible problems have a property which they call *divertibility*. Divertibility is a man-in-the-middle attack on identification protocols, but can also be employed for blinding the corresponding non-interactive signature.

Three-move identification protocols of the structure

$$\begin{aligned}
\text{commitment } a &: \text{ } signer \rightarrow receiver \\
\text{challenge } c &: \quad signer \leftarrow receiver \\
\text{response } s &: \quad signer \rightarrow receiver
\end{aligned}$$

can be turned into signatures using the technique of Feige and Shamir [9], by calculating the challenge as hash of the message to be signed and the given commitment, i.e. $c = H(m, a)$.

Blind signatures based on divertible three-move witness-indistinguishable identification protocols (the notion of witness-indistinguishability is also due to Feige and Shamir [10]) have been proven to be secure in the random oracle model for an ℓ that is poly-logarithmicly bounded in the security parameter [17, 2].

While this limitation would render the blind signatures based on identification protocols impractical, there is one general technique to improve their security, which we will discuss in the next section, but there are two other results:

- A new blind signature was presented by Abe [1], which can be proven to be secure in the random oracle model for an ℓ polynomially bounded in the security parameter, however this is at the cost of reducing perfect blindness to computational blindness.
- Schnorr [20,21] has recently presented a new generic parallel attack against Schnorr blind signatures, that is not covered by [17]. He showed that the witness indistinguishable Okamoto-Schnorr blind signature does not protect

better against this attack than a plain Schnorr blind signature does. Furthermore, it was proven that Schnorr blind signatures are provably secure in the random oracle and generic model. However, the generic model assumes an ideal group, where group operations are done by a group oracle.

The Schnorr blind signature: An example for divertibility is the blind signature based on the Schnorr signature [19] as shown in figure 2.

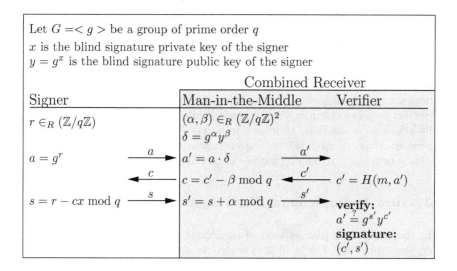

Let $G = \langle g \rangle$ be a group of prime order q
x is the blind signature private key of the signer
$y = g^x$ is the blind signature public key of the signer

		Combined Receiver	
Signer		Man-in-the-Middle	Verifier
$r \in_R (\mathbb{Z}/q\mathbb{Z})$		$(\alpha, \beta) \in_R (\mathbb{Z}/q\mathbb{Z})^2$	
		$\delta = g^\alpha y^\beta$	
$a = g^r$	$\xrightarrow{\ a\ }$	$a' = a \cdot \delta$	$\xrightarrow{\ a'\ }$
	$\xleftarrow{\ c\ }$	$c = c' - \beta \bmod q$	$\xleftarrow{\ c'\ }\ c' = H(m, a')$
$s = r - cx \bmod q$	$\xrightarrow{\ s\ }$	$s' = s + \alpha \bmod q$	$\xrightarrow{\ s'\ }$ **verify:** $a' \stackrel{?}{=} g^{s'} y^{c'}$ **signature:** (c', s')

Fig. 2. A Schnorr blind signature based on the divertible identification protocol.

The system parameters of a Schnorr blind signature consist of a group G of prime order q and a generator g of G. The private key of the signer is $x \in \mathbb{Z}/q\mathbb{Z}$ and the corresponding public key is $y = g^x$. The signer first commits to a random value $r \in_R \mathbb{Z}/q\mathbb{Z}$ and sends the commitment $a = g^r$ to the signature receiver, who blinds the commitment to $a' = ag^\alpha y^\beta$. The challenge is computed as $c' = H(m, a')$ and blinded to $c = c' - \beta \bmod q$. The blinded challenge c is sent to the signer, who returns the response $s = r - cx \bmod q$. Finally, the signature receiver unblinds the response to $s' = s + \alpha \bmod q$. The pair (c', s') is a valid signature for the message m.

2.4   Enhancing the Security of Blind Signatures

While the results on the security of blind signatures based on identification protocols are ambiguous, there is a general technique, which is due to Pointcheval [16] that can enhance the security of blind signatures. This add-on allows to overcome the limitation to poly-logarithmic many interactions with the signer to keep the protocol provably secure. However, the attacker must be limited to a parallel synchronized attack: for all parallel interactions with the signer, the indices of the interactions must always be in the same order.

The idea is to always issue two blind signatures in parallel, however the signer randomly selects one protocol execution to be aborted right before the signature is finally issued. Then the signature receiver has to prove that the aborted protocol has been executed correctly. Therefore, the signature receiver uses a perfect hiding commitment on his blinding parameters and the messages to be signed for both protocol executions and sends them to the signer before the protocols are started. For the aborted protocol the signature receiver has to present the committed values to the signer, who may now check that the corresponding challenge was built correctly. Only then the other protocol execution will be continued.

This generic enhancement, which is based on the cut-and-chose paradigm, is at the cost of two additional messages and additional computation, which depends on the signature scheme. Furthermore, a synchronization between all parallel protocol executions is necessary. While this synchronization may be easily achieved, it may also be object to a denial of service attack: If a signature receiver delays to open the requested commitment, no other parallel blind signature protocol started afterwards can be finished until this one has timed out.

3   How to Implement Blind Signatures

In this section we discuss how to implement blind signatures as an abstract cryptographic tool. Our goal is to design an abstraction layer that enables easy replacement of each implemented blind signature algorithm with any other.

3.1   Communication and Interoperability

To enable interoperability of different implementations of abstract blind signatures, we have to take the following general conditions into account:

- A *context* for the blind signature protocol is necessary, including a prior agreement on a common algorithm and on the key pair to be used, if several key pairs are possible.
- The exchanged messages must have a standardized format that integrates raw *protocol data* and some *control information*.

The context is essentially application dependant and should be set up in an authenticated manner. Therefore, we have to negotiate the context outside of the basic protocol and the abstract blind signature is always used by another communication protocol. We suggest a token based approach for blind signatures. Tokens are protocol elements that can be generated and consumed by the abstract blind signature API (application program interface), however the exchange of tokens is up to the application. Such an token based approach is also used by e.g. the Generic Security Service (GSS) [13].

Having a token based approach has three advantages:

1. Any kind of application dependant control information (status and error codes) can easily be integrated into the exchanged messages
2. We do not have to take care for a standardized message format as this is dependant on the current application. However, a standardized encoding is still required for the algorithm specific protocol data. We suggest to use an encoding that is similar to the corresponding standardized signature algorithm, which normally is DER encoded ASN.1 syntax.
3. We can make blind signatures a useful part in complex protocols. For such an integration, explicit knowledge of the content of a token is necessary and a general model for abstract blind signatures is required.

3.2   A General Model for Blind Signatures

To set up a general model for blind signatures, we have analyzed the two major sources for blind signatures as introduced in section 2. We have excluded the security enhancing technique discussed in section 2.4 from our model as this could easily be build on top of our model using the provided tokens.

We will distinguish blind signatures as *deterministic blind signatures* and *randomized blind signatures*.

Deterministic Blind Signatures: This category contains blind signatures that result from (homomorphic) trapdoor one way functions. Those blind signatures consist of only three operations in two protocol moves:
1. The client prepares a hashed and padded message, blinds the message and sends the blinded message to the server.
2. The server signs the blinded message and sends the signature back to the client.
3. The client removes the blinding from the signature.

Currently, the RSA blind signature is the only member of this category.

Randomized Blind Signatures: This category contains blind signatures that result from three-move identification protocols. They consist of four operations in three protocol moves:
1. The server first commits to a secret value and sends the commitment to the client.
2. The client blinds the commitment and creates a challenge by hashing the message and the blinded commitment together. Then the challenge is blinded and sent to the server.
3. The server computes a response and sends it back to the client.
4. The client unblinds the response.

Besides the blind signatures based on three-move identification protocols the blind versions of other randomized digital signatures, modified DSA and ElGamal signatures, can also be subsumed under this type of blind signatures.

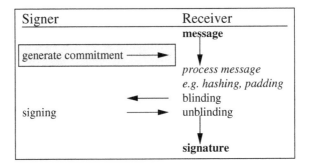

Fig. 3. An integrated model for blind signatures.

Both types of blind signatures can be easily integrated in a single, intuitive model that is shown in figure 3.

This model enforces to check, whether the used blind signature is randomized. In this case an additional protocol step is required, where the signer generates a "commitment token" that is consumed by the client. Afterwards, both types of blind signatures process the same steps:

Blinding: The signature receiver processes the message to be signed and generates a "blinded message token".

Signing: The signer uses the "blinded message token" to generate the "blinded signature token".

Unblinding: The signature receiver removes the blinding from the "blinded signature token" and returns the signature.

3.3 Limitations of the General Model

Our general model seems to be a good abstraction for blind signatures based on trapdoor one way functions, three-move identification protocols, and related constructions like ElGamal, DSA, and Nyberg-Rueppel.

However, in this model it is impossible to integrate blind signatures that have a different structure or require additional steps. This is not a drawback of our model, as this is necessary for security reasons, as discussed in section 2:

1. It is difficult to prove a blind signature to be secure. Trapdoor one way functions and three-move identification protocols are well-elaborated concepts and turned out to be very practical in designing secure digital signatures and corresponding blind signatures.
2. Blind signatures should never be used as a black box. Explicit knowledge of the properties and limitations of a blind signature is required for its correct usage.

Therefore, we do not recommend the usage of blind signatures that are based on other sources.

4   Integration into the Java Cryptography Architecture

The Java Cryptography Architecture (JCA) provides a powerful framework for abstract cryptographic services. We show how to extend this framework to similarly support blind signatures as an abstract cryptographic service.

4.1   The Java Cryptography Architecture

The JCA provides a framework for abstract cryptographic services that are *proxies* for the exchangeable algorithms implementing this cryptographic service, the *service providers*. Thus, the application only interacts with an instance of the proxy that delegates all operations to the selected service provider. Every proxy provides a static method getInstance(String algorithm[,String provider]), that returns an instance of the proxy class itself that is correctly set up to use a service provider for the passed algorithm name.

4.2   Integrating Blind Signatures

To extend the JCA with a blind signature service, we have to introduce the new type of abstract service to the JCA. Fortunately, this is no problem, as the JCA is not restricted to the services already given, and new ones can be added.

We have added the abstract blind signature proxy BlindSignature and the corresponding service provider interface BlindSignatureSpi to the framework. The blind signature proxy is defined very similar to the signature proxy, however two parties are distinguished, the *server* who issues a blind signature and the *client* who receives the signature. In the following, we will present some methods of the blind signature proxy.

void initServer(PrivateKey key[,SecureRandom random])
  Initializes the proxy as server using the given private key for signing. Optionally, the application may pass its own source or randomness to the proxy.
void initClient(PublicKey key[,SecureRandom random])
  Initializes the proxy as client using the given public key for blinding messages or for verifying signatures. Optionally, the application may pass its own source or randomness to the proxy.
void update(byte[] message)
  Passes the message that will be blindly signed or whose signature will be verified to the client proxy. This method may also be called for each message part, if the message has multiple parts.
byte[] getBlindedMessage([BlindingParameter param])
  Generates and returns the "blinded message token" from the messages passed via the update method. Optionally, the application may pass its own blinding parameter to the client proxy.
BlindingParameter getBlindingParameter()
  Returns the blinding parameter currently used by the client proxy.

```
byte[] sign(byte[] blindedMessage)
```
Generates and returns the "blinded signature token".
```
byte[] unblindSignature(byte[] blindedSignature)
```
Removes the blinding from the "blinded signature token" and returns the signature.
```
boolean verify(byte[] signature)
```
Returns true, if the given signature is valid for the messages passed via the update method and false otherwise.
```
boolean isRandomized()
```
Returns true, if the implementation of the blind signature is randomized and false otherwise.

The following methods are only available to randomized blind signatures:

```
byte[] getCommitment()
```
Returns the "commitment token". A new commitment is generated, if the proxy is initialized as server. Otherwise, if the proxy is initialized as client, the currently used commitment is returned, e.g. after blinding this is the blinded commitment.
```
void setCommitment(byte[] commitment)
```
Consumes the "commitment token" that has been generated by the corresponding server proxy.
```
KeyPair getCommitmentKeyPair()
```
Returns the current commitment as key pair, where the public key holds the commitment and the private key holds the corresponding secret values. The representation of commitments in the form of key pairs has the advantage that keys can be used with most other cryptographic objects of the JCA.

A simple fragment of code issuing a blind signature in an already established context is shown in figure 4.

```
Client                                   Server

if (bsig.isRandomized()){                if (bsig.isRandomized()){
                                           byte[] cmt = bsig.getCommitment();
  byte[] cmt = receive();    ◄─────────    send(cmt);
  bsig.setCommitment(cmt);                }
}
bsig.update(message);
byte[] blMsg = bsig.getBlindedMessage();
send(blMsg);                   ─────────►  byte[] blMsg = receive();
                                           byte[] blSig = bsig.sign(blMsg);
byte[] blSig = receive();      ◄─────────  send(blSig);
byte[] sig = bsig.unblindSignature(blSig);
```

Fig. 4. Issuing a blind signature

5   Conclusion

The goal of this paper was to aid the development of privacy enabled applications using blind signatures as a cryptographic tool in a secure, flexible, and exchangeable manner.

We gave an abstraction of blind signatures to a general model and showed how to integrate this model into the framework of the Java Cryptography Architecture. Our implementation of several blind signature algorithms has proven to be quite fast and very practical in several applications.

Several attempts have been made to prove the security of blind signature algorithms. Although recent results encourage to trust in the security of blind signatures, there are still some open questions. Thus, it is even more important to be able to immediately replace a blind signature algorithm with another algorithm in case the used algorithm turns out to be insecure.

References

1. M. Abe. A secure three-move blind signature scheme for polynomially many signatures. In *Advances in Cryptology – EUROCRYPT 2001*, volume 2045 of *Lecture Notes in Computer Science*, pages 136–151. Springer-Verlag, 2001.
2. M. Abe and T. Okamoto. Provably secure partially blind signatures. In *Advances in Cryptology – CRYPTO 2000*, volume 1880 of *Lecture Notes in Computer Science*, pages 271–286. Springer-Verlag, 2000.
3. M. Bellare, C. Namprempre, D. Pointcheval, and M. Semanko. The power of RSA inversion oracles and the security of Chaum's RSA-based blind signature scheme. In *Financial Cryptography '01 Pre-proceedings*, pages 258–277. Springer-Verlag, 2001.
4. M. Bellare and P. Rogaway. Random oracles are practical: a paradigm for designing efficient protocols. In *1st ACM Conference on Computer and Communications Security – CCS '93*, pages 62–73. ACM Press, 1993.
5. D. Chaum. Blind signatures for untraceable payments. In *Advances in Cryptology – CRYPTO '82*, pages 199–203. Plenum, 1983.
6. J. L. Camenisch, J-M. Piveteau, and M. A. Stadler. Blind signatures based on the discrete logarithm problem. In *Advances in Cryptology – EUROCRYPT '94*, volume 950 of *Lecture Notes in Computer Science*, pages 428–432. Springer-Verlag, 1995.
7. T. ElGamal. A public key cryptosystem and a signature scheme based on discrete logarithms. *IEEE Transactions on Information Theory*, 31(4):469–472, 1985.
8. A. Frier, P. Karlton, and P. Kocher. The SSL 3.0 protocol. Internet Draft, 1996.
9. A. Fiat and A. Shamir. How to prove yourself: Practical solutions to identification and signature problems. In *Advances in Cryptology – CRYPTO '86*, volume 263 of *Lecture Notes in Computer Science*, pages 186–194. Springer-Verlag, 1987.
10. U. Feige and A. Shamir. Witness indistinguishable and witness hiding protocols. In *22nd Symposium on Theory of Computing – STOC '90*, pages 416–426. ACM Press, 1990.
11. P. Horster, M. Michels, and H. Petersen. Meta-message recovery and meta-blind signature schemes based on the discrete logarithm problem and their applications. In *Advances in Cryptology – ASIACRYPT '94*, volume 917 of *Lecture Notes in Computer Science*, pages 224–237. Springer-Verlag, 1995.

12. A. Juels, M. Luby, and R. Ostrovsky. Security of blind digital signatures. In *Advances in Cryptology – CRYPTO '97*, volume 1294 of *Lecture Notes in Computer Science*, pages 150–164. Springer-Verlag, 1997.
13. J. Linn. Generic security service application program interface, version 2. RFC 2078, 1997.
14. National Institute of Standards and Technology (NIST). The Digital Signature Standard. FIPS PUB 186, 1994.
15. T. Okamoto and K. Otha. Divertible zero-knowledge interactive proofs and commutative random self-reduciblity. In *Advances in Cryptology – EUROCRYPT '89*, volume 434 of *Lecture Notes in Computer Science*, pages 134–149. Springer-Verlag, 1990.
16. D. Pointcheval. Strengthened security for blind signatures. In *Advances in Cryptology – EUROCRYPT '98*, volume 1403 of *Lecture Notes in Computer Science*, pages 391–405. Springer-Verlag, 1998.
17. D. Pointcheval and J. Stern. Provably secure blind signature schemes. In *Advances in Cryptology – ASIACRYPT '96*, volume 1163 of *Lecture Notes in Computer Science*, pages 252–265. Springer-Verlag, 1996.
18. R. Rivest, A. Shamir, and L. Adleman. A method for obtaining digital signatures and public key cryptosystems. *Communications of the ACM*, 21(2):120–126, 1978.
19. C.P. Schnorr. Efficient signature generation by smart cards. *Journal of Cryptology*, 4(3):161–174, 1991.
20. C.P. Schnorr. Security of DL-encryption and signatures against generic attacks, a survey. In *Public-Key Cryptography and Computational Number Theory 2000*. Walter De Gruyter, 2001.
21. C.P. Schnorr. Security of blind discrete log signatures against interactive attacks. In *3rd International Conference On Information And Communication Security – ICICS 2001*, Lecture Notes in Computer Science. Springer-Verlag, 2001.

FAucS: An FCC Spectrum Auction Simulator for Autonomous Bidding Agents

János A. Csirik[1], Michael L. Littman[1], Satinder Singh[2], and Peter Stone[1]

[1] AT&T Labs – Research
180 Park Ave.
Florham Park, NJ 07932
{janos,mlittman,baveja,pstone}@research.att.com
[2] Syntek Capital
423 West 55th Street
New York, NY 10019
satinder.baveja@syntekcapital.com

Abstract. We introduce *FAucS*, a software testbed for studying automated agent bidding strategies in simulated auctions, specifically the United States FCC wireless frequency spectrum auctions. In addition to the complexity of these auctions, which provides ample opportunities for intelligent approaches to bidding, this type of auction has huge commercial importance, each bringing in billions of dollars to governments around the world. We implement straightforward sample agents in *FAucS* and use them to replicate known beneficial bidding strategies in this type of auction. We then discuss potential in-depth studies of autonomous bidding agent behaviors using *FAucS*. The main contribution of this work is the implementation, description, and empirical validation of the *FAucS* testbed. We present it as a challenging and promising AI research domain.

1   Introduction

In recent years, governments around the world have used spectrum auctions as a mechanism for allocating rights to radio spectrum. These auctions have generated extremely large revenues, often with billions of dollars at stake.

The United States' Federal Communications Commission (FCC) has already engaged in more than 30 such auctions, altering the rules from auction to auction in the hopes of maximizing revenue and reducing opportunities for tacit, mutually beneficial agreements among participants [12]. The result is a complex set of rules that require sophisticated strategizing on the part of auction participants. To the best of our knowledge, participants in these auctions have always generated their strategies and bids manually, even though all bids are submitted and acknowledged online.

Recent work in the field of artificial intelligence has introduced the possibility of creating autonomous bidding agents to participate in auctions. In particular, the first trading agent competition (TAC) was held in Boston in July, 2000 [13].

L. Fiege, G. Mühl, and U. Wilhelm (Eds.): WELCOM 2001, LNCS 2232, pp. 139–151, 2001.
© Springer-Verlag Berlin Heidelberg 2001

TAC agents acted as simulated travel agents and had to procure goods for their clients in different types of auctions, bidding against other autonomous agents. ATTac-2000, our entry in TAC, finished in first place [11]. TAC was very successful at attracting many competitors from around the world by creating an artificial domain that was simple enough to understand quickly, but complex enough to prevent a trivial winning strategy. However, one potential criticism of TAC is that the domain was not realistic enough to generate meaningful, scalable agent strategies.

This paper introduces spectrum auctions as a complex and realistic domain for exploring general autonomous bidding strategies. Our simulator, *FAucS*, is faithful to the FCC regulations for the most recent FCC auction, Auction 35, which involved 422 licenses in 195 markets and ran from December 12th, 2000 to January 26th, 2001. *FAucS* allows autonomous bidding agents and humans to participate simultaneously in mock auctions. We introduce several implemented bidding strategies and use *FAucS* to replicate some of the observed strategic bidding opportunities in past auctions such as budget stretching.

The main contribution of this work is the implementation, description, and empirical validation of the *FAucS* testbed. We present it as a challenging and promising AI research domain.

The remainder of the paper is organized as follows. Section 2 introduces the spectrum auction domain and our FCC spectrum auction simulator, *FAucS*. Section 3 discusses the strategies used by our sample bidding agents. Section 4 reports the results of a set of simulations. Section 5 suggests future uses for *FAucS*, Section 6 describes related work, and Section 7 concludes.

2   FCC Spectrum Auction Simulator

The goods available in the FCC spectrum auctions are a set of *licenses*, or blocks of spectrum; each in a *market*, or region of the United States. In Auction 35, licenses were 10 or 15 megahertz in size, and each of the 195 markets had between 1 and 4 licenses available. A total of 422 licenses and more than 80 bidders were involved.

2.1   Overview

To a first approximation, the rules of the auction are straightforward (official rules are presented in FCC document DA 00–2038). All of the FCC spectrum auctions, including Auction 35, use a simultaneous multiple round (SMR) system. In an SMR auction, all goods are available at the same time, and bidding occurs in discrete rounds. After each round, each bidder's bids are announced publicly. The *provisionally winning bids* are also announced: These are the highest bid received up to that point on each license. (In case of a tie, the first bid submitted to the FCC's system wins.) The auction ends immediately after the first round with no new activity. Each license is then sold to its provisional winner, for a price equal to the provisionally winning bid.

2.2   Allowable Bids

The amount that can be bid on a particular license is constrained to be an element of a small fixed set. If the license has attracted no bids yet, this set consists only of a *minimum bid price* as pre-announced by the FCC. Once the license has attracted at least one bid, the acceptable bids are those that top the provisionally winning bid by 1 to 9 times the *increment*, which is a value between 10% and 20% of the provisionally winning bid. The increment is calculated by the FCC using an exponential smoothing formula, which tends to make the increment high or low depending on whether the number of bids the license is drawing is high or low. We refer to any bid other than the 1-increment bid as a *jump bid*.

The bid increment rule was added to prevent bidders from communicating with one another via the low-order (i.e. relatively insignificant) digits in the bids.

2.3   Eligibility Constraints

The most important rules that make FCC spectrum auctions different from other auctions concern *eligibility constraints*. The rules are intended to prevent bidders from sitting out during the early rounds of bidding and delaying placing their serious bids until late in the auction. It was feared that such a strategy might be employed and would result in lower FCC revenues and an unnecessarily long auction.

For the purposes of the eligibility rules, each license is assigned a number of *bidding units*. The number of bidding units per license ranges from 2,500 (Minot, ND) to 15,906,000 (New York City), and it correlates with the population of the corresponding market. For each round of the auction, each bidder has a certain *eligibility* and *activity*, both of which are expressed in terms of bidding units.

Activity(b,r): A bidder b's activity for a round r is defined as the total number of bidding units in the licenses where b has (a) placed a bid in the current round; or (b) held the provisionally winning bid as of the end of the previous round.

Eligibility(b,r): b's eligibility in round r is a quantity that controls the allowable activity for that round. Eligibility is defined as follows:

Eligibility(b,r) = Min(Eligibility($b,r-1$),Activity($b,r-1$)/.80)

The eligibility in the first round can be chosen by the bidders themselves (it is directly proportional to the deposit they put down). In each round, each bidder's activity is constrained to be no higher than its eligibility. If a bidder submits a set of bids such that the activity is less than 80% of the eligibility, its eligibility is reduced[1]. Thus, once eligibility is lost, it cannot be recovered.

---

[1] This constant starts at 80% and is increased by the FCC to 90% and then 98% as the auction draws near its end.

2.4 Withdrawals and Waivers

Bidders are also allowed a small number of *bid withdrawals*, but the rules governing doing so are so punitive[2] that withdrawals play little role in recent FCC spectrum auctions and in our simulations.

Additionally, bidders are allowed up to five *activity waivers*. A bidder using an activity waiver in a certain round ensures that their eligibility will not be reduced in that round, even if its activity is low. These waivers are intended to ensure that equipment failures and the like do not put bidders in impossible situations, since a bidder with no provisionally winning bids could reduce its eligibility to zero by not bidding in a single round of the auction, and thereby shut itself out completely from the rest of the auction[3]. Activity waivers have potential strategic uses. In real FCC spectrum auctions, bidders tend to save up most of their activity waivers until they are almost ready to drop out.

2.5 *FAucS*

Our FCC spectrum auction simulator, *FAucS*, models all of the above rules in their entirety. It uses a client-server architecture with the server and the bidding agents (clients) all written in Perl and using TCP sockets to communicate with each other. The software is highly customizable in that it

- Reads in license files defining the goods that are available for sale;
- Can model a wide range of rules used by the FCC in past auctions or considered by the FCC for future auctions via simple comand-line parameters.
- Allows for the automatic inclusion of arbitrary numbers of parameterized agents;
- Allows humans and agents (or only humans) to simultaneously participate in a simulated auction;
- Allows for tracking FCC spectrum auctions as they happen;
- Allows for loading data from a partially completed auction, real or simulated, and finishing it off with the participation of various bidding agents and/or humans;
- Was designed so as to be easily extensible to combinatorial auctions such as those planned in the future by the FCC.

Typical auctions last between 100 and 150 rounds, with Auction 35 lasting 101 rounds. In real life, they take several weeks, or even months to complete. We have completed auctions involving humans using *FAucS* that have completed within a day, and agent-only auctions with more than 60 licenses and about 10 agents complete in 15 to 20 minutes[4]. A good deal of this time is typically agents

---

[2] A withdrawn provisionally winning bid must still be paid unless another bidder matches that price on the license. Thus, bid withdrawals are a potentially very expensive way of freeing up eligibility.

[3] The FCC will automatically grant bidders activity waivers (if they have any left) in any round in which they weren't heard from.

[4] Times are on a multiprocessor, 270Mhz SGI workstation.

waiting for each other to finish their bidding, since a round can only advance when all agents have placed their bids.

3   Prototype Autonomous Bidding Agents

In this section, we present sample autonomous bidding agents for use in *FAucS*. These agents are not meant to be realistic in all regards, but are rather intended to demonstrate the full functionality of *FAucS* and the challenging nature of the problem it presents. As such, the agents incorporate several approximations to fully realistic (i.e. human-like) behavior. We point out the elements that represent approximations throughout.

First, we define the utility measure we use to evaluate bidding agents. Second, we present a sub-problem essential to all intelligent bidding strategies. Third, we describe the basic agent (BA), which uses a strategy designed to maximize the bidder's utility without any regard to the constraints of the other bidders. Fourth, we describe the budget-stretching agent (BSA), which actively tries to force other agents to spend more money in some markets in order to reduce their abilities to bid in others.

3.1   Agent Utilities

Merrill Lynch & Co. analyzed the wireless communications industry and estimated that each megahertz of spectrum is worth

- $2 per person in markets with fewer than 750,000 people (144 markets from McCook, NE to Worcester, MA)
- $4 per person in markets with between 750,000 and 2,500,000 people (33 markets from Syracuse, NY to Pittsburgh, PA), and
- $6 per person in markets with more than 2,500,000 people (18 markets from Tampa, FL to New York, NY) [6].

Following this basic insight, we imagine that each bidder has a dollar value for obtaining a license in a given market that is related to the size of that market, and a somewhat lower value for obtaining a second license in the same market. We use the following terms:

Market Value(m,b): the dollar worth (possibly 0) of a single license in market m to bidder, b.

Secondary market value(m,b): the dollar worth (possibly 0) of a second license in m to b.

Supply(m): The number of licenses for sale in market m.

Demand(m): The number of non-zero market and secondary market values in market m among all the bidders.

Budget(b): The total dollar amount available to bidder b. b can never have outstanding bids in excess of this amount.

For the purposes of this paper, no bidder has a non-zero value for a third license in a market. The precise market values vary among the agents within a range but are commonly known: we use a private-value, complete-information model[5].

In the absence of other constraints, the expected final price of a market in which supply is greater than or equal to demand will be the minimum bid price. The final price of a market with supply of k and demand greater than k is within one bid increment of the $(k + 1)$st highest market value. Note that multiple licenses in the same market are sold independently; they can and do sell for different prices[6].

At the end of the auction, the total of the market values and secondary market values of the licenses a bidder won, minus the cost of those goods, is the bidder's *utility*:

$$\text{Utility} = \text{Total value} - \text{Total cost}.$$

Each bidder seeks to maximize its utility, which can be done by winning as much market value as possible at as low a price as possible.

3.2   The Allocation Sub-problem

In the absence of budget or eligibility constraints, bidders can be quite successful with the strategy of simply bidding in each market in which the ask price is less than the bidder's value. The presence of the additional constraints make the basic bidding strategy somewhat more complex. This section describes a constrained allocation problem and our solution to it. The resulting algorithm is then used by the bidding agents described in later sections.

The allocation sub-problem is this: given a set of licenses, each with a utility, a number of bidding units, and a cost; a maximum total number of bidding units (eligibility); and a maximum total cost (budget), find the subset of licenses with maximum total utility subject to budget and eligibility constraints.

Ignoring the eligibility constraint, the allocation sub-problem is precisely the classic "knapsack" problem. The standard exact dynamic-programming solution to knapsack computes a table with one entry for each possible integer value from 0 to the total utility of all licenses. In the FCC auction domain, however, the total can easily be in the billions of dollars. We developed a refined version, which only creates table entries for totals that are actually encountered during the search for an optimal solution.

To find a subset of licenses that obeys both budget and eligibility constraints, our allocation algorithm calls the knapsack solver to find a set of licenses with maximum total utility subject only to the budget constraint. If the resulting set violates the eligibility constraint, the algorithm repeats the optimization using a reduced budget (one dollar less than the cost of the previous optimal solution).

---

[5] The complete-information aspect is not entirely realistic: In real auctions, the bidders only have rough ideas of each others' market values.

[6] The licenses represent different frequency bands. Some real bidders exhibit preferences among the bands [2]. For the purposes of the experiments in this paper, we consider licenses in the same market to be of identical value to the agents.

This process terminates eventually with a solution that satisfies both budget and eligibility constraints.

In general, the procedure described above can produce solutions that are arbitrarily worse than optimal. However, we found that, in practice, the first solution produced by the algorithm generally satisfied the eligibility constraint and was therefore an optimal allocation.

3.3   Basic Agent

Our sample bidding agent algorithm is summarized in Table 1. The quantities in Steps 2 and 3 are computed as follows.

Remaining eligibility: subtract from the bidder's current eligibility the bidding units tied up in licenses of which it is provisional winner;

Remaining budget: subtract from the bidder's total budget the money tied up in licenses of which it is provisional winner;

Current values for markets: use the market value or the secondary market value, depending on the number of licenses in the market in which the bidder is already provisional winner;

Current costs for each market: find the two least expensive licenses in each market.

This basic agent strategy is myopic in that it assumes, at each bidding round, that the bidder will win all licenses of which it is provisional winner, and that it could win any other license for a 1-increment bid. For choosing the desired licenses in each round (Step 4 in Table 1), the bidder uses the allocation algorithm described in Section 3.2

Once the set of desired licenses was determined, the basic agent always bids (Step 5 in Table 1) at the 1-increment price (no jump bids) for those and only those licenses. In a single-good ascending auction, this strategy is optimal [7]. However, in SMR auctions, and particularly in the presence of budget constraints, other bidding strategies may be more beneficial. One such strategy is described next.

Table 1. High-level overview of our basic agent (BA) algorithm.

REPEAT (once per round)
1. Get market prices from server
2. Compute remaining budget and eligibility
3. Compute current values and costs of markets
4. Choose desired licenses within constraints
5. Submit bids to server
UNTIL game over

3.4 Budget-Stretching Agent

Budget constraints "provide incentives to ... try to reduce opponents' budgets in early sales in order to lower subsequent sale prices." [7]. To demonstrate this effect within the spectrum auction scenario, we created an agent that aggressively bids in markets in which its opponents are interested in order to raise the prices of licenses in those markets and reduce their competitiveness.

Specifically, BSA acts identically to BA except for in Step 5 of Table 1, at which point it does the following.

1. Submit all bids that BA would submit.
2. Compute the **stretchable markets**—those in which the agent has no market value and in which the total demand of all bidders is equal to the supply. This computation can be done once at the beginning of the auction and stored.
3. In each stretchable market:
   - Let **OPlimit** be the smallest market value for a license in the market among bidders with demand in that market.
   - Compute:
     - **BSAlimit** = OPlimit/1.2
     - **NJmin** = BSAlimit/1.4
     - **NJmax** = BSAlimit/1.2
   - Bid at the largest possible price p such that $p <$ NJmin OR ($p >$ MJmax AND $p <$ BSAlimit)

Figure 1 illustrates this strategy. Notice that BSA relies on knowing the demands and values of the other bidders: We are assuming a complete-information scenario.

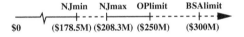

Fig. 1. A general picture of the budget-stretching strategy (numbers in parentheses correspond to the example in the text). The agent avoids bidding at prices covered by a dashed line. Subject to that restriction, it bids at the maximum allowable price.

To understand the purpose of budget stretching, consider the following example with two agents and 2 markets, each of which has only 1 license available:

Agent S (*stretcher*): budget $250M, market 1 value $300M
Agent V (*victim*): budget $525M, market 1 value $300M, market 2 value $300M.

If both agents use the BA strategy, **V** will win the license in market 1 for (within one bid increment of) $250M and the license in market 2 for the minimum bid price (since there's no competition). **S** will win neither license.

However, assuming that **V** follows the BA strategy, **S** can win the market 1 license. Early in the auction, it can raise the price of the market 2 license to just below $300M (the opponent's budget limit, OPlimit). Care must be taken such that the next lowest acceptable bid is still under $300M so that **V** can still afford it. **V** will then spend (close to) its limit on that license, leaving **S** to win the license in market 1 for $225M.

Recall that the bid increment can be as high as 20% of the current price. Thus, **S** must bid on the license in market 2 for no more than OPlimit/1.2 = $250M (the BSAlimit). Additionally, if its final bid is only a single increment over the previous price (i.e., not a jump bid), **V** will place the same bid and have a chance of winning the license at the lower price. Therefore, **S**'s best strategy is to plan such that it can reach a price of close to the BSAlimit with a final bid that is a jump bid. In particular, if the going price is ever between BSAlimit/1.4 (NJmin for "no jump minimum") and BSAlimit/1.2 (NJmax), then there will be no jump bids available below the BSAlimit level in the next round. Thus, in this example, **S** bids in the early rounds at the highest price possible covered by a solid line in Figure 1. Due to the jump bids, the market 2 license rises in price much faster than does the market 1 license, and, after a few rounds, **V** steps in and wins the license at a price close to its $300M budget.

In general, budget stretching can be effective in markets such that the agent has no demand and total demand is equal to supply, the stretchable markets (observe that market 2 in the above example is stretchable). Without budget stretching, the agents with demand in that market win the licenses at the minimum bid price. With budget stretching, agents with demand in the market win the licenses at a significantly higher price, close to their market values. Even though the prices are high, the bidders still win the licenses because the budget stretching happens in the early rounds, so they can still all afford to bid for the licenses, as they do according to the BA strategy[7].

4   Empirical Results

This section describes a set of simulated auctions we ran to illustrate a known bidding strategy: budget stretching. The primary purpose of this experiment was to verify the potential usefulness of *FAucS* for studying autonomous agent bidding strategies in a complex, realistic domain. However, the parameter choices are all justified by data from Auction 35. In this sense, the experiments provide a way of quantifying the potential benefits of strategies that were known to be good ideas in principle.

4.1   Test Auction Setup

In our runs, we included only the largest 62 markets from Auction 35 (this is the subset of the top 100 U.S. markets that are available in Auction 35), as these

---

[7] The opponent agents could come up with a better response to budget stretching. BSA is designed to exploit weaknesses in BA.

constitute a large majority of the value in the auction. There were 155 licenses available in these markets. We began by defining a set of five "big bidders," intended to emulate the presence of five national companies participating in Auction 35[8]. We also included 4 "small bidders" in each market with smaller market values. These small bidders represent regional companies that are budget-constrained and are only interested in specific markets. They essentially served to raise the minimum final prices to more realistic levels. Market values and baseline budgets were randomly selected from a constrained distribution so as to realistically represent the Auction 35 scenario.

4.2   Sample Experiment: Budget Stretching

To study budget stretching in our simulation, we ran bidder 3 with the BSA strategy[9]. With our randomly generated market values, bidder 3 had 8 stretchable markets.

We compared the bidders' utilities in runs in which they all used the BA strategy against runs in which bidder 3 used the BSA strategy (65 runs of each). Table 2 gives the mean utility for each bidder under the BA and BSA conditions, along with the increase (positive) or decrease (negative) in utility and whether the difference is statistically significant ($p < .05$ by a two-sided t-test).

Table 2. Comparison of average utilities (65 runs) between runs in which all agents used the basic agent (BA) strategy and runs in which bidder 3 used the budget-stretching (BSA) strategy. Use of the BSA strategy improved bidder 3's utility substantially.

Bidder	BA	BSA	Δ	Sig.
0	437M	490M	12.2%	yes
1	457M	403M	-11.7%	yes
2	231M	176M	-23.5%	yes
3	**306M**	**385M**	**25.9%**	**yes**
4	162M	141M	-12.9%	no

Not surprisingly, the biggest change in utility is the increase for bidder 3. Budget stretching was quite successful in this case, improving bidder 3's score by almost $80 million. All other bidders were hurt, except bidder 0, who also enjoyed a significant improvement in utility. Although bidder 0 is budget-stretched in some markets, it benefits fortuitously from the fact that some of its competitors no longer have enough capital to compete with it in some of its most valuable markets: it more than makes up for its losses in 15 different markets with significant gains across 21 markets. For comparison, bidder 3 has small

---

[8] AT&T Wireless, Cingular Wireless, Sprint PCS, Verizon Wireless, and Voicestream.
[9] We selected bidder 3 since it has the largest number of stretchable markets.

losses in 4 markets and gains in 14 (5 of them larger in magnitude than the largest loss) as a result of budget stretching. The gains of bidder 3 and bidder 0 both result in large part from a significant saving in a single big market (Los Angeles and San Francisco, respectively).

Bidder 0's benefits derive from a complex set of situations that would be difficult to predict in advance. This fact points out one of the strengths of the simulation approach enabled by *FAucS*—it makes it possible for us to examine the effects of complicated interactions in auction dynamics that would be difficult, if not impossible, to predict by direct analytic methods alone.

5   Potential Uses for *FAucS*

The agents presented in this paper are straightforward agents meant to suggest the potential uses of *FAucS*. We anticipate that *FAucS* will be useful for a wide variety of future studies, both by ourself and by other researchers. Potential directions for future bidding agents include those designed to study

- the development of stable strategies;
- inference under incomplete information;
- strategic uses for activity waivers; and
- communication via bid signaling.

Furthermore, as *FAucS* was developed so as to be easily extensible to combinatorial auctions, it can also be used to study agent bidding strategies in such cases.

One of the original motivations behind *FAucS* was our desire to create a tool to aid human bidders who are participating in multi-unit simultaneous auctions. It can be used to study on-going auctions in depth and to project future scenarios by modeling the other participants as agents.

Another exciting potential use for *FAucS* is as the substrate for a competition such as TAC [13], which would undoubtedly lead to a set of competitive agent strategies.

Finally, *FAucS* can be used to study bidding interactions between autonomous bidding agents and human bidders.

6   Related Work

Although there has been a good deal of research on auction theory, especially from the perspective of auction mechanisms [7], studies of autonomous bidding agents and their interactions are relatively few and recent. The Trading Agent Competition [13], briefly described in Section 1, is one example. Our first-place team at TAC [11] used adaptive bidding agents to successfully avoid the most contentious, and thus expensive, markets. However, TAC involved simplified bidding scenarios that were not particularly realistic and that in some cases dramatically affected agent strategies [5]. FM97.6 is another auction test-bed, which is based on fishmarket auctions [9]. Automatic bidding agents have also been created in this domain [3]. Outside of, but related to, the auction scenario, automatic shopping and pricing agents for internet commerce have been studied within a simplified model [4].

FAucS addresses a much more complex scenario than has been previously studied with autonomous bidding agents: the FCC spectrum auctions. Spectrum auctions have been analyzed retrospectively [12,2], but little is known about them from a theoretical perspective.

As suggested by the results presented above, perhaps the most challenging aspect of spectrum auctions is the presence of budget constraints. As noted by Benoit and Krishna [1], "Traditionally, auction theory ... assumes that bidders have unlimited budgets ...." They argue that even with just 2 goods for sale, and complete information about the goods' values and the bidders' budgets (as assumed by our budget-stretching strategy), budget constraints complicate auctions sufficiently to warrant study.

Indeed, Benoit and Krishna [1] study such a scenario—extending previous research involving just 2 bidders—and find that sequential auctions are more advantageous to the seller than simultaneous auctions (Benoit and Krishna [2] discusses why the FCC chose to use sequential auctions), and that budget constraints can arise endogenously in addition to externally. That is, agents can do better if they choose to be budget constrained, provided that the other agents are aware of this constraint and adjust their strategies accordingly. Pitchick [8] also studies budget-constrained bidders in sequential auctions, finding that the order of sale can affect price.

Our study reported in this paper significantly extends this budget-constraint research to consider multiple bidders, multiple goods, and private values (bidders value goods differently) for the goods in simultaneous, multiple-round auctions. We retain the constraint that bidders have complete knowledge of each other's values for the goods.

7   Conclusion and Future Work

This paper introduces *FAucS* as a rich and realistic simulator for studying autonomous bidding agents in a complex, real-world domain. We have illustrated its usefulness via quantitative experiments using prototype agents in one randomly generated, competitive scenario over a series of runs. The chosen scenario is closely modeled after the most recent FCC spectrum auction, Auction 35.

Our on-going research agenda includes more agent development and experimentation in this new domain. In related research, we have studied abstract mechanisms for agents to issue and receive such signals in a game-theoretic scenario [10].

The BSA strategy relies on the other agents all using the BA strategy. Our research agenda includes using *FAucS* to explore potential responses to BSA as well as competitive equilibria in this domain. BSA also relies on the agent having complete information about the market values of all the other agents. Although bidders do have some knowledge of each other's values in general, we plan to investigate strategies that are less dependent on this assumption.

FAucS currently reflects all of the details of the United States FCC wireless frequency spectrum auction 35. However, it is implemented in such a way as to be easily modifiable to facilitate human and autonomous agent bidding in other FCC spectrum auctions including future combinatorial auctions that will allow bidders to bid on packages of licenses instead of simply single licenses.

Acknowledgements. We thank Mark Bradner and Tim Schaffer of AT&T Wireless for sharing their insights on FCC spectrum auctions.

References

1. J. P. Benoit and V. Krishna. Multiple object auctions with budget constrained bidders. *Review of Economic Studies*, March 2000. In press, available at http://econ.la.psu.edu/~vkrishna/research.html.
2. Peter C. Cramton. The FCC spectrum auctions: An early assessment. *Journal of Economics and Management Strategy*, 6(3):431–495, 1997.
3. Eduard Gimenez-Funes, Lluis Godo, Juan A. Rodriguez-Aguiolar, and Pere Garcia-Calves. Designing bidding strategies for trading agents in electronic auctions. In *Proceedings of the Third International Conference on Multi-Agent Systems*, pages 136–143, 1998.
4. Amy Greenwald and Jeffrey O. Kephart. Shopbots and pricebots. In *Proceedings of the Sixteenth International Joint Conference on Artificial Intelligence*, pages 506–511, 1999.
5. Amy Greenwald and Peter Stone. Autonomous bidding agents in the trading agent competition. *IEEE Internet Computing*, 5(2):52–60, March/April 2001.
6. Jessica Hall. U.S. carriers likely to be choosy in wireless auction. Reuters Newswire, November 2000.
7. Paul Klemperer. Auction theory: A guide to the literature. *Journal of Economic Surveys*, 13(3):227–86, July 1999.
8. Carolyn Pitchick. Budget-constrained sequential auctions with incomplete information. Unpublished manuscript. Under revision November 2000., 1996.
9. Juan A. Rodriguez-Aguilar, Francisco J. Martin, Pablo Noriega, Pere Garcia, and Carles Sierra. Towards a test-bed for trading agents in electronic auction markets. *AI Communications*, 2001. In press. Available at http://sinera.iiia.csic.es/~pablo/pncve.html.
10. Peter Stone and Michael L. Littman. Implicit negotiation in repeated games. In *Proceedings of The Eighth International Workshop on Agent Theories, Architectures, and Languages (ATAL-2001)*, August 2001.
11. Peter Stone, Michael L. Littman, Satinder Singh, and Michael Kearns. ATTac-2000: An adaptive autonomous bidding agent. In *Proceedings of the Fifth International Conference on Autonomous Agents*, pages 238–245, 2001.
12. Robert J. Weber. Making more from less: Strategic demand reduction in the FCC spectrum auctions. *Journal of Economics and Management Strategy*, 6(3):529–548, 1997.
13. Michael P. Wellman, Peter R. Wurman, Kevin O'Malley, Roshan Bangera, Shou-de Lin, Daniel Reeves, and William E. Walsh. A trading agent competition. *IEEE Internet Computing*, 5(2):43–51, March/April 2001.

A Dynamic Programming Model for Algorithm Design in Simultaneous Auctions

Andrew Byde

HP Labs
Bristol, UK

Abstract. In this paper we study algorithms for agents participating in multiple simultaneous auctions for a single private-value good; we use stochastic dynamic programming to derive formal methods for optimal algorithm specification; we study a number of algorithms of complementary complexity and effectiveness, and report preliminary tests on them. The methods and analysis in this paper extend naturally to more complicated scenarios, such as the purchase of multiple complementary goods, although different problem areas bring their own challenges with respect to computational complexity.

1 Introduction

As the quantity of business done on-line rises, there is not only a need for infrastructure to support e-transactions, but also a need to understand how best to select trading partners from among many options. Agents need tools, rules and algorithms to help them optimize their choices within fleeting time-spans, so as to balance risk against potential payoff: A multiplicity of relatively frictionless trading opportunities requires tools to help traders understand what constitutes a good deal, and what does not.

To study optimal rational practice in such environments, we start by looking at auctions, which are already a common trade mechanism, and benefit from often having simple formal specifications. It is our belief that the methods and analysis in this paper extend naturally to more complicated scenarios, such as the purchase of multiple complementary goods, although different problem areas bring their own challenges with respect to computational complexity. In future work we will seek to explore this problem from the perspective of service composition.

The organization of this paper is as follows: In the remainder of this section we discuss the applicability of existing theory to the problem under consideration, and we discuss certain assumptions which are intrinsic to the rest of the paper. In Section 2 we discuss the Dynamic Programming formulation of the agent's decision problem. In Section 3, we discuss some alternative algorithms to be tested against the DP algorithm; in Section 4 we report preliminary work towards empirical investigations of algorithm effectiveness. Section 5 is for Conclusions.

L. Fiege, G. Mühl, and U. Wilhelm (Eds.): WELCOM 2001, LNCS 2232, pp. 152–163, 2001.

1.1   Auction Theory

Bidding strategies for agents participating in auctions have traditionally been studied from a Game Theoretic perspective, mostly in order to address questions of economic design (see e.g. [8] or [7] for an overview).

There are several problems with the existing literature on auction theory as it applies to the sort of real-life simultaneous on-line auctions described above.[1]

1. **Lack of information**. In practice an agent knows very little about its environment compared to typical assumptions. For example, it will typically have no idea what other agents are participating in the auctions in which it desires to trade, and will have no idea what other auctions those agents may themselves be engaged in. Given the fact that many auction participants consider anonymity important, an agent may not even know if two observed bids are from the same opponent.

2. **Rationality**. The problem domain, even in simplified form, is sufficiently large as to make the set of strategies that a given agent may chose to follow intractable. This makes the Nash-equilibrium calculations that are the core of most game-theoretic analyses unfeasible in practice, especially given the lack of information described in (1). An agent cannot realistically hope to solve for equilibrium strategy except in very simple circumstances, and even if the equilibrium calculations could be solved, there is no guarantee that the other agents involved would be able to calculate it.

3. **Simultaneity**. Auction theory typically considers complete auctions, possibly in sequence. The novelty here is that we consider parallel games, which end asynchronously and overlap in time. One could argue that such a multitude of auctions is simply a more complicated auction. In that case, such auctions have not hitherto been considered, and so we consider them here.

1.2   Belief Modeling

Despite our comments regarding lack and uncertainty of information, if an agent is to behave non-trivially, then it needs *some* beliefs regarding (for example) the auctions in which it is participating, or the other agents participating in those auctions.

In this paper we choose to focus on closing price distributions, since they are (assumed to be) directly observable, and hence unambiguous. To be precise, to each auction i, and each price p we assign a number $\delta P_i^{price}(p)$, the agent's belief regarding the prior probability of auction i closing at price p, and write $P_i^{price}(p)$ for the prior probability that auction i will close at price greater than or equal to p, $P_i^{price}(t) = \sum_{t' \geq t} \delta P_i^{price}(t)$ We assume that these probabilities $P_i(t)$ are mutually independent with respect to i.

The main reason for assuming independence is to simplify the model enough to make it practical. The model can be improved by conditioning closing price probabilities on the number or set of auctions open at each moment in time, on

---

[1] See [1] for a discussion of the application of Game Theory to automated negotiation.

historically observed prices and on the agent's behaviour. However, the larger a model is, the longer it takes to build it up from market observations, and the more computationally complex it is. Thus more complicated models are intrinsically less dynamic than simpler models, and the marginal increases in effectiveness derived from an improved belief model could easily be outweighed by losses in effectiveness due to low responsiveness to changing market conditions. In practice the beliefs regarding these probabilities would be built up using some weighted average from observations of actual closing prices.

The main disadvantage of this approach is the fact that an agent should be able, in principle, to use more sophisticated information - such as beliefs regarding the population of opponents - to improve the expected return on its choices. The main reason for restricting attention to closing prices is that most other forms of belief - such as opponent models - require inference over the space of strategies in order to be used (or derived from observed bids). As mentioned in (2) above, we consider this inference highly problematic in general, and so we avoid it.

It may be that there are effective methods for doing this inference, or for deriving models which are predictive of market behaviour without inferring strategy at all. Such methods are not considered here.

1.3   Assumptions

We assume that there is a finite set of auctions S labeled with integers, and a global time variable t which will also be measured using integers, and which is used to synchronize the progress of the auctions. We assume that the decision process is finite, and write K for the largest time at which anything can possibly happen; if the agent has a deadline, this forms a suitable value for K.

The auctions studied in this paper will be English auctions, proceeding in rounds, in which prices may only rise by a fixed increment in each round, and which terminate upon inactivity:

1. Except in the first time step, there is always a participating agent which holds the "active" bid (or "is active").
2. If, at a given time step, no agents shout, then the good is awarded to the agent that is active, and the auction closes;
3. otherwise, the price is increased by a fixed amount (which may depend on time), and one of the agents which shouted is chosen at random to be "active".
4. An active agent may not bid.

It follows that the price in any given auction is a fixed function of time. We write the price in the ith auction at time t as $x_i(t)$.

For a specified agent, we implicitly assume a quasi-linear model for utility, whereby the utility to the agent of purchasing any number of goods at total price x, at time t, is given as

$$u(t, x) = v(t) - x,$$

where the intrinsic value $v(t)$ that the agent places on obtaining 1 or more goods can vary in any way with respect to time. Thus the agent has no incentive to purchase more than one good, and all goods are identical. The framework can be adapted to more complicated utility structures a lá [4]; we shall address such questions in future work.

2 Dynamic Programming Framework

The problem of optimizing decisions in the above context can be framed using Dynamic Programming by identifying the states in which an agent may find itself, and the actions it can take in each state.

States and Actions. For a single auction, the variety of potential states is clear. Besides the time variable t, either the auction is *closed*, or it is open and the agent is *inactive*, or it is open and the agent is *active*. We refer to these possibilities more compactly as C, I, and A. The state space for a given auction is thus $\{0, \ldots K\} \times \{C, I, A\}$. An agent only has options if the auction is open and the agent is inactive, in which case the set of actions is *bid, nobid*.

The state space for the simultaneous auction case is the product over those auctions which are concurrent, of the individual state spaces: Let S_t be the set of auctions with non-zero probability of being open at time t. Then

$$\mathcal{S} = \{(t, s) : t \in \{0, \ldots K\}, s \in Map(S_t, \{C, I, A\})\}$$

with an extra state *done* appended to designate completion of the task.

Transition Probabilities. The planning regarding which states are likely to follow which state-action pairs is performed relative to the beliefs that the agent holds. In this paper we assume that the agent maintains beliefs regarding closing price distributions. These beliefs determine the probability of a given auction moving from an open to a closed state. In addition the agent must maintain beliefs regarding the probability of obtaining the active bid at a given price, if bidding. As before, the theoretical interest of such beliefs would be enhanced if we were to allow correlations between auctions, or to build up models of the opposition which is generating potential bidding conflicts; we choose not to do so for the same reasons as before.

Thus the agent has a function $P_i(t)$ which gives the a-priori probability that auction i will be open at time t, and $Q_i(t)$ which gives the a-priori probability that a bid at time step t in auction i[2] will be *blocked*, resulting in the agent *not* obtaining the winning bid. This will be known as the "blocking" probability.

---

[2] Given that the auction is still open

It follows that we have the following transition probabilities for a single auction i:

$$\mathcal{P}((t, A) \rightarrow (t+1, C)) = \mathcal{P}((t, I), nobid \rightarrow (t+1, C)) = \frac{P_i(t) - P_i(t+1)}{P_i(t)},$$

$$\mathcal{P}((t, A) \rightarrow (t+1, I)) = \mathcal{P}((t, I), nobid \rightarrow (t+1, I)) = \frac{P_i(t+1)}{P_i(t)}, \qquad (1)$$

$$\mathcal{P}((t, I, bid) \rightarrow (t+1, I)) = Q_i(t),$$

$$\mathcal{P}((t, I, bid) \rightarrow (t+1, A)) = 1 - Q_i(t),$$

and all others zero. The probability of a given multiple-auction state transition is the product over the individual auctions of the corresponding individual state transition probabilities, and the plan ends when there is a transition from *active* to *closed* in any auction.

Rewards. The agent is rewarded only on a terminal transition, i.e. one in which one or more auctions change from being *active* to *closed*. If the transition is $(t, s) \rightarrow (t+1, s')$, then the reward is calculated to be the immediate reward generated by the profit and loss of the set of transactions at time t, minus the expected payments on active bids in s': $s^{-1}s's^{-1}$

$$v(t) - \sum_{i \in s^{-1}(A) \cap s'^{-1}(C)} x_i(t) - \sum_{i \in s'^{-1}(A)} \frac{P_i(t+1) - P_i(t+2)}{P_i(t+1)} x_i(t+1).$$

3   Algorithms

In this section we specify three algorithms designed to purchase a good of fixed private value in multiple simultaneous English auctions.

The first algorithm is the most obvious (perhaps):

GREEDY:
Unless *active* in some auction, bid in whichever auction has
the currently lowest price (greatest utility).

Some of the properties of greedy algorithms like this one were explored in [10]. GREEDY is extremely easy to code, and does not depend on *any* beliefs about the auctions in which it participates, but is myopic about the long-term effects of its actions. In particular, two obvious problems with GREEDY are that it tends to jump out of an auction whenever a new auction opens, irrespective of the likelihood of getting the good at this new low price; and that it cases where there are good auctions opening in the future, it does not know to *stop* bidding in an auction and wait for the better one.

The second algorithm we will discuss is designed to overcome these faults:

```
HISTORIAN:
(1) If active, don't bid.
(2) Among the auctions which are either open or have not yet
opened, determine the auction with the greatest expected
utility.
(3) If it is possible to bid in this auction, do so;
(4) otherwise, if the current best utility is better than
the future best utility, bid in the current best auction.
```

HISTORIAN overcomes the tendency of GREEDY to jump into a new auction, regardless of expected payoff, in step (3), where it will choose to bid in the auction of greatest expected utility, if possible. This step, in combination with (4) allows HISTORIAN to rationally leave on-going auctions. In the case of consecutive auctions, it will stay in the first until it is indifferent between the current offer and the expected return in the future. Thus, in theory at least, HISTORIAN is a significant improvement on GREEDY. Of course, there is a price to pay: beliefs must be maintained about auction prices, in order to decide whether future auctions are more promising than current ones or not.

Last, but not least, these two algorithms will be compared to the algorithm that simply solves the Dynamic Programming problem described in Section 2.

Having described the states, actions and rewards that make up a Markov decision process, its solution via dynamic programming is standard: To each state, a value is assigned, which is interpreted as the expected total reward due to the agent if the optimal policy is followed, and this value is calculated in one of several ways.

In this case, since the state space is finite and a-cyclic with respect to histories, the value function can be determined by a straight-forward inductive process: It is zero for states with time component K, and for all other states is computed recursively as the maximum, with respect to action, of the expected value of the possible subsequent states.

```
OPTIMAL:[3]
(1) Calculate and store the value function V(t,s) for all
states (t,s).
(2) In any state, bid in whichever auction the corresponding
optimal policy specifies.
```

This algorithm can be customized to re-plan or not in the event of unexpected auction openings, or in the event of an auction remaining open when the agent believed it would certainly be closed. The choice of whether to re-plan or not will depend on how resource intensive calculation of the value functions is.

---

[3] It should be stressed that the name OPTIMAL only has meaning relative to the assumptions that were made in Section 1.3. In particular, if the beliefs the agent holds are inconsistent with the behaviour in a given auction, we cannot expect this algorithm to give optimal performance.

4   Testing

To test the relative effectiveness of the algorithms specified in Section 3 we propose a full range of analysis: formal mathematical analysis; simulation of "realistic" decision problems that an agent might be expected to encounter; implementation in agents that compete in simulated economies; deployment into real products that are tested in actual marketplaces. Each transition from formality to deployment re-introduces factors which were removed from the model in order to make it tractable; whether these factors are significant enough to undermine algorithmic efficiency remains to be seen.

In this section we report preliminary results at the level of decision problem simulation:

We generate specifications of $x_i(t)$, the price functions for each auction, $v(t)$, the valuation of the agent, and the probabilities $P_i(t)$, $Q_i(t)$ which govern the transition probabilities. Each non-DP algorithm is taken as a fixed policy, with respect to which we calculate the value function in the usual way; for OPTIMAL we calculate the optimal policy, and its corresponding value function.

4.1   Experimental Setup

In these experiments, all auctions share common price and blocking distributions, and have prices rising by one unit per unit time.[4] For the closing price distribution we choose the distribution of the second highest of n uniform random variables on $[x_{min}, x_{max}]$. The point is that if n agents each have valuation selected at random from $[x_{min}, x_{max}]$, and compete in a single English auction using their dominant strategy, the closing price will have this distribution. A formula for the probability that any given auction closes at price greater than or equal to x is thus defined to be

$$P^{price}(x) = 1 - n\left(\frac{x - x_{min}}{x_{max} - x_{min}}\right)^{n-1} + (n-1)\left(\frac{x - x_{min}}{x_{max} - x_{min}}\right)^{n}, \quad (2)$$

where $x \in [x_{min}, x_{max}]$, and x_{min}, x_{max}, n are constants.

Likewise, if there were n opponents, each with valuation picked uniformly at random between x_{min} and x_{max}, the blocking probability would be

$$Q^{price}(x) = \sum_{j=1}^{n} \frac{1}{j}\binom{n}{j}\frac{(x - x_{min})^{n-j}(x_{max} - x)^{j}}{(x_{max} - x_{min})^{n}} \quad (3)$$

In these experiments, x_{min}, x_{max} and n were chosen to be 0, 20.0 and 4 respectively.

The private information of an agent consists of a valuation v for the good, which we assume independent of time, and a deadline time by which the good

---

[4] These assumptions, can be seen as *homogeneity* assumptions: it doesn't matter which auction is which. These properties favour the greedy algorithm by removing variations which HISTORIAN and OPTIMAL would otherwise exploit.

must have been purchased, which is the "end-of-time" K from Section 2 beyond which the agent need not reason. In these experiments it was chosen to be 50.

Given the constants v, K, M and n, each instance of the decision problem is then generated by selecting an opening-time sequence t_i, after which P_i and u_i are given by

$$x_i(t) = \begin{cases} x_{min} & \text{if } t < t_i \text{ or } t > t_i + x_{max} - x_{min} \\ t - t_i + x_{min} & t \in [t_i, t_i + x_{max} - x_{min}] \end{cases}$$

$$P_i(t) = \begin{cases} 1 & t < t_i \\ P^{price}(t - t_i) & t \in [t_i, t_i + x_{max}] \\ 0 & t > t_i + M \end{cases} \tag{4}$$

$$Q_i(t) = \begin{cases} 1 & t < t_i \\ Q^{price}(t - t_i) & t \in [t_i, t_i + x_{max}] \\ 0 & t > t_i + M \end{cases}$$

Auction opening times t_i were chosen at random from the interval $[0, K - (x_{max} - x_{min})]$, in experiment A, and at random from the interval $[-(x_{max} - x_{min}), K]$ in experiment B, the quantitative difference being that in the second cases auctions may already be open when the agent begins trading, and may remain open beyond the agent's deadline.

4.2   Results

We have chosen to display results relative to the performance of OPTIMAL, since this algorithm can be seen as a benchmark in this context.

Average and Worst-case performance. The data in tables 1 and 2, and figure 1 show that HISTORIAN is indeed more effective than GREEDY, and that they both become less effective relative to optimal as the degree of simultaneity increases. For experiment B, the worst-case effectiveness is significantly lower than average in cases where the agent has only an average endowment[5]; when the agent is rich, the difference is not so great. For this experiment, although HISTORIAN out-performs GREEDY, the difference is not large.

On the other hand, for experiment A, where auctions can open at any time during, or before, the agent's task window, the worst-case scenario is considerably worse than it was for experiment B, and particularly so for GREEDY. For some configurations, namely ones in which, in the first few periods there is only a single auction open, which happens to have high prices, GREEDY does very badly indeed. By comparison, HISTORIAN does much better in the worst case, although

---

[5] The price and blocking distributions assume 4 opponents with valuations drawn at random from $[0, 20]$, thus a valuation of 10 means that the agent has an "average" endowment. An endowment of 20 in this context is large, since it means that the agent can guarantee a purchase in any auction if it so wishes.

Table 1. Average and minimum relative efficacy for experiment A

	n	2	2	3	3	4	4
	v	10	20	10	20	10	20
Historian	min	0.539	0.697	0.443	0.572	0.399	0.494
	avg	0.959	0.953	0.889	0.914	0.853	0.870
Greedy	min	0.424	0.095	0.351	0.075	0.205	0.068
	avg	0.943	0.806	0.862	0.737	0.826	0.658

Table 2. Average and minimum relative efficacy for experiment B

	n	2	2	3	3	4	4
	v	10	20	10	20	10	20
Historian	min	0.539	0.781	0.382	0.681	0.332	0.621
	avg	0.851	0.891	0.730	0.803	0.653	0.753
Greedy	min	0.539	0.757	0.382	0.659	0.332	0.604
	avg	0.843	0.849	0.720	0.776	0.645	0.736

not much better on average. Thus we can see the chief advantage of HISTORIAN over GREEDY as being that it provides better worst-case returns.

With respect to the agent's valuation, for experiment A, the sub-optimal algorithms were less effective in cases of higher endowment; for experiment B the opposite was true. This makes sense in the context of the fact that experiment A is risker, because optimal behaviour involves both avoiding potential loss, and choosing the auctions with high return. With higher endowment, the value of choosing well is reduced, so that non-optimality of the algorithm is relatively less significant. In risky circumstances, however, a higher endowment means that there is more at stake.

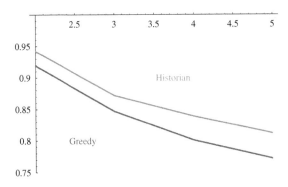

Fig. 1. The average effectiveness of GREEDY and HISTORIAN relative to that of OPTIMAL vs. number of auctions, for experiment A, $v = 10$

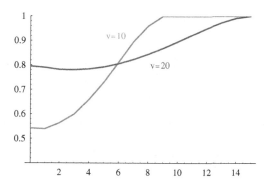

Fig. 2. The effectiveness of HISTORIAN relative to difference in start times, for the 2 auction case.

Degree of Simultaneity. As well as improving relative to the non-optimal algorithms when the number of auctions increases, OPTIMAL is also better when there is a high degree of overlap: Figure 2 plots the relative efficacy of HISTORIAN against the difference in starting times for the 2-auction case of experiment B, with $v = 10$ and $v = 20$.

First consider the $v = 10$ curve. At one extreme, when the difference is of size 10 or greater, the auctions are essentially consecutive: They are open on a common region, but on that region, the earlier one will necessarily have a price higher than the agent's valuation. At this extreme, HISTORIAN performs optimally. At the other extreme, when the two auctions have identical starting times, the optimal policy is to bid in both auctions at the same time, up to price 8. In doing so, OPTIMAL exposes itself to the risk of over-purchase: if it should obtain both active bids, and then not be out-bid in either, then it will have over-spent. On the other-hand, this turns out to be very unlikely, whereas the likelihood of winning *one* auction, while small, is considerably higher. The ability to calculate whether it is worthwhile to expose oneself to such risks in the pursuit of their possible gains is a large contributing factor to OPTIMAL's success.

Of course, it is not always best to bid in all auctions at the same time. When $v = 20$, the optimal policy for two totally simultaneous auctions is to bid in both up to price 13, then in only one from time 14 to time 18, in which region the risk is obviously too high to justify the increased likelihood of purchasing the good cheaply.

4.3   Relevant Work

Dynamic Programming has been applied to the context of agent strategies before, see e.g. [2].

In particular, Boutilier et al. [4,3] analyse the case of a series of sealed bid auctions for goods with complementarities, but the auctions are consecutive, not concurrent; this work is distinct from theirs in that the agent makes decisions during the course of the auctions, and may switch back and forth between them. This work follows on from [10], which developed out of [9].

[6] uses a belief-based modeling approach to generating appropriate bids in a double auction. Their work is close in spirit to ours, in that it combines belief-based learning of individual agents' bidding strategies with utility analysis. However, it is applied to a single double auction marketplace, and does not allow agents to bid in a variety of auctions. [11] uses a more sophisticated learning mechanism that combines belief-based learning with reinforcement learning. Again, the context for this is a single double auction marketplace. Unlike Gjerstad's approach, this focuses on learning the distribution of the equilibrium price. Finally, [5] is clearly relevant. They consider the development of bidding strategies in the context of the Spanish fishmarket tournament. Agents compete in a sequence of Dutch auctions, and use a combination of utility modeling and fuzzy heuristics to generate their bidding strategy. Their work focuses on Dutch rather than English auctions, and on a sequence of auctions rather than potentially parallel auctions. However, the insights they have developed may be applicable in our domain also. We hope to investigate this further in the future.

5   Conclusions and Future Work

We have specified three algorithms for use in multiple simultaneous auctions, of which GREEDY is almost trivial, HISTORIAN uses beliefs in a relatively light-weight way, and OPTIMAL finds the best policy subject to the various assumptions made in Section 1.3

The results of the preliminary experiments we have run engender several observations:

1. In many cases, the performance of GREEDY is far from dismal. On average, for example, in the 4-auction case above, GREEDY was 73% efficient relative to the optimal solution, and better for fewer auctions. On the other-hand, that extra 27% could be worth a lot of money in the right circumstances.
2. As well as modest improvements in average performance, the chief advantage of HISTORIAN over GREEDY in its worst-case performance. As can be seen from Table 1, in the wrong circumstances, GREEDY can do very badly indeed. HISTORIAN can also do badly, but performs much better in such corner cases.
3. As well as another improvement in average performance, the chief advantage of OPTIMAL over HISTORIAN is its ability to reason about exposure to over-purchasing, and hence to maximize its probability of obtaining cheap goods. Of course we must concede that there are probably more efficient ways to reason about such exposure than via Dynamic Programming.

Among the many directions for future work, some are derived immediately from these observations:

1. Most obviously, there is a large amount of empirical work to do. These experiments only scratch the surface of the analysis necessary to understand the algorithms under consideration.

2. We will add a fuller understanding of risk to the framework, from the point of view of a utility defined over bargains. At the same time, we intend to experiment with situations in which the beliefs the agent has are inconsistent with the actual dynamics of the auctions in which it is participating.
3. We will apply this English auction framework to the sort of problem addressed in [2], namely that of purchasing multiple goods, among which the agent has complementarities.

There are other directions that lie further into the future, but which are important to consider because they lie at the heart of the analysis. Principally they are to widen the framework to the case of correlated closing prices, and to consider the effects that arise when these algorithms are used not just against a static model, but "in anger".

References

1. K. Binmore and N. Vulkan. Applying game theory to automated negotiation. *Netnomics*, 1:1–9, 1999.
2. C. Boutilier. Sequential optimality and coordination in multi-agent systems. In *Proc. IJCAI 99*, 1999.
3. C. Boutilier, M. Goldszmidt, and B. Sabata. Continuous value function approximation for sequential bidding policies. In *Proc. UAI '99*, 1999.
4. C. Boutilier, M. Goldszmidt, and B. Sabata. Sequential auctions for the allocation of resources with complementarities. In *Proc. IJCAI '99*, 1999.
5. P. Garcia, E. Giminez, L. Godo, and J. Rodriguez-Aguilar. Possibilistic-based design of bidding strategies in electronic auctions. In *Proc. 13th Biennial European Conference on Artificial Intelligence*, 1998.
6. S. Gjerstad and J. Dickhaut. Price formation in double auctions. *Games and Economic Behaviour*, 22(1):1–29, 1998.
7. P. Klemperer. Auction theory: A guide to the literature. *Journal of Economic Surveys*, 13(3):227–286, July 1999.
8. R. P. McAfee and J. McMillan. Auctions and bidding. *Journal of Economic Literature*, 25:699–738, June 1987.
9. C. Preist, C. Bartolini, and I. Philips. Algorithm design for agents which participate in multiple simultaneous auctions. In F. Dignum and U. Cortes, editors, *Agent Mediated Electronic Commerce III*, Lecture Notes in AI. Springer Verlag, September 2001.
10. C. Preist, A. Byde, and C. Bartolini. Economic dynamics of agents in multiple auctions. To appear at Autonomous Agents 2001, 2001.
11. N. Vulkan and C. Preist. Automated trading in agents-based markets for communication bandwidth. In *Proc. UKMAS*, 1999.

User Modelling for Live Help Systems

Johan Aberg, Nahid Shahmehri, and Dennis Maciuszek

Department of Computer and Information Science
Linköpings universitet, S-581 83 Linköping, Sweden
{johab,nahsh}@ida.liu.se
Phone, Fax: +46-13-281465, +46-13-282666

Abstract. We have explored the role of user modelling in live help systems for e-commerce web sites. There are several potential benefits with user modelling in this context: 1) Human assistants can use the personal information in the user models to provide the users with efficient support tailored to their personal needs; 2) Assistants can be more comfortable in their supporting role; 3) Consultation resources can be saved, and thus, financial savings can be made for the e-commerce company. A user modelling approach has been implemented and deployed in a real web environment as part of a live help system. Following the deployment we have analysed consultation dialogue logs and answers to a questionnaire for participating assistants. This paper elaborates on these results, which show that assistants consider user modelling to be helpful and that consultation dialogues can be an important source for user model data collection. Based on lessons learned from the study, future directions for research and development are carefully analysed and laid out.

1 Introduction

It has been shown that customer service has a positive influence on e-commerce. For example, in [22] it is suggested that customer service has a positive effect on user attitudes toward Internet catalogue shopping. Further, it has been suggested that customer service is of great importance for a web site's credibility [11]. Still, the current state of practise in customer service for e-commerce is limited and in need of improvements [15,21].

In our previous work we have introduced a general model for customer service for web sites [1], now referred to as a model for *live help*[1]. The model features a combination of human assistants and computer-based support. We propose a flexible user interface where users can select how they want to interact with the system. For example, users can choose whether they only want computer-based customer service or if they prefer to chat with human assistants via text chat, voice chat, or other means of interaction. In our model, we also aim at providing personalised customer service by employing user modelling.

---

[1] Originally we used the term *web assistant system*. However, similar system have recently begun to appear on e-commerce sites, commonly referred to as live help systems. To avoid future confusion we now refer to our work using this newly adopted terminology.

L. Fiege, G. Mühl, and U. Wilhelm (Eds.): WELCOM 2001, LNCS 2232, pp. 164–179, 2001.

There are several potential benefits with user modelling for live help systems. Knowledge about the user can allow a human assistant to provide high quality and personalised support to the individual user [12]. User modelling can also allow human assistants to be more comfortable in their supporting role, simply because the information in the user model can make them feel familiar with the user. Further, user models can make help sessions more efficient and the dialogues smoother, because the assistants do not have to ask the user for the same information over and over. In [6] an example is presented illustrating the potential financial savings to be made for a company employing a kind of live help system, due to the shorter dialogue time: assuming a modest 20 second reduction per help session, a large company can save \$1.5M per year, under realistic conditions.

We have studied our proposed model in a two-step project. In step 1 we explored the value of our model in an e-commerce setting, and we conducted an exploratory usability study based on a limited prototype implementation designed for communication between a user and an assistant [1]. In general, the user feedback was very positive, and we found indications that a user modelling tool would be of help for assistants. Thus, we decided to continue our study in a second step.

In step 2, our main aim was to test the technical feasibility of the live help model. To do this we implemented an instance of the full model and deployed it at an existing web site for a three-week period.

This paper is an extension of a previous short paper [4], presented at the ACM conference on electronic commerce[2]. The focus of this paper is on the study of the user modelling component that was part of step 2. We explore the value and feasibility of user modelling for live help systems. Apart from testing technical feasibility we focus on two main questions: 1) What are the subjective opinions of assistants towards the concept of such a user modelling tool? 2) What kind and amount of user model data can be collected from consultation dialogues, and what are the linguistic characteristics for the dialogues? We are also looking into future directions for research and development in some detail, based on the lessons learned from our study.

Positive feedback from assistants regarding question 1 means that this kind of user modelling can be a valuable component of a live help system. Negative feedback on the other hand means that we must question the value of user modelling for live help systems. The importance of acquiring user model data is highlighted by question 2. Consultation dialogues have the potential to be a rich source for user model data acquisition, and can be a complement or a replacement for other sources such as product ratings or registration forms. The linguistic characteristics of the dialogues are of importance for the automatic extraction of user data.

This paper is structured as follows. In section 2 we give a brief overview description of the live help system, and in section 3 we provide a detailed pre-

---

[2] The present paper provides a much more detailed presentation of the results. We have also added the treatment on future directions.

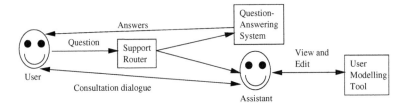

Fig. 1. Overview of the live help model

sentation of our user modelling approach. Section 4 describes the field study involving the user modelling system and section 5 presents the results. In section 6 we comment on limitations of the study, and in section 7 we present related work. Section 8 analyses three important directions for future work, and section 9 concludes the paper.

2   Live Help System

An overview illustration of our live help model is presented in Figure 1. The support router is responsible for deciding whether the user needs computer-based support or support by a human assistant. The computer-based support is a question-answering system. If the support router connects the user to a human assistant they can have a real-time consultation dialogue. A user modelling tool for supporting the assistant is also part of the model.

In our implementation of the model the support router always routes the user through the question-answering system before connecting to a human assistant. The question-answering system is implemented using an information retrieval approach with frequently asked questions (FAQs) [2]. The user modelling component is the focus of this paper and will be further described in the next section.

The user's support process is initiated when the user asks a question in natural language. The question is fed to the automatic question-answering system. FAQ items which closely match are returned as potential answers to the question. If the user indicates that the returned answers are not satisfactory, the support router will connect the user to a human assistant with expertise matching the topic of the question. If all the appropriate assistants are currently busy, the user can choose to wait in a queue. Once an assistant is available the user is connected to that assistant and can proceed with a consultation dialogue via textual chat.

The implemented live help system has been evaluated from the users' point of view in [3]. The findings are very encouraging, particularly when it comes to users' attitudes.

3   User Modelling Approach

Information about a user is stored in a predefined attribute hierarchy, in an overlay style. A user's model is displayed for an assistant as soon as a consultation dialogue begins. The assistant can then make use of the information in the model to tailor the consultation to that individual user. No automatic inference is made on the data in the user model, although the assistant is of course free to make inferences as a part of his or her interpretation of the user data. The assistant can also update the model by filling in attribute values based on what is learned from the consultation dialogue with the user. Further, some basic demographic information (age, gender, and country) is automatically inserted in the user model via questions in a registration phase for the live help system (not shown in Figure 1).

We have chosen a simple approach, and there are two reasons for this. First, we look into the general value of this kind of user modelling tool. If we get positive results we can continue to explore technical issues and more advanced designs in a next step. Second, our aim to evaluate the system in a field study requires a simple system that voluntary assistants can take up with minimal instructions and training.

To find out what kind of user attributes would be most useful for the assistants, we ran a user poll at the web site of our field study (the site is called Elfwood and is in the art and literature domain). In the poll, we asked what kind of questions users wanted to ask in a live help system. Most users wanted help with art creation or help with finding interesting art and literature.

Based on the poll results, we decided to let the detail level of the attribute hierarchy roughly correspond to the number of questions expected for that attribute category. Our assumption was that a detailed attribute structure would be most useful for categories where a large number of related questions was expected. The user model attribute hierarchy is illustrated in Figure 2. The bracketed numbers in the figure correspond to the number of times that user data occurred in the consultation dialogues. The relevance of these numbers is discussed in section 5.1.

The tool for viewing and editing a user model is shown in Figure 3. Each attribute is displayed as a rectangular button with the attribute name as a label. Attributes without a corresponding value are shown in grey in the figure. An attribute that has been given a value is shown in black, with the actual value written after the attribute name. The detail level of the display can be adjusted by the assistant by expanding or contracting branches in the tree. By clicking on an attribute button, an editor window is brought up, where the assistant can create a value or change an existing value. The value can be chosen from a predefined value set or be created as an arbitrary text string. Textual comments can also be associated to a value. This feature can be used for explaining a given value.

A user's skill or interests may change over time and therefore it is important for the system to be able to handle this temporal aspect of user modelling. In order to deal with this a history feature is used. An assistant can update an

Personal data (10) - Age (5), Gender, Country (6), Occupation (1), Name (36),
                        Conversation style
Elfwood data (3) - Elfwood member (54), Link to art (41), Link to stories (10)
Art skill (10)
    Art media (2)
        Wet - Ink, Oil paint, Watercolour (2), Acrylics
        Dry - Pencil (7), Coloured pencil (1), Charcoal, Conte, Pastel
        Digital (2) - Adobe Photoshop (8), MetaCreations Painter, Paintshop Pro (2),
                Graphics tablets (4), 3D programs
    Art objects (6) - Humans (6), Animals, Buildings, Nature
    Art styles (2) - Realism (1), Anime/Manga (7), Impressionist, Art nouveau
    Art techniques (13) - Perspective, Sketching (3), Detail drawing
Writing skill (9)
    Writing styles (1) - Humour, Serious writing, Fantasy (3), Sci-fi (2), Horror
    Writing technical (1) - Grammar, Characters, Setting, Plot, Point of view
Elfwood skill
    Site navigation - Pictures, Stories
    Member functions - Intranet, Tour creation, Picture upload, FARP (creation)
    User functions - Text search, Attribute search, FARP (usage), FantasyHoo
Computer skill (1) - Internet (1), Scanners (3), MS Windows (1), Linux, Unix

Fig. 2. The complete user model attribute hierarchy

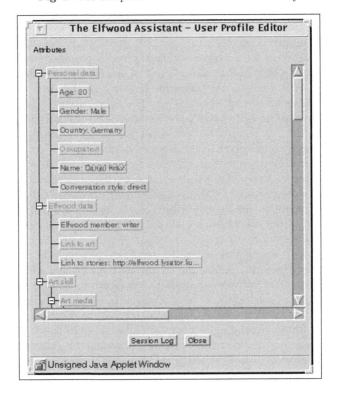

Fig. 3. Screen shot from the user model viewer

attribute that already has been assigned a value. The old value is then stored in a history file associated with that particular attribute. The history file is shown in the attribute editor.

A somewhat controversial design decision was to hide the user model from the users in the sense that users had no tool available for viewing or updating their own models. The reason was purely technical. We thought that adding such tools to the users' web clients would make the help system more complex and error prone, and thus risk that users lose interest in using the system. Still, we recognise the many advantages of making the user models public (e.g. [8]) and consider this as an important aspect of our future work. The design decision should not affect the results in this paper since our focus is on the assistants' subjective impressions of the tool concept.

Kass and Finin [17] analysed user modelling for natural language systems. Several dimensions for categorising user models were discussed. According to these dimensions our approach to user models can be classified as follows. Our models are *individual*, *dynamic*, and intended for *long term* and *descriptive* usage. A *single* user is modelled by a *single* user model. Our user models are mainly intended for *providing help and advice* for the user, and for *providing output to the user*. Further, the information in a user model can be classified into several categories. We model *capabilities* and *knowledge and belief*. We also model what we call personal data, such as name and age of a user.

4   Field Study

The overall research objective in step 2 has been to test the technical feasibility of our live help model. Therefore, a field study, where the system is tested in a real environment, is a natural research method. Consequently, the user modelling part of the live help system is also evaluated in this way. The field study consisted of two parts: system deployment for data collection, and data analysis.

4.1   Environment

The live help system has been attached to an existing web site for a period of three weeks. The site, called Elfwood, is a non-profit site with a focus on art and literature, where amateur artists and writers can exhibit their material. At the time of writing around 9400 artists and 1900 writers exhibit their work in the fantasy and science fiction genre. The artists and writers are members of the site with access to an extranet for updating their own exhibition galleries. A part of the site is devoted to teaching art, and offers a large number of feature articles on different topics.

Elfwood has around 14,500 daily visitor sessions (many are by non-members), where each session averages approximately 35 minutes. About 60% of the sessions are conducted by users from the US. The remaining users are mainly from Europe and Canada.

We mainly supported three types of user tasks. 1) Learning how to create art and literature related to fantasy and science fiction. 2) Searching for interesting art and literature at Elfwood. 3) Member activities, such as uploading new art and literature, and the management of each member's exhibition area.

We chose Elfwood as the environment for our study for two reasons. First, we wanted a site with a reasonable number of users and user traffic, and with a user community that would allow the recruitment of suitable assistants. Second, we wanted to test our system in a low risk environment where unexpected system problems would not have large financial consequences. This meant that we could not go for an e-commerce site at this early stage of the research. Still, we acknowledge the importance of continuing research in real e-commerce settings in the future.

4.2   Participants

Voluntary assistants participated in the study from their home or work environment. They were recruited some months before the field study began and they were all Elfwood members. In the end 30 persons with proper expertise served as assistants. The live help system was not designed to allow multiple simultaneous consultation dialogues for assistants, so no assistant helped more than one user at a time.

During the field study, 636 users registered with the system, and 129 of these users worked through the system to have consultation dialogues with assistants.

4.3   Data Collection and Analysis

In this study we have used two main data sources, namely the logs of the consultation dialogues and a questionnaire for the assistants. While our current focus is on the subjective opinions of assistants, it is also desirable to study the users' perspective. Such a study can best be pursued by conducting a controlled experiment including a control group without user modelling.

Dialogue analysis. During the three weeks of the data collection period a total of 175 consultation dialogues took place. We have analysed the dialogue logs in order to answer the following questions. 1) *How much user model data, and what type of data can be collected from help dialogues?* 2) *In what conversational circumstances does the user provide user model data?* 3) *What are the chat language characteristics for the consultation dialogues?*

In investigating these questions we evaluate how useful consultation dialogues can be as a source of acquiring information about the user. We are also looking for conversational strategies to aid assistants in optimising the amount and quality of user model data that can be acquired. Further, knowledge about the different conversational circumstances in which user model data comes up, and knowledge about the chat language characteristics, is of importance for the automatic extraction of this data.

The following paragraph illustrates the start of the dialogue part of a log file. We logged the exact time that each utterance reached the chat server. We also logged the times when the assistant began a typing session on the keyboard. (This information was used as an awareness cue in the user interface.)

```
<time> 0:30:31 <chat starts>
<assistant id> *****
<time> 0:30:41 <assistant typing>
<time> 0:30:41 <assistant> hi
<time> 0:30:56 <assistant typing>
<time> 0:31:1 <user> Hi.
<time> 0:31:15 <assistant> May I ask your name first?
<time> 0:31:20 <user> I can't think of any good ideas for backgrounds for my
drawings.
<time> 0:31:24 <assistant typing>
<time> 0:31:39 <user> My user or name or my real first name?
```

The methods we have used for investigating each question are as follows. For question 1 we have simply counted the number of times that a user made a statement about himself or herself. We have also matched the type of the statement to the existing hierarchy of user model attributes. Note that only statements of potential long term interest for the tasks that we intended to support are counted. Issues of only short term interest need not be collected for the user model since they have no future value. Thus certain data, for example, data related to the user's short term goals, is not considered.

For question 2 we have followed the work of Elzer and colleagues [10]. They identified four different conversational circumstances for user model data collection from dialogues. *Reject-Solution* (Rej-Soln) is when a user rejects a proposed solution and motivates the rejection by giving a piece of personal information. *Volunteered-Background* (Vol-Back) occurs when the user provides some personal data as part of a problem description. *Volunteered* (Vol) happens when a user volunteers personal information in a conversation without being prompted to do so. *Question-and-Answer* (Q-A) is when the user gives some personal information in response to a question from the system (an assistant in this case). We classified each utterance containing user model data according to these circumstances and summarise the results quantitatively.

For question 3 we have considered the language characteristics mainly in terms of grammar, spelling, and message order.

Assistant questionnaire. In order to also get a subjective view from the assistants, we employed a questionnaire. This questionnaire contained items related to various aspects of the user modelling system. All 30 assistants who had participated in the field study received the questionnaire by e-mail just after the data collection period was over. We received 22 answers. Unfortunately, only 14 of these were answered completely, which corresponds to a response rate of roughly 47%. The respondents were from North America (64%), Europe (29%), and Oceania (7%). The assistants were from different age groups: 10-19 (43%), 20-29 (36%), 30-39 (14%), and 40-49 (7%). A total of 57% were female. All respondents had at least 3 years of Internet experience. Most assistants used dial-up connection to the Internet (57%), while some used a cable modem (21%), and

Table 1. Conversational circumstances statistics

Circumstance	Total no. occurrences	Dialogue average
Q-A	134 (50.8%)	0.77
Vol	67 (25.4%)	0.38
Vol-Back	51 (19.3%)	0.29
Rej-Soln	12 (4.5%)	0.07
All circumstances	264	1.51

others had a direct cable access (21%). The responding assistants participated in 7.4 consultation dialogues on average.

There were two types of questions in the questionnaire. The first type asked the respondent to rate a statement using a 1 to 10 scale. The second type listed a number of alternative statements and asked the respondent to rank their relative importance. For each question, the respondent was asked to explain the answer.

5   Results

5.1   Dialogue Analysis

How much user model data, and what type of data can be collected from help dialogues? We found a total of 264 user statements containing personal information that could be used for user modelling purposes. In this total we do not count information about a user that is out of the scope of the tasks for the live help system. There were 175 consultation dialogues in total, which means that each dialogue revealed on average 1.51 pieces of information about a user. Regarding the type of user model data that can be collected from consultation dialogues we present the distribution over the attribute hierarchy in Figure 2 (note that the figure appears a few pages back). The numbers in brackets that appear after some of the attributes correspond to the number of times that related user model data occurred in the dialogues. In some cases user model data did not fit into any of the most specific attributes. Then we placed the data in the least general attribute that fit with the data. For example, a user's e-mail address does not fit into any of the sub-attributes of "Personal data", and thus we placed the data in "Personal data".

In what conversational circumstances does the user provide user model data? We found no pieces of information given by a user that did not fit into the set of conversational circumstances previously described. This indicates that they are fairly complete. Statistics from the conversational circumstance analysis is summarised in Table 1. Note that more than 50% of the user data comes from a question by an assistant. This indicates that assistants have an important role to play in user model data collection. *What are the chat language characteristics for the consultation dialogues?* We observed that the dialogue language is notably informal. The fact that messages are sent as a whole, and not character by

Table 2. Questionnaire results about the user modelling system

Statement	Mean	S. dev.
In general the user models were (no help=1, helpful=10)	6.93	2.95
The amount of time available to view user model data during a help session was (on average) (too limited=1, enough=10)	7.79	2.91
How did the value of a user model change as more data was added to it? (less helpful=1, more helpful=10)	8.29	2.09
The number of times that a user model gave me wrong assumptions about a user were (few=1, many=10)	1.57	0.85
Extracting information from a help conversation for insertion in the user model was (hard=1, easy=10)	5.79	2.94

character, means that there is a time lag between a message being written and a message being read. Also, a certain space between two related messages may be filled by other information. The answer to a question or the rejection of a solution can reach the recipient right away or several lines later, with a "gap" of unrelated text in between. Furthermore, answers and rejections need not occur in the same order as their questions and solutions. Another striking aspect of the dialogues is that they are generally full of misspelled words, grammar mistakes and incomplete sentences. These results have implications for automatic information extraction, and we discuss this issue further in section 8.1.

5.2   Assistant Questionnaire

In Table 2 we present selected results from the rating statements in the assistant questionnaire. The statements left out of the presentation were all concerned with the usability of particular functions of the user modelling tool. Since our focus here is on the concept of this kind of user modelling tool and not on the actual implementation, they are of limited interest in this context.

Through ranking statements in the questionnaire, we learned that the most useful attributes were the Personal data attributes, the Elfwood data attributes, and the Art skill attributes. The Personal data attributes were useful in the sense that the assistants could know the user's name and thus have a more personal dialogue. One assistant also mentioned that he sometimes tailored his help based on the Age attribute by using the heuristic: old users are more experienced than young users.

An additional source of user information available at Elfwood was the members' own display of art and literature. Two Elfwood data attributes in the user models represented links to such user info. Links to a user's art or literature proved very valuable for the assistants as it gave a concrete indication of the user's art or writing skill.

It is important to analyse how the user modelling system was helpful to the assistants. For this purpose we consider the reasons given by the assistants who considered the system to be helpful. Not all these assistants elaborated on their answer, but five of them said that user modelling helped them tailor the help to the individual needs of the user. Another assistant said that the user model data made the dialogues smoother. Yet another assistant said that reviewing the user model reminded her to ask the user questions that were helpful.

6   Limitations

A main limitation of our study is that the data collection period only lasted for three weeks. Consequently, the number of users who used the system more than once was limited. Only 26 out of the 129 users used the system more once, and thus only a small number of users had updated information in their user model. This means that the subjective opinions of the assistants must be interpreted with some care, since they have a somewhat limited experience with user models containing more information than the Age, Gender, and Country attributes that are present in all models. Another limitation is the low response rate for the assistant questionnaire. This could imply that the results are not representative for all the assistants.

Some of the assistants only got to assist first-time users with empty user models (except for the Age, Country, and Gender attributes). They gave low scores on the question about the helpfulness of user models, stating that the models never contained any helpful information. If we disregard the scores from these three assistants and recompute the mean and standard deviation for the corresponding questionnaire statement, we get a mean of 8.27 and standard deviation of 1.35 instead. This gives a stronger indication of the potential helpfulness of user modelling for assistants.

In summary, these limitations mean that we must consider our results as indications and not as proofs. A natural further step would be to use controlled experiments to statistically test the value of user modelling, both for users and for assistants.

7   Related Work

Since the initiation of our work, there have been commercial moves toward live help systems. Companies such as LivePerson, FaceTime, Cisco, and Blue Martini, to name a few, now offer commercial systems for human assistance in web sites. These systems have recently been adopted by hundreds of e-commerce sites. This trend confirms the importance of the kind of studies reported in this paper.

The commercial systems now available are clearly similar in spirit to our system. Also, the vendors have realised the potential of user modelling for live help systems. Still, to our knowledge there is limited prior research on user modelling in this context. One exception is the paper by Fridgen and colleagues [12]. They argue for the importance of customer models in the financial services industry, and suggest a process for establishing customer models and deducing user-specific actions. They also discuss different categories of user information that should be modelled. The paper thus complements our work in a nice way. The project reported is at an initial stage, and no evaluation is provided.

It is important that the user modelling system does not influence the dialogues too much. In [7] a study of a bank call centre is presented. It is shown that the assistants' interaction with the computer system shape the dialogue to a large extent. The assistants' task of smoothly integrating their computer support into the consultation dialogues requires skill.

Work has been done on user modelling in automated dialogue systems [17,23, 16,10]. The user modelling requirements for automated dialogue systems and for live help systems are somewhat different. For automated dialogue systems, data about a user's short term goals, for example, can be highly relevant in order to interpret the user's question. In contrast, for a live help system it is not important to model this data since the human assistant can interpret the user's question, using his or her human intelligence and domain knowledge. For live help systems, it is most important to model data about the user that is valid over several help sessions. Such data includes the user's preferences, knowledge, and beliefs, as well as personal data. Another difference is the necessity of visualisation of user model data for assistants in live help systems. Note however, that visualisation can also be important for automated dialogue systems using user models (at least for long term models) to allow the users to see their models.

8   Future Directions

8.1   Information Extraction

Manual extraction of user model data can be cumbersome, as indicated in the assistant questionnaire results. Having the system relieve human assistants of this task would further improve live help in terms of efficiency and convenience for assistants. The company could save time and money, and the assistants could avoid unnecessary stress. When examining a consultation dialogue, either during chat or its log file, an assistant usually does the following: 1) Discover phrases that reveal information about the user. 2) Associate each phrase with attributes in the user model hierarchy. 3) Update those attributes' values in the individual user model.

Automation of this process is a natural language processing problem. Considering the unstructured language of chat dialogues though, in-depth grammatical and semantic understanding, as performed in automated dialogue systems [16, 10], is currently not feasible. Also considering that our sought-for long term, skill-related information is comparatively vague in nature, in-depth understanding is not necessary either. One solution is *information extraction* (IE). IE algorithms understand natural language texts only partially, but with the clear intention of discovering and storing specific information [9].

Consider the following sample dialogue lines taken from a log file.

```
<assistant> a digital drawing tablet would suit you very nicely..
  [...]
<user> I do have one but, but strangly I prefer a mouse it works better for me
for some reason.
```

Read by a human assistant, he or she could 1) discover the user model phrases
I do have one, I prefer a mouse, and it works better for me, 2) associate the first phrase with the attribute Graphics tablets, and the others with
Digital, 3) update the user's model with the information that he or she owns
a graphics tablet, and that his or her preferred digital drawing instrument is
the mouse. Altogether, this involves solving three *tasks* of IE: recognising the
domain entity name mouse *(named entity recognition)*; replacing the anaphoric
terms one and it by their referred-to entity names digital drawing tablet
and mouse respectively *(coreference resolution)*; making out the relevant descriptions around each entity name, associating the phrases with attributes, and
updating those attribute values with respect to their previous values *(template
element construction)*.

From the dialogue analysis we observe: 1) Conversational circumstances play
an important role in resolving coreferences. In the example above, replacing
one with the entity name it refers to, shows how, in a Rej-Soln circumstance,
reference and referred-to entity name appear in a "rejection/solution pair" of
phrases. 2) The dialogue language style has implications for IE parsing. The
example includes the misspelling strangly, the repeated word but, and a missing
sentence separator between mouse and it. IE parsing needs to tolerate these.

All in all, we are enhancing our implemented user modelling tool by integrating a real-time, easily portable IE module. Its basic design will either follow Ragnemalm's *keyword based interpretation* approach [18], or the regular grammar
driven "FASTUS" *partial parsing* approach [13]. An evaluation of two prototype
implementations will reveal, if the user model acquisition task is best handled
by focusing on keywords in the context of other keywords, or by recognising well
specified grammar fragments.

8.2   Inference

Data collection for user models typically occurs incrementally, with little pieces
of information added over several user interaction sessions. Therefore a user
model usually contains limited information, and consequently inference would
be valuable. Inference is a process of reasoning under uncertainty that aims at
extending and generalising collected user data. For live help systems, inference
can be done either by the human assistants or in some automatic way. Doing the
inference manually has the disadvantage that it may be time consuming, and demand quite some effort from the assistants. Also, there is a risk of inconsistency.
Thus, automatic inference should be investigated as an alternative.

Automatic inference on user model data has been studied previously to some
extent in traditional user modelling research. However, before attempting to
design an approach for this particular kind of application we should consider the
special characteristics that may distinguish it from previous research:

– Explainability. Since the user models are being used by human assistants,
  explainability is of great importance. An assistant needs to be able to trust
  the user model data in order to feel comfortable in using it as a basis for

the consultation. The inference system needs to be able to explain the inferences to the assistant whenever the assistant is in doubt about some piece of information.

- Justifiability. The inference system needs to be able to justify inferences. For example, assume that an assistant recommends a user to purchase an expensive product, based on some piece of inferred information about the user. The assistant would then likely have to justify the recommendation to convince the user. Justifiability is somewhat different from explainability, as pointed out in [14]. Even if the inference system could explain some inferred data, the explanation may not be sufficient to justify an action taken based on the inferred data.
- Handling different value types. When assistants update a user model they may want to go outside the scope of predefined (numerical) attribute values by providing a new qualitative value. This can be of importance when special cases occur and the predefined values do not fit. Also, the assistants may want to explain an attribute's value by giving a textual description of why the value fits the user. The inference system needs to be able to handle these different types of qualitative and quantitative values.

One of the earliest attempts to apply inference to user models was the so-called *stereotype* approach [19,20]. Later, more general approaches to dealing with reasoning under uncertainty have been applied to user modelling. In [14], Anthony Jameson considers three common approaches, namely *bayesian networks*, *Dempster-Shafer theory of evidence*, and *fuzzy logic*. Given the requirements presented above, the suitability of each possible approach to inference needs to be analysed with care, before a solution is attempted. Of course, the particularities of the application at hand must also be taken into consideration. We see this as an important direction for future work.

8.3 Privacy

User modelling in general, and perhaps for e-commerce in particular, raises privacy issues. Several studies have shown that users consider privacy to be of great importance for e-commerce (see e.g. [5]). We informed the users in our field study that they were being modelled, and how the collected data would be used. Of course, they were given the possibility to opt out. We believe that for user modelling to really be useful it is vital that users are informed of the ongoing data collection process, and how the data will be used. The users should also be allowed to be in control of the information that is kept about them. One idea for implementing this is to require web sites to have the user's digital signature on the user model, before being allowed to use it. We consider this an interesting issue for future work.

9   Conclusions

We conclude by considering the two initial questions raised in the introduction. First, the questionnaire results showed that the assistants in fact considered user modelling to be helpful for assisting users. Second, the analysis of the consultation dialogues showed that much important user information of various kinds can be gained through such dialogues. We also identified requirements for automatic extraction of user data.

In section 4.1 we argued for why we did not test our live help system in an e-commerce environment. Still, it is interesting to discuss the generalisability of our results on user modelling towards e-commerce web sites. A fundamental property for user modelling to work in any web site, is to have a large rate of users who frequently return to the web site. Further, our test site was a community oriented web site. Thus, our results are most likely to carry over to the kind of e-commerce web sites that gather a community of users that keep coming back. Amazon is an example of such an e-commerce site that has managed to get the users involved in providing feedback on the products, and created a community of reviewers. Also note that, as we have shown previously [1,3], a live help system improves users' attitudes toward the site, and it alone may create a "community feeling" and encourage users to revisit the site.

Live help systems are here to stay. The questions we have considered in this paper represent the beginning of one branch of research on live help systems. In our analysis on future directions we have considered three issues that deserve thorough study. There are also other issues of importance: What are the conversational strategies that work best for acquiring user model data? What kind of user data is most important to model, for different kinds of web sites? How can the user models be integrated with the computer-based support?

References

1. Johan Aberg and Nahid Shahmehri. The role of human Web assistants in e-commerce: an analysis and a usability study. *Internet Research: Electronic Networking Applications and Policy*, 10(2):114–125, 2000.
2. Johan Aberg and Nahid Shahmehri. Collection and Exploitation of Expert Knowledge in Web Assistant Systems. In *Proceedings of the 34th Hawaii International Conference on System Sciences*, Maui, Hawaii, USA, January 3-6 2001.
3. Johan Aberg and Nahid Shahmehri. An Empirical Study of Human Web Assistants: Implications for User Support in Web Information Systems. In *Proceedings of the CHI Conference on Human Factors in Computing Systems*, pages 404–411, Seattle, Washington, USA, 2001.
4. Johan Aberg, Nahid Shahmehri, and Dennis Maciuszek. User Modelling for Live Help Systems: Initial Results. In *Proceedings of the Third ACM Conference on Electronic Commerce*, Tampa, FL, USA, 2001. In press.
5. Mark S. Ackerman, Lorrie Faith Cranor, and Joseph Reagle. Privacy in E-Commerce: Examining User Scenarios and Privacy Preferences. In *Proceedings of the ACM Conference on Electronic Commerce (EC'99)*, pages 1–8, Denver, Colorado, USA, 1999.
6. Howard G. Bernett and Areg Gharakhanian. Call Center Evolution: Computer Telephone Integration and Web Integration. *The Telecommunications Review, MitreTek Systems*, pages 107–114, 1999.

7. John Bowers and David Martin. Machinery in the New Factories: Interaction and Technology in a Bank's Telephone Call Centre. In *Proceedings of the Conference on Computer-Supported Cooperative Work*, pages 49–58, Philadelphia, PA, USA, 2000.

8. R Cook and J Kay. The justified user model: a viewable, explained user model. In *Proceedings of the Fourth International Conference on User Modeling*, pages 145–150, 1994.

9. Hamish Cunningham. Information Extraction – a User Guide (updated version). Department of Computer Science, University of Sheffield, UK, April 1999.

10. Stephanie Elzer, Jennifer Chu-Carrol, and Sandra Carberry. Recognizing and Utilizing User Preferences in Collaborative Consultation Dialogues. In *Proceedings of the Fourth International Conference on User Modeling*, pages 19–24, 1994.

11. BJ Fogg, Jonathan Marshall, Othman Laraki, Alex Osipovich, Chris Varma, Nicholas Fang, Jyoti Paul, Akshay Rangnekar, John Shon, Preeti Swani, and Marissa Treinen. What Makes Web Sites Credible? A Report on a Large Scale Quantitative Study. In *Proceedings of the CHI Conference on Human Factors in Computing Systems*, pages 61–68, Seattle, WA, USA, 2001.

12. Michael Fridgen, Jürgen Schackman, and Stefan Volkert. Preference Based Customer Models for Electronic Banking. In *Proceedings of the 8th European Conference on Information Systems*, pages 789–795, Vienna, Austria, 2000.

13. Jerry R. Hobbs, Douglas Appelt, John Bear, David Israel, Megumi Kameyama, Mark Stickel, and Mabry Tyson. FASTUS: A Cascaded Finite-State Transducer for Extracting Information from Natural-Language Text. In *Finite State Devices for Natural Language Processing*, pages 383–406. MIT Press, Cambridge, MA, USA, 1996.

14. Anthony Jameson. Numerical Uncertainty Management in User and Student Modeling: An Overview of Systems and Issues. *User Modeling and User-Adapted Interaction*, 5:193–251, 1996.

15. Sirrka L. Jarvenpaa and Peter A. Todd. Consumer Reactions to Electronic Shopping on the World Wide Web. *International Journal of Electronic Commerce*, 1(2):59–88, 1997.

16. Robert Kass. Building a User Model Implicitly from a Cooperative Advisory Dialog. *User Modeling and User-Adapted Interaction*, 1(3):203–258, 1991.

17. Robert Kass and Tim Finin. Modeling the User in Natural Language Systems. *Computational Linguistics*, 14(3):5–22, September 1988.

18. Eva L. Ragnemalm. *Student Modelling based on Collaborative Dialogue with a Learning Companion*. PhD thesis, Department of Computer and Information Science, Linköpings universitet, S-581 83 Linköping, Sweden, 1999.

19. Elaine Rich. Users are individuals: individualizing user models. *Int. J. Man-Machine Studies*, 18:199–214, 1983.

20. Elaine Rich. Stereotypes and User Modeling. In W. Wahlster and A. Kobsa, editors, *User Models in Dialog Systems*, pages 35–51. Springer Verlag, 1989.

21. Peter Spiller and Gerald L. Lohse. A Classification of Internet Retail Stores. *International Journal of Electronic Commerce*, 2(2):29–56, 1998.

22. Leo R. Vijaysarathy and Joseph M. Jones. Print and Internet catalog shopping. *Internet Research: Electronic Networking Applications and Policy*, 10(3):191–202, 2000.

23. W. Wahlster and A. Kobsa, editors. *User Models in Dialog Systems*. Springer Verlag, 1989.

Multidimensional Recommender Systems: A Data Warehousing Approach

Gediminas Adomavicius[1] and Alexander Tuzhilin[2]

[1] New York University, Courant Institute of Mathematical Sciences,
Computer Science Department, New York, NY 10012, USA
adomavic@cs.nyu.edu
[2] New York University, Stern School of Business,
Information Systems Department, New York, NY 10012, USA
atuzhili@stern.nyu.edu

Abstract. In this paper, we present a new data-warehousing-based approach to recommender systems. In particular, we propose to extend traditional two-dimensional user/item recommender systems to support multiple dimensions, as well as comprehensive profiling and hierarchical aggregation (OLAP) capabilities. We also introduce a new recommendation query language RQL that can express complex recommendations taking into account the proposed extensions. We describe how these extensions are integrated into a framework that facilitates more flexible and comprehensive user interactions with recommender systems.

1 Introduction

As recognized by various researchers [7,8,20], recommender systems constitute an important component of many e-commerce applications by allowing companies to develop long-lasting personalized relationships with their customers. The problem of providing personal recommendations over various marketing channels, including e-mail, the Web and mobile communication devices, attracted substantial research activities in the e-commerce community within the past few years [4,7,8,11,20]. Most of this research focused on recommending items to users, such as movies or books to customers. These recommendation mechanisms are usually based on collaborative filtering [5,19,21], content-based filtering [14,15, 18] or a combination of these two methods [2,3,17].

However, in many e-commerce applications, such as recommending vacation packages, restaurants, or Web content to customers, it may not be sufficient to recommend items to users (or users to items). For example, customer preferences for specific vacation packages can depend significantly on the time of the year: a particular customer may prefer to go on vacation to the Caribbean in the winter, but not in the summer. Therefore, to provide useful recommendations in such applications, we propose to support *multiple dimensions*, such as users, items, time, and place. Also, it may not be sufficient in many applications to recommend individual items to individual users but rather categories of items to certain types of users, such as action movies to college students. Therefore, we

L. Fiege, G. Mühl, and U. Wilhelm (Eds.): WELCOM 2001, LNCS 2232, pp. 180–192, 2001.

propose to support *aggregation hierarchies* for various dimensions and provide recommendation capabilities at different levels of aggregation. Moreover, while some of the existing recommender systems support profiles of users and items [2, 15,17,18], multidimensional recommender systems require more extensive profiling capabilities, such as the ones developed in [1]. Therefore, we also propose to support more extensive *profiling* capabilities in multidimensional recommender systems. Finally, traditional two-dimensional recommender systems usually provide recommendations of one or two particular types, i.e., recommend top N items to a user or top M users to an item. Moreover, these types of recommendations are typically *"hard-wired"* into recommender engines by a software vendor. However, in many multidimensional applications, it is important to be able to provide more extensive and flexible types of recommendations that can be requested by the user "on the fly." For example, we may want to recommend top 3 action movies that are not longer that 2 hours and only to those people whose favorite movie genre is action movies. To provide such extensive and flexible recommendation capabilities, we introduce a new *recommendation query language* (RQL) that allows users to express complex recommendations that can take into account multiple dimensions, aggregation hierarchies, and extensive profiling information.

We would like to point out that all the capabilities described above, including multiple dimensions, aggregation hierarchies, profiling, and a query language, are not stand-alone features but comprise components of a *multidimensional recommendation model* and are unified into one integrated approach. This approach is based on the data warehousing paradigm [10,12], because it provides the support for multiple dimensions and because hierarchies provide recommendation capabilities at multiple aggregation levels, as OLAP-enabled data warehousing systems do.

As will be described in the paper, a multidimensional recommender system consists of two components: (a) a *recommender engine* that estimates new recommendation ratings based on the already available set of ratings, and (b) a *query engine* that allows the users to express different types of recommendations "on the fly" in a flexible manner. In this paper, we focus on presenting the proposed multidimensional recommendation model and the query language. Implementation of a particular recommendation engine, including the issue of selecting a rating estimation function for specific application domains, is orthogonal to the description of the multidimensional recommendation model and the query language; it will be presented separately.

In summary, the contributions of this paper lie in the development of a multidimensional recommendation model based on the data warehousing paradigm, supporting

- multiple dimensions, aggregation hierarchies, and profiling capabilities;
- a flexible method for users and e-commerce applications to interact with a recommender system via a query language, that allows the users to express an extensive class of recommendations "on the fly" as their needs arise;

– a specific recommendation query language, called RQL, that supports multidimensional recommendations.

2   Multidimensional Recommendation Model

Traditionally, collaborative, content-based, and hybrid recommender systems deal with applications that have two types of entities, *users* and *items* (e.g., movies, Web pages). In order to provide recommendations, an initial set of ratings specifying how users liked items is either explicitly specified by the users or is implicitly inferred by the system. For example, in case of the MovieCritic [16] recommender system, John Doe may assign a rating of 7 (out of 13) for the movie "Gladiator," i.e., set $R_{movie}(John\ Doe,\ Gladiator) = 7$. Based on these initial ratings, a recommender system tries to determine the ratings of the items yet unspecified by the users by estimating the rating function R

$$R : Users \times Items \rightarrow Ratings .\quad\quad\quad (1)$$

for the (user, item) pairs that have not been rated yet. In the traditional two-dimensional recommender systems, a rating function (1) can be implemented as a matrix specifying rating $R(i, j)$ of item j by user i.

As mentioned in Section 1, some applications, such as travel, restaurants, and dynamic Web content presentation, do not fit well into the traditional two-dimensional user/item approach since they require extra dimensions, such as time, to model their inherent additional complexities. In this section, we describe the *multidimensional* approach to recommendations.

Multiple Dimensions. In this paper we propose to extend the traditional two-dimensional approach to multiple dimensions. More formally, given dimensions $D_1, D_2, \ldots, D_n$, we define a *recommendation space* to be $\mathcal{S} = D_1 \times D_2 \times \ldots \times D_n$. Let *Ratings* be a rating domain representing the set of all possible rating values. Then, the rating function R is defined as:

$$R : D_1 \times D_2 \times \cdots \times D_n \rightarrow Ratings .\quad\quad\quad (2)$$

For example, in the two-dimensional case described in (1), the recommendation space is $\mathcal{S} = Users \times Items$. Moreover, let $\mathcal{S} = Users \times Content \times Time$ be the recommendation space for the personalized Web content application, where a user assigns a score to a content seen at a certain time. For example, user John Doe assigned rating 8 to the stock reports on weekday evenings, i.e., $R_{content}(John\ Doe,\ "Stock\ Report",\ weekday\_\ evening) = 8$. Other examples of multidimensional applications include recommending food to customers in restaurants, i.e., $\mathcal{S} = Users \times Restaurant \times Food$, and purchasing agent applications – recommending the products to buy to customers, including when and where, i.e., $\mathcal{S} = Users \times Products \times Time \times Place$.

While most traditional recommender systems provide recommendations only of one particular type, i.e., "recommend top N items to a user," multidimensional recommender systems offer many more possibilities. For example, in the personalized Web content application described above, one could ask for the "top N content items for each user/time combination" or the "top N times for each user/item combination," or the "top N user/time combinations for each item." Therefore, having recommender systems support multiple dimensions allows us to apply recommender technologies in a much more diverse set of applications than the traditional two-dimensional recommender systems and to obtain new types of recommendations.

Profiling Capabilities. The initial approaches to recommender systems [5,19, 21] operated on a two-dimensional matrix of ratings and provided very limited profiling capabilities. This was the case because unknown rating estimations were based *only* on the known ratings, and neither user nor item profiles have been used for this purpose.

More recent approaches to recommender systems utilized some profiling capabilities. For example, Pazzani [17] describes how to use certain demographic information of users in the collaborative setting. Also, some content-based approaches used keywords for providing recommendations [15,18]. More recently, Ansari et al. [2] proposed a hybrid approach to rating estimation that uses limited profiling information about *both* users and items.

We propose to significantly extend profiling capabilities of a recommender system and view it as a *recommendation warehouse* consisting of multidimensional cubes for storing the ratings, as well as comprehensive profiles representing elements of each dimension. These profiles can contain a set of various attributes describing each dimension. For example, for the "user" dimension, a profile may include attributes such as the name, the address and the phone number of each user, as well as his/her preferences (e.g. a favorite drink), and behavioral characteristics, such as the largest purchase made at a Web site. Similarly, for a "Web content" dimension, a profile may include information about the Web content type (e.g., politics, finance, weather, sports, science), the length of the content item (e.g., how long is the news article), and the presence or absence of the important keywords in the content item. Such profiles can be stored as records in relational tables, one record for each profile and a separate table for each dimension, as will be discussed in detail in Section 4.

Profiles allow us to provide more complex recommendations. Instead of the standard recommendation of "top N items to a user," we can now use the available profiling information to provide more targeted recommendations, such as recommending "top 3 action movies with either Sylvester Stallone or Arnold Schwarzenegger that were released within last 5 years." We will demonstrate in Section 3 how these profiling capabilities can be incorporated into a query language that can express such recommendations.

Aggregation Capabilities. While OLAP-like aggregation capabilities have been used in some e-commerce applications, including the storing and analysis of Web usage data [6,22], these capabilities have not been utilized in recommender systems. This is unfortunate, since various dimensions may have hierarchies associated with them. For example, *Products* dimension has standard industrial product hierarchy and *Time* dimension has a temporal hierarchy, e.g., minutes, hours, days, months, seasons, etc.

Given these hierarchies, recommender systems can provide more complex recommendations that deal not only with individual items, but also with *groups* of items. For example, we may want to know not only how individual users like individual movies, e.g., $R_{movie}(JohnDoe, Gladiator) = 7$, but also how they may like categories of movies, e.g., $R_{movie}(JohnDoe, action\_movies) = 5$. Similarly, we may want to group users and other dimensions as well. For example, we may want to know how graduate students like "Gladiator", e.g., $R_{movie}(graduate\_students, Gladiator) = 9$.

More generally, given individual ratings in the multidimensional cube, we may want to use hierarchies to compute aggregated ratings. For example, assume that movies can be grouped based on their genres and assume that we know how John Doe likes each action movie individually. Then, as shown in Figure 1, we can compute an overall rating of how John Doe likes action movies as a genre by aggregating his individual action movie ratings, i.e.,

$$R_{movie}(JohnDoe, action) := AGGR_{x.genre=action} R_{movie}(JohnDoe, x) \ . \quad (3)$$

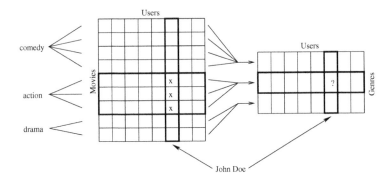

Fig. 1. Aggregation capabilities for recommender systems: aggregating the ratings.

Most traditional OLAP systems use similar aggregation operation (known as roll-up) that often is a simple summation of all the underlying elements. Such approach, however, is not applicable to recommender systems because ratings usually are not additive quantities. Therefore, more appropriate aggregation functions *AGGR* for recommender systems are *AVG, MAX, MIN,* and *AVG of TOP k.* For example, the cumulative rating of action movies can be computed for John Doe as

$$R_{movie}(JohnDoe, action) := AVG_{x.genre=action} R_{movie}(JohnDoe, x) \ . \quad (4)$$

In summary, the aggregation-based approach described in this section provides for more complex recommendations that include recommending *groups* of items, users, and elements of other dimensions.

Estimating the Ratings. An important research question is how to estimate unknown ratings in a multidimensional recommendation space. More specifically, the rating function R in (2) is defined initially as a partial function on $\mathcal{S}$, where domain $dom(R) = H \subset \mathcal{S}$ and is defined by explicit ratings specified by the users or is obtained implicitly using various proxies to user ratings [9,13]. As in traditional recommender systems, the key problem of multidimensional systems is *extrapolation* of the rating function from the initial (partial) domain H to the whole recommendation space $\mathcal{S}$, i.e., estimation of $R(x_1, \ldots, x_n)$ for the points $(x_1, \ldots, x_n) \in \mathcal{S} - H$ based on the initial recommendation ratings defined on H.

There are many methods proposed for estimating ratings in traditional two-dimensional recommender systems. These methods are classified into three broad categories: collaborative, content-based, and hybrid. Overview of these methods are presented in [5,17]. However, not all of these methods can be directly extended to the multidimensional case. An example of a particular two-dimensional technique that has a straightforward extension to the multidimensional case is the method proposed by Ansari et al. [2] that, as demonstrated in [2], outperformed several previously known collaborative filtering methods.

In particular, the method proposed by Ansari et al. [2] combines the information about users and items into a single hierarchical regression-based Bayesian preference model that uses Markov chain Monte Carlo techniques for exact estimation and prediction. In particular, this Bayesian preference model allows statistical integration of the following types of information useful for making recommendations of items to users: a person's expressed preferences (ratings), preferences of other consumers, expert evaluations, item characteristics, and characteristics of individuals. For example, in case of recommending movies, this information may include known movie ratings, gender and age of users, movie genres, movie reviews by critics. While the approach presented in [2] is described in the context of traditional two-dimensional recommender systems, it can be directly extended to combine information about more than two dimensions by letting regressions include additional variables that describe characteristics of other dimensions, and not just items and users.

We would like to point out that the problem of selecting specific multidimensional rating function (2) is *orthogonal* to the multidimensional model described in this paper. Since different rating estimation functions may work better in different applications, we do not attempt to provide a single one-size-fits-all function for all possible applications. Instead, we let the domain expert select a specific rating estimation function (2) that is most suitable for the application at hand. This is achieved in our model by providing the `DEFINE ESTIMATOR` and the `ESTIMATE` commands as a part of the data definition component of the Recommendation Query Language (RQL) that will be introduced in Section 3. These commands are specified by the user, e.g. system administrator, and define a particular rating estimation function for an application at hand (DEFINE ESTIMATOR command) as well as compute actual ratings (ESTIMATE command).

3   Recommendation Query Language (RQL)

As mentioned in Section 1, unlike traditional recommenders, multidimensional recommender systems provide for more complex types of recommendations. Moreover, these types of recommendations may need to be expressed *directly* by the users (such as customers and business analysts) and by various e-commerce systems (e.g., shopping bots), rather than being "hard-wired" into the recommender system directly by the vendor. This motivates the need for a flexible query language that allows users to express ad hoc recommendations in the same manner as SQL allows to express ad hoc database queries. In this section we introduce such a language, called RQL, through a series of examples.

Data Definition Language. The purpose of the data definition language of RQL is to define various components of a recommendation warehouse, such as dimensions, cubes, and rating estimation methods. Dimensions of the recommendation warehouse, such as *User*, *Product*, and *Time*, are defined in RQL with the DEFINE DIMENSION command. Also, the RQL command DEFINE CUBE is used for defining multidimensional cubes of ratings. These commands are similar to the data cube definition commands in traditional data warehousing/OLAP languages.

Using RQL, we can define the warehouse for a traditional movie recommendation application, consisting of two dimensions and a matrix of ratings, as follows:

```
DEFINE DIMENSION User ( UserId, LastName, FirstName, Gender, Age )
DEFINE DIMENSION Movie ( MovieId, Title, Genre, Length, Director, Year)
DEFINE CUBE MovieRecommender ( User, Movie ) WITH MEASURES ( Rating )
```

Notice, that each dimension is represented by a name and is described with a list of attributes characterizing each element of the dimension.[1] In other words, each element of a dimension is represented by a profile, as described in Section 2. A data cube is defined by DEFINE CUBE command that utilizes previously defined dimensions (*User* and *Movie* in this example) and uses the *Rating* measure specified with the WITH MEASURES clause. Although most traditional recommender systems use a single measure, multiple measures can also be used, as will be demonstrated with Query 3 later in this section. In fact, multiple recommendation criteria may even be desired in some applications, such as recommending a restaurant. For example, a popular Zagat restaurant guide rates restaurants according to four criteria: food, decor, service, and cost. The following is an example of the data warehouse for a vacation recommender system that is described with more than two dimensions and more than one measure:

---

[1] Each attribute also has a data type associated with it in the data warehouse (e.g., *Length* INTEGER), but we omit it in this paper for the sake of simplicity and clarity.

```
DEFINE DIMENSION Customer ( CustId, LastName, FirstName, Gender, Age )
DEFINE DIMENSION Vacation ( VacationId, Destination, Length, Price )
DEFINE DIMENSION Time ( TimeId, Month, Season )
DEFINE CUBE      VacationRecommender ( Customer, Vacation, Time )
          WITH MEASURES ( Rating, Profit )
```

The DEFINE DIMENSION and DEFINE CUBE commands specify the structure of a recommendation warehouse. In addition to this, we need to populate it with the recommendation ratings. Therefore, the recommendation warehouse has to support various rating insertion and estimation methods. User-specified ratings are inserted into the warehouse using INSERT and LOAD commands. Functions for estimating the unknown ratings based on the initial user-specified ratings are defined with the command

DEFINE ESTIMATOR *estimator_name* AS *module_name*

where *estimator_name* is the name of the rating estimation function defined by this statement and *module_name* denotes a software module (e.g., a program file) that computes this function. In addition, RQL provides the ESTIMATE command

ESTIMATE *measure_name* IN *cube_name* USING *estimator_name*

that computes the unknown values for the measure *measure_name* in the cube *cube_name* using the estimation function *estimator_name* previously defined with the DEFINE ESTIMATOR command.

Querying Capabilities. Recommendation queries are expressed in RQL with the RECOMMEND command, the use of which is illustrated with a series of examples below. These examples are based on the movie and vacation recommendation warehouses defined earlier in this section. The first example shows the "standard" type of recommendation supported by most of the current recommender systems.

Query 1 *Recommend top 5 yet unseen movies to each user:*

RECOMMEND Movie TO User BASED ON Rating SHOW TOP 5
    FROM MovieRecommender

This query retrieves all estimated (i.e., new) user/movie ratings from cube *MovieRecommender* specified in the FROM clause, groups them by the user, and returns 5 highest-ranked movies for each user, as specified by the SHOW subclause. The BASED ON subclause specifies that *Rating* measure should be used to rank movies.   □

Notice, that the above query can be very easily modified to recommend users to movies, instead of movies to users. The next example illustrates selection capabilities of RQL.

Query 2 *To each user who is from New York, recommend the top 3 movies, including the previously seen ones, that are longer than two hours:*

RECOMMEND Movie TO User BASED ON Rating
        USING ALL SHOW TOP 3
     FROM MovieRecommender
     WHERE Movie.Length > 120 AND User.City = 'New York'

Instead of retrieving ratings from the whole *MovieRecommender* cube, we use WHERE clause to restrict it to include only the movies that are longer than 2 hours and only the users that are New Yorkers. Also, the ALL keyword in the USING subclause specifies that *all* ratings from the (restricted) cube should be taken into consideration. If USING subclause is omitted, by default only the estimated (i.e., new) ratings are being retrieved.   □

The next example shows how multiple measures are supported in RQL as well as how measure values can be restricted.

Query 3 *Recommend to each user the top three most profitable vacations, that are also highly rated (the rating of at least 8):*

RECOMMEND Vacation, Time TO User BASED ON Profit
        SHOW TOP 3 WITH Rating ≥ 8
     FROM VacationRecommender

Here we use both measures defined in *VacationRecommender* cube (see DEFINE CUBE example in the beginning of this section). We use *Rating* in the WITH subclause to include only vacations that are highly rated, and we use *Profit* to rank the alternatives before returning the results.   □

The next example introduces the aggregation capabilities of RQL and also illustrates additional selection capabilities.

Query 4 *Recommend movie genres to each user that has previously seen "Gladiator," but only if the rating for this genre is above 8:*

RECOMMEND Movie AGGR BY Genre TO User BASED ON AVG(Rating)
        WITH AVG(Rating) > 8
     FROM MovieRecommender
     WHERE User HAS (Movie.Title = 'Gladiator')

The AGGR BY keyword specifies that movie *genres* should be recommended rather than individual movies. Also, in this query we use the AVG (average) function to aggregate and rank the ratings. In addition, we restrict the aggregate ratings so that only the ones, that are greater than 8, are considered. The HAS operator allows to specify restrictions based on what users have previously done. In particular, "User HAS (Movie.Title = 'Gladiator')" restricts the set of all users to include only the ones who have already seen "Gladiator."[2] Also notice, that we do not use the SHOW subclause in this query to include only *top k* movie genres for each user. Therefore, this query retrieves *all* genres that satisfy all its restrictions.   □

---

[2] include only users who *rated* this movie (i.e., the rating is *known*, not estimated).

In general, the syntax of the RECOMMEND statement is

```
RECOMMEND dimension_list_1 TO dimension_list_2
         BASED ON rank_measure
         USING measure_type_restrictions      // optional
         SHOW measure_rank_restrictions       // optional
         WITH measure_value_restrictions      // optional
     FROM cube_name
   WHERE dimension_restrictions               // optional
```

The semantics of the RECOMMEND statement is the following. First, the cube *cube_name* specified in the FROM clause is restricted using *dimension_restrictions* from the WHERE clause. The WHERE clause is optional. The resulting subcube is then processed by the RECOMMEND clause. The *dimension_list_1* argument specifies the dimensions that should be recommended, whereas *dimension_list_2* specifies the dimensions that should receive the recommendations. These two dimension lists must be disjoint. Also, any dimension in these lists can be "aggregated" based on some of its attributes, as illustrated in Query 4. The BASED ON subclause specifies the measure by which recommendations are ranked. The USING, SHOW, and WITH subclauses allow to put various restrictions on the measures before returning recommendation query results, as illustrated in Queries 1-4.

RQL, as described above, can be used either directly by the "power-users" or as a query language embedded in general programming languages. However, it may be difficult for the naive users to formulate recommendation requests using RQL syntax. Therefore, as in the case of many DBMSes, various GUI-based tools could be developed that let the naive end-users express their queries using intuitive graphical means.

4   Implementation

As in the case of OLAP systems, multidimensional recommendation model can be implemented in one of the following ways. First, as in the case of MOLAP systems (e.g., Hyperion Essbase), it can support proprietary data structures for cube storage and proprietary RQL query processing methods. Alternatively, as in the case of ROLAP systems (e.g., MicroStrategy Intelligent Server), the multidimensional recommendation model can be implemented via the relational data model and SQL. The main differences of implementing proprietary recommendation methods for data storage and operations versus using the existing database technologies are similar to the differences between the two OLAP approaches: it is a tradeoff between the efficiency and performance of the MOLAP model and the extensibility, openness and standardization of the ROLAP model [10].

As an initial approach that would test our ideas and methods, we decided to follow the ROLAP-based approach that maps the data model into the relational model, and map our multidimensional recommendation model into the relational data model and the Recommendation Query Language into SQL. Besides other benefits mentioned above, it also made the implementation of our prototype multidimensional recommender system simpler than if we had to design and implement our own system for data storage and management. The main drawback of this decision is inefficiency, since some recommendation queries may become quite complex after the translation into SQL and their processing by a standard relational DBMS can be slow. As a part of the future research, we plan to investigate the possibilities of implementing RQL using the MOLAP approach, i.e., by developing our own, potentially more efficient, methods of data storage and management for multidimensional recommendation warehouses.

Following many relational OLAP approaches, we map our multidimensional data model into a specific relational design called the *star schema*. Each dimension is represented by a single relational table, which consists of columns that correspond to attributes of the dimension. Individual records in such a table represent the profiles of the elements of the dimension (e.g., user profiles, content profiles). The multidimensional cube of ratings is represented by a single fact table, where each record represents an "entry" in a multidimensional cube. That is, a record in the fact table contains pointers (or *foreign keys*) to the corresponding element of each dimension.

The current implementation of the system consists of two components: (a) *recommender engine* that populates the recommendation cube with ratings, and (b) *query engine* that supports RQL queries.

Recommender Engine. As mentioned in Section 2, we can use various multidimensional rating estimation methods, including the one proposed by Ansari et al. [2]. Currently, we are working on implementing several of these methods and on comparing their performance (both recommendation accuracy and computational complexity). The results of this work will be reported separately.

Query Engine. To query the resulting relational data model, we translate RQL queries into corresponding SQL queries and run them in the relational database. The results of SQL queries are then processed and returned to the end-user. We would like to point out that, while we can ultimately use standard database query languages, such as SQL, to retrieve recommendations, we still need RQL because it allows to express recommendation queries at a higher level of abstraction than SQL and facilitates a clear separation between practical and conceptual aspects of recommender systems. For example, consider Query 4, which is expressed in RQL very intuitively and concisely. The SQL version of this query would be:

```
SELECT UserId, Genre, AVG(Rating)
   FROM MovieRecommender R, Movie M
   WHERE R.MovieId = M.MovieId AND R.RatingType = 'estimated' AND
         R.UserId IN ( SELECT DISTINCT UserId
                       FROM MovieRecommender RR, Movie MM
                       WHERE RR.MovieId = MM.MovieId AND
                       MM.Title = 'Gladiator' AND RR.RatingType = 'known' )
   GROUP BY UserId, Genre HAVING AVG(Rating) ≥ 8
   ORDER BY UserId, AVG(Rating), Genre
```

As we can see from this example, RQL is a declarative and easy-to-use tool to query multidimensional recommender systems, since it allows to manipulate multidimensional recommendation data in a natural and intuitive way.

Following the ideas described in this section, we implemented a prototype recommendation system that stores all the data (e.g., cubes, dimensions) in a relational database management system and uses SQL for data manipulation. The recommender engine stores the implementations of rating estimation functions that are used with the particular application. Interactions with the recommendation system are made using RQL.

5   Conclusions and Future Work

In this paper, we presented a multidimensional recommendation model that is based on the data warehousing paradigm. It extends traditional two-dimensional recommender systems by supporting multiple dimensions, hierarchical aggregation, and extensive profiling capabilities. Moreover, our model supports Recommendation Query Language (RQL) that allows the users to express a comprehensive class of recommendations "on the fly" as their needs arise. Users and e-commerce applications can interact with multidimensional recommender systems using RQL in an interactive and flexible way. Furthermore, we presented a prototype recommendation system that implements the proposed multidimensional recommendation model.

One of the defining features of our approach lies in separating our recommendation model from the underlying implementation (relational model in our case). This is in line with traditional approaches utilized in several data models, such as entity-relationship and some of the object-oriented and OLAP models, and constitutes one of the important advantages of our approach. Moreover, this separation of the model from the underlying implementation allowed us to introduce a declarative query language that can express complex recommendations in a concise, intuitive, and implementation-independent manner.

The multidimensional approach to recommender systems presented in this paper needs to be explored further in order to realize its full potential. In particular, we plan to examine various estimation functions for the DEFINE ESTIMATOR operator proposed in Section 3 and compare the performance for different choices of these functions and across different application domains. Moreover, we plan to study by how much they improve recommendation accuracy in comparison to two-dimensional recommender systems. Another topic of future research is the development of data structures and algorithms that directly implement our data model and RQL, rather than mapping them into the relational data model and SQL. This should provide performance improvements for our model. We also plan to work on real-time issues pertaining to our model and plan to utilize some of the methods developed in the OLAP systems such as on-the-fly materialization of data cubes and their incremental updates.

References

1. G. Adomavicius and A. Tuzhilin. Expert-driven validation of rule-based user models in personalization applications. *Journal of Data Mining and Knowledge Discovery*, 5(1/2):33–58, 2001.
2. A. Ansari, S. Essegaier, and R. Kohli. Internet recommendations systems. *Journal of Marketing Research*, pages 363–375, August 2000.
3. M. Balabanovic and Y. Shoham. Fab: Content-based, collaborative recommendation. *Communications of the ACM*, 40(3):66–72, 1997.
4. P. Baudisch, editor. *CHI'99 Workshop: Interacting with Recommender Systems*, May 1999. http://www.darmstadt.gmd.de/rec99/.
5. J. S. Breese, D. Heckerman, and C. Kadie. Empirical analysis of predictive algorithms for collaborative filtering. Technical Report MSR-TR-98-12, Microsoft Research, May 1998.
6. A. Buchner and M. Mulvenna. Discovering internet marketing intelligence through online analytical web usage mining. *SIGMOD Record*, 27(4):54–61, 1998.
7. *Communications of the ACM*, 40(3):56–89, 1997. Special issue on Recommender Systems.
8. *Communications of the ACM*, 43(8):26–158, 2000. Special issue on Personalization.
9. A. Caglayan, M. Snorrason, J. Jacoby, J. Mazzu, R. Jones, and K. Kumar. Learn sesame - a learning agent engine. *Applied Artificial Intelligence*, 11:393–412, 1997.
10. S. Chaudhuri and U. Dayal. An overview of data warehousing and OLAP technology. *ACM SIGMOD Record*, 26(1):65–74, 1997.
11. H. Kautz, editor. *Recommender Systems. Papers from 1998 Workshop. Technical Report WS-98-08*. AAAI Press, 1998.
12. R. Kimball. *The Data Warehouse Toolkit*. John Wiley & Sons, Inc., 1996.
13. J. A. Konstan, B. N. Miller, D. Maltz, J. L. Herlocker, L. R. Gordon, and J. Riedl. GroupLens: Applying collaborative filtering to Usenet news. *Communications of the ACM*, 40(3):77–87, 1997.
14. K. Lang. Newsweeder: Learning to filter netnews. In *Proceedings of the 12th International Conference on Machine Learning*, 1995.
15. R. J. Mooney, P. N. Bennett, and L. Roy. Book recommending using text categorization with extracted information. In *Recommender Systems. Papers from 1998 Workshop. Technical Report WS-98-08*. AAAI Press, 1998.
16. Movie Critic. http://www.moviecritic.com.
17. M. Pazzani. A framework for collaborative, content-based and demographic filtering. *Artificial Intelligence Review*, pages 393–408, December 1999.
18. M. Pazzani, J. Muramatsu, and D. Billsus. Syskill & Webert: Identifying interesting web sites. In *Proceedings of the National Conference on Artificial Intelligence*, 1996.
19. P. Resnick, N. Iakovou, M. Sushak, P. Bergstrom, and J. Riedl. GroupLens: An open architecture for collaborative filtering of netnews. In *Proceedings of the 1994 Computer Supported Cooperative Work Conference*, 1994.
20. J. B. Schafer, J. A. Konstan, and J. Riedl. E-commerce recommendation applications. *Journal of Data Mining and Knowledge Discovery*, 5(1/2):115–153, 2001.
21. U. Shardanand and P. Maes. Social information filtering: Algorithms for automating 'word of mouth'. In *Proceedings of the Conference on Human Factors in Computing Systems (CHI'95)*, pages 210–217. ACM Press, 1995.
22. J. Srivastava, R. Cooley, M. Deshpande, and P.-N. Tan. Web usage mining: Discovery and applications of usage patterns from web data. *SIGKDD Explorations*, 1(2):12–23, 2000.

A Multi-criteria Taxonomy of Business Models in Electronic Commerce

Andreas Bartelt and Winfried Lamersdorf

University of Hamburg, VSYS, Vogt-Kölln-Straße 30, D-22527 Hamburg
{bartelt|lamersd}@Informatik.Uni-Hamburg.DE

Abstract. Looking at the ongoing evolution in electronic commerce there are more and more business models becoming significant. E-shops, e-auctions or e-tendering are not the only possibilities for a company to be active in electronic commerce. This article presents many relevant business models and systematically classifies them. Mainly the classification is based on the type of business subjects like suppliers, customers and mediators and their active or passive role as initiators and carrier of a business model. Another basis for the classification is the breakdown of the concept of electronic commerce and an explicit modeling. This allows to build up a taxonomy using multiple criteria and the presentation and subsumption of individual business models. The taxonomy can be used to analyze and enhance existing systems and business models as well as to develop new internet strategies for companies. An example of the implementation of the business model *e-portal* concludes the article.

1 Introduction

The variety of business scenarios is one reason for the success of individual companies today. The activities in electronic commerce are also part of this variety. However, companies like established firms and internet-oriented start-up's have different requirements in electronic commerce. So the innovative possibilities need to be designed and customized at an individual level. We provide insights and help with these problems by presenting a systematic multi-criteria taxonomy for reference models, advances in modelling for the electronic business domain and a classification scheme for the business models. This provides help at the development of a successful internet strategy. In this context the detailed representation of single areas and models of the electronic commerce domain offer a practical consolidation of the subject matter.

1.1 Electronic Business

Under the ongoing development of a scientific realm the concepts / notions get manifold and also more detailed. Especially the notions are getting more exact. Talking of electronic commerce the notions are currently used with changing semantics and are overlapping each other. This is often caused by intensive marketing activities. The notion of 'Electronic Commerce' (EC), which is used since years as a conglo-

L. Fiege, G. Mühl, and U. Wilhelm (Eds.): WELCOM 2001, LNCS 2232, pp. 193-205, 2001.
© Springer-Verlag Berlin Heidelberg 2001

merate with great publicity, should be defined more exactly and delimited from other notions. This is necessary as there are new notions like 'Electronic Business' (EB) which is now used as a comprehensive word for all electronically handled business activities. A subset of electronic business is the area of 'Electronic Cooperation' (ECoop) which is getting greater attention today, e.g. by the business model of virtual companies or collaboration platforms. Another subset is 'Electronic Information' (EI), which covers all processes in electronic business, which are primarily devoted to the mediation and transportation of information to customers. Important examples from this actually intensively pursued area are web-directories / catalogues, digital libraries and content management systems. In the context of this overall classification „*Electronic Commerce*" (EC) now is used again with the original sense – the electronic trade, where suppliers and costumers, eventually also mediators are involved and exchange goods or services for an equivalent value (money). By now, electronic commerce is the most important force in electronic business. Fig. 1 shows today's common notions in the field of electronic business.

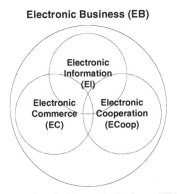

Fig. 1. Notions in Electronic Business (EB)

Concrete activities in electronic commerce can be characterized through business models, like Timmers suggest them for electronic markets [14, 15]. He defines a business model as 'an architecture for the product, services and information flows, including a description of the various business actors and their roles; and a description of the potential benefits for the various business actors; and a description of the sources of revenues' [14]. There has been only little work done to define an e-business model in a formal way. Alt and Zimmermann [1] highlight the need for a better understanding of business models in electronic business in their introduction to the special section on business models in the ten-year anniversary issue of the international journal on Electronic Markets. The same issue contains an article from Essler et al. [6] who emphasize interactivity in their modelling efforts. O'Daniel [11] introduces a value-added model in the same issue. Other relevant work comes from Gordijn et al. [8], who already define a semi-formal value-port based model (e^3-VALUE).

In this article, Timmers' modelling approach is continued, enhanced, and a classification scheme is developed for the business models of electronic commerce in order to show the peculiarity of certain groups of business models. The scheme considers at the same time, which economy subjects (supplier, customer or mediator/trader) initiate and carry a business model, and in which manner (active or passive) they communicate with their trade partners. The relevant models introduced by Timmers and further actual business models are discussed and assigned to the classification scheme. More emphasis is given to the business models carried by the customers as their importance had risen substantially in the mean time (cf. [2]).

2   A Classification of Business Models in Electronic Commerce

An abstract classification in electronic business was already presented in the introduction. *Electronic Business* (EB) can be subdivided into the areas of *Electronic information* (EI), *Electronic Commerce* (EC) and *Electronic Cooperation* (ECoop). Besides this classification usually only superficial classifications are used. Activities are only classified into the areas of Business-to-Consumer (B2C) and Business-to-Business (B2B), using the economy types of the participants as criteria. But further combinations and groups already get relevant. Examples are Consumer-to-Consumer (e.g. eBay), or groups like administration and government. A detailed classification of the business models seems necessary.

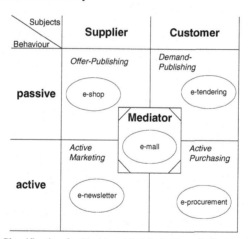

Fig. 2. Classification for Business Models (with typical examples)

Fig. 2 shows a possible structure for a classification of business models. Some business models are placed in the classification to show examples. The business models are classified at first after which (economy-) *subjects* carry the model. The most important subjects in electronic commerce are supplier and customer. For example the business model of an e-shop is carried characteristically by the subject *supplier*. Other relevant economy subjects can be mediators. A second classification criterion (*behaviour*) describes whether supplier or customer initiates the trade transactions. The subject can behave active or passive in the communication with its trade partners. Push-models like an e-newsletter may have active character. The customer may be contacted and then gets the information active delivered as a subscriber. An e-shop generates a passive offer; the supplier waits until a customer enters its shop, informs himself about the products, and initiates an order. A *mediator* is a subject that acts as an agent between the supplier and the customer. He can behave either *active* or *passive* to the supplier as well as to the customer. So there are four possibilities for the positioning of a mediator in the classification scheme. For example an e-mall, that is a union of several e-shops, is characteristically *passive* to the customers and also *passive* to the suppliers. This classification clarifies the position of a business model in electronic commerce.

3   Modelling in Electronic Business

Currently there is no systematic presentation and modelling technique for business models in Electronic Business. Based on Timmers [14] the modeling of actors and a phase model for trade transactions is presented. Also the possible revenue sources are analysed. Additionally function modules for applications in Electronic Business are discussed, which evolve as a basis for the implementation of systems for business models.

3.1 Modelling of Actors and Their Roles

To model the most important actors in a business model, their roles and their relations to one another, a graphical diagram based interaction-oriented language is used. This schematic and clearly arranged presentation technique was chosen for better comprehensibility.

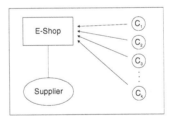

Fig. 3. Modeling Example: E-Shop

Fig. 3 shows the example of a scenario for the business model *e-shop*. A supplier usually carries this business model. The supplier presents it's products and services. Customers can access the offers and initiate trade transactions. The meaning of the graphical elements is now described in detail:
- the roles of the actors are marked with small circles
- possible roles are suppliers (S), customers (C) and mediators (M)
- the role of the actor / economy subject which carries the business model is marked with an ellipse
- software systems are shown with a rectangle
- basic connections between the elements are shown by simple lines
- the action of one actor contacting another is shown by arrows; the contact may lead to a trade transaction

3.2 Phase Model for Trade Transactions

Trade transactions can be subdivided into multiple phases. A simple and broadly accepted phase model spans the three phases of *search*, *negotiate* and *fulfil* (cf. [10]). To better understand the weaknesses and strengths of a business model in its support of trade transactions, it is investigated in which way and how much a business model supports each single phase. To gain more insights a more detailed model is used. It's adapted from Guttman et al. [9], who have developed the model on top of several descriptive theories and models to capture consumer buying behaviour.

Table 1. Phase Model for Trade Transactions

No.	Phase	Abbr.
1.	Need Identification	NI
2.	Product Brokering	PB
3.	Merchant Brokering	MB
4.	Negotiation	N
5.	Purchase and Delivery	PD
6.	Product Service and Evaluation	SE

Table 1 shows the six phases or stages of the model. As every model this is a simplification and single phases could overlap each other or become specialized forms in the concrete scenario. Nonetheless this helps to establish reference business models, which describe what phases are typically supported in an e-business model.

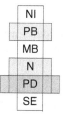

Fig. 4. Trade Transaction Phases of an E-Shop

The example in Fig. 4 shows the phase model for an e-shop to provide a better understanding. The width of the blocks (resp. their shading) stands for the level of support, which is provided from a business model for a specific trade transaction phase. In this example the phases NI, MB and SE are only poorly supported, while the phases PB and N have typically good support. The phase PD should have excellent support by every e-shop, since the functions of purchasing and the organization of the delivery are most naturally to the character of an e-shop.

3.3 Revenue Sources in Electronic Business

Revenue sources are an integral part of an e-business model [15]. They are the basis for the economy of a business model and determine the direct incomes. In the internet economy revenues can also be generated by other sources than *sales of products and services*. There are sources like the marketing of *contacts* and *information* [13]. Actors could use their *contacts* to customers, e.g. for advertising purposes. Visitors of web sites generate *information*, which can also be used as a revenue source. Derived user profiles and web statistics may be used under the restrictions of legal standards for the protection of data privacy. Fig. 5 shows the three major groups of revenue sources.

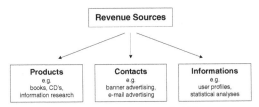

Fig. 5. Revenue Sources (cf. [13])

This revenue sources may be adapted nearly to all business models. The real usage and the revenue allocation depend on the real scenario and are tightly coupled with the price formation of the suppliers offers.

3.4 Functional Modules for E-business Applications

E-business models contain functional modules, which can be identified and re-used in other models. Specific modules can be replaced by other modules, which have the same type. For example the module for *price discovery* may use module instances that use static prices, a discount system or an auction mechanism. By exchange and combination of such functional modules new business models can be created. The software implementation of functional modules can be accomplished, e.g. by component technology. In the following an e-catalogue / e-shop is taken as example. An e-catalogue is a reduced form of an e-shop, which is restricted to the marketing functions. Some possible modules of an e-catalogue are the *catalogue function*, *product presentation*, *search function*, and *available to promise*. An e-shop should contain additional modules for the purchase order processing. For example a *basket*, the *e-payment* functions, *logistics*, and *security functions* (e.g. encoding). Modules can be *required* to form a specific e-business model or can be *optional*. Using the viewpoint of modules and components it is possible to substantiate e-business models even further.

4   Important Business Models for Electronic Commerce

In this section, business models of electronic commerce are presented, which have already reached broad economic relevance or show a clear trend for major relevance in the future. In this paper only some of these models can be presented in detail. A broader range can be found in [2]. The models are integrated into the classification scheme developed in section 2. As a basis for the presentation typical instances of the models are identified, which help to develop so called reference models. These reference models can be combined with other models and can be customized easily to help implement a solution for a concrete real world scenario.

4.1 Business Models of Offer Publishing

The business models of this group are carried by the *suppliers*, who act only in a *passive* way to the customers. The suppliers publish their offers and wait for orders from the customers. Besides *electronic product catalogs* the most prominent business model of this group is the *e-shop*. The e-shop has already been used as an example in the modelling section above. See Fig. 3 and Fig. 4 for details. An e-shop is used by companies to distribute their products and services using the internet. The main functionalities provided are *marketing* and *purchase order processing*. See [3] for a detailed discussion on these subjects.

4.2 Business Models of Demand Publishing

The business models in the group of demand publishing are carried by the *customers*. The customers publish their demands, sometimes making use of mediators, and wait for the offers of the suppliers (*passive*). In the past these models were not suitable due to the relative high costs. But based on the cost savings from e-business solutions today, such business models seem to be promising now. A typical business model in this group is *e-tendering / e-sourcing* (Fig. 6).

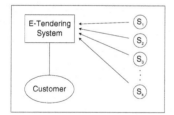 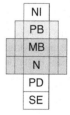

Fig. 6. E-Tendering / E-Sourcing

Examples of the e-tendering business model which make use of mediators are the Deal Assistant (www.Dealassist.com) and eWanted (www.eWanted.com), which currently use reverse auctions in the C2C area.

4.3 Business Models of Active Marketing

The business models of active marketing are carried again by the *suppliers*, but the suppliers contact the possible customers in an *active* manner. The suppliers provide information about their products, the prices or other conditions in an active manner. This marketing often uses the e-mail channel and may lead to undesirable effects like spamming. But there are many positive applications like active cross-selling mechanisms or alerting services about new products and prices. Also the *E-CRM* (customer relationship management) business model, which may have an emphasis on the service and evaluation phase, can be positioned in the group of active marketing. The *e-newsletter* (Fig. 7) is a typical example of active marketing in the information phase. When a customers register with additional profile information, or the information are derived from other sources, customized content can be provided in a personalized way to the customer.

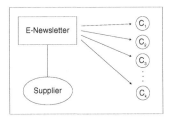
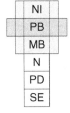

Fig. 7. E-Newsletter

4.4 Business Models of Active Purchasing

In the group of active purchasing the *customers* carry the business models, investigate *active* and communicate *active* with the suppliers. An innovative example are *shopping agents* [9], which automatically search for products and services in the name of the customer and under certain circumstances also buy the goods. An example is Jango (www.jango.excite.com), which evolved from the Netbot project [5]. A preliminary stage of shopping agents are *offer comparison services*. But shopping agents are designed as autonomous flexible software agents [16,17]. Due to a lack of adequate technologies shopping agents are not spread today. A more practical business model in the active purchasing group is *e-procurement*, where customers access the electronic commerce systems of suppliers using the service functions of an own e-procurement system.

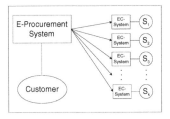
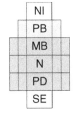

Fig. 8. E-Procurement

Currently basic e-procurement systems are used by big companies to reduce their procurement costs. The functions support internal processes, e.g. authorization issues, as well as external procurement processes. Business messaging, EDI or XML based, is an important interoperability issue in this context.

4.5 Business Models of Mediators

The business models for mediators and marketplaces are presently only ambiguously and fuzzy defined. Many of the already introduced business models can also be operated by a mediator and there are many possibilities to customize the reference e-business models. With the beginning of electronic commerce the concept of disinter-mediation, which fosters direct contacts between customers and suppliers, has become more relevant. But the process of bringing together the commerce partners can still be accomplished in various cases at a lower cost with a mediator. Also the mediator may allow to add some useful value-added services in the process. For mediators, various e-business models exist like the 3rd party marketplace [15], online exchanges, e-auctions [16], or full featured e-malls [2]. In the following the business model of an *e-portal* and the case study of the *PublicationPORTAL* will be described.

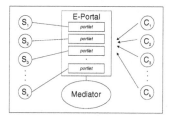
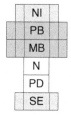

Fig. 9. E-Portal

E-portals (Fig. 9) support users with search and information discovery functions for the access to the manifold information on the internet. E-portals give access to information on products and trade partners in the phases of product brokerage and merchant brokerage. The suppliers present their information and services in so called portlets, small areas inside a web-portal. System portlets provide functions for user convenience. Also the trade transaction phases of need identification and evaluation are typically supported. E-portals can be seen as a preliminary stage to marketplaces, which also allow and support to carry out the trade transactions, including settlement issues.

To further define the hype word 'portal' an e-portal can be defined as *a fixed start and return point in the web, which is personalized to the user*. Portals help users to cope with the information overload of the web. Portals do this by personalization of their information to individual users, by specialization to user groups, by specialization and expertise on special themes and by presenting a broad range of prepared information. E-portals are also predestinated to integrate other business models from electronic commerce or electronic information.

Looking from the viewpoint of *electronic information*, the processing of information is central. Fig. 10 shows a phase model [4] where at first information sources are *registered*, then the *content is opened up* for later access and usage, an *archive* stage can preserve information, the *search and discovery* phase provides meta information to the user and finally the *delivery* phase gives the user access to the desired information.

Special variants of the e-portal business model that appeared in this chronological order are *consumer-portals, portals special to a line of business, intranet-portals* and *enterprise-information-portals (EIP). Consumer-portals* like 'Yahoo!' are highly used start pages into the web with services like search engines, directories, unified messaging, news from many areas, shopping-malls and auctions. Another variant are portals, which are special to a *line of business*. These are vertical portals that develop a high expertise in the area. *Intranet-portals* support employees through information and services specialized for the company. E*nterprise-information-portals (EIP)* join the functionalities of intranet-portals and the outward representation and communication of a company.

E-Portal

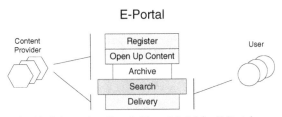

Fig. 10. Information Centric Phase Model for E-Portals

The implementation of portals requires complex web-technology and the integration of heterogeneous information and service sources. Different vendors try to create standard software for portals. Examples are *Viador, Oracle, BEA* and some other major commercial vendors. An example for an open-source framework is *Jetspeed* from the Apache group.

5   The PublicationPORTAL: Mediating Information and Services in Digital Publishing

Portals are mediators for suppliers and consumers and primarily provide integrated access to the technical implementation of the various business models of suppliers for the consumers. This applies also for the business models in the area of electronic information [4].

Applications of the business models from the area of electronic information, like digital libraries or content providers, help to cover the information demands that arise at work, in private life and in science. However large problems exist in the efficient utilization and development of the information market. A typical user has only a marginal overview of the information sources and services. The *PublicationPORTAL* [18] addresses these problems and offers an effective solution based on the mediation strengths of the business model of an *e-portal*, which was already presented above.

The *PublicationPORTAL* aims at the support of users that can be divided into different roles including authors, editors, publishers, distributors, librarians and readers. The users can be separated furthermore into the orthogonal categories of customers and providers. Providers use the Portal to promote their services exactly to the desired audience by specifying their *service types* and *offers*. Customers on the other hand are using the Portal as a starting point to achieve their domain specific goals. The *PublicationPORTAL* guides them using a process that is divided into three steps and assembles a generic procedure to accomplish different objectives in the application domain of e-publishing. The three steps are *orientation and mediation, integration,* and *access and utilization.*

In the first *orientation and mediation* phase, a mediation of task-related services based on individual characteristics and preferences of customers is done guiding users of different skills to a set of providers that together accomplish the desired goal. Here customers find out about the necessary processes, the related services and finally the most favourable providers ready available.

The second *integration* phase of the Portal guides the user in combining sub-services as to establish value chains. These combinations are deduced from the objectives and preferences as well as formerly chosen *service types* and providers, leading to optional or necessary additional services. Furthermore, coupling and coordination of partial services are supported on system level.

If concrete services are to be taken into account, this conventionally leads to proprietary procedures of use, including repeatedly registrations and different user interfaces. Where registering over and again is just inconvenient, different user interfaces can lead to severe failure due to semantically incompatibility. To cope with this, the *PublicationPORTAL* offers means for the support of *access and utilization*, which include initialisation, calling, and interactive control of services in a generic homogeneously fashion. An important part of this is semi automatic generation of generic Web interfaces (portlets) for categories of services. For further convenience, the phase can be backed by persistent customer profiles, enabling automatic service configuration and single-sign-on capabilities.

Individual user characteristics generally have an effect on support functions of a portal, as the elements of the three phases could be combined in a variable fashion. They can be utilized to optimize the way assistance is carried out. Thus, temporary as well as persistent personalization is a desired feature of the *PublicationPORTAL*, backed by profile gathering and accounting. Beside its influence on the essential phases of assistance, personalization allows for some nice tools like bookmark lists or individual desktops. In order to allow the users to use services and composite-service in a semi automatic manner, we work on a broker architecture, which is mainly based on concepts of type management and automated negotiation for services. Fig. 11 shows the web interface of the prototype that was implemented using the framework *Jetspeed*, an open source project from the Apache group.

The project is supported as part of the Global Info initiative of the German Federal Ministry of Education and Research (BMBF) [7]. It's the goal of the initiative to support the basic change in the scientific information infrastructure. Scientists should have efficient access to all the worldwide available electronic and multimedia information, that are digitally stored in distributed information systems, by their work place computers.

6   Conclusion

Current activities of companies in e-business change permanently and become very manifold. Therefore a systematic analysis of the basic structures in combination with the real usage of business models is important. As a result a multi-criteria taxonomy of e-business models has been presented. The modelling methods for e-business models were enhanced and concretely used. A case study with the e-business model *e-portal* has shown a real world scenario. The new classification and modelling methods help to analyse existing e-business models and to select and design e-business models for real world scenarios.

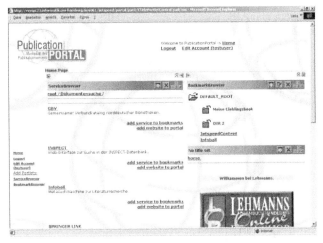

Fig. 11. PublicationPORTAL Prototype

References

1. Alt, R., Zimmermann, H.-D.: Introduction to Special Section – Business Models, in: EM - Anniversary Edition: Business Models, Electronic Markets, Vol. 11, No. 1, 04/2001, 2001.
2. Bartelt, A., Lamersdorf, W.: Geschäftsmodelle des Electronic Commerce: Modellbildung und Klassifikation, in: Verbundtagung Wirtschafsinformatik 2000, Shaker, pp. 17-29, 2000.
3. Bartelt, A., Meyer J.: A practical guideline to the implementation of online-shops, in: SRDS '99, WELCOM '99, 18:348-353, IEEE, Oct. 1999, Lausanne, Switzerland, 1999.
4. Bartelt, A., Zirpins, C., Fahrenholtz, D.: Geschäftsmodelle der Electronic Information: Modellbildung und Klassifikation, in: Proceedings of the 31. Jahrestagung der deutschen Gesellschaft für Informatik und der Österreichischen Computer Gesellschaft, accepted for publication, 2001.
5. Doorenbos, R. B., Etzioni, O., Weld, D. S.: A scalable comparision-shopping agent for the world-wide web, in: Proceedings of Agents '97, 1997.
6. Essler, U.; Whitaker, R.: Re-Thinking eCommerce Business Modeling in terms of Interactivity, in: Electronic Markets, Vol. 11, No. 1, 04/2001, 2001.
7. GlobalInfo: Globale Elektronische und Multimediale Informationssysteme für Naturwissenschaft und Technik, http://www.global-info.org, access 20.12.2000, 2000.
8. Gordijn, J., Akkermans, H., van Vliet, H.: Value Based Requirements Creation for Electronic Commerce Applications, in: HICSS 2000, Maui, Hawaii, IEEE, 2000.
9. Guttman, Robert H.; Moukas, Alexandros G.; Maes, Pattie: Agents as Mediators in Electronic Commerce, in: Electronic Markets, 05/98, 1998.
10. Merz, M.: Electronic Commerce: Marktmodelle, Anwendungen und Technologien. Dpunkt.verlag, Heidelberg, 1999.

11. O'Daniel, T.: A Value-Added Model for Electronic Commerce, in: Electronic Markets, Vol. 11, No. 1, 04/2001, 2001.
12. Reck, M.: Trading-process characteristics of electronic auctions. Electronic Markets, 7(4):17-23, 1997.
13. Skiera, B., Lambrecht, A.: Erlösmodelle im Internet, in: Herrmann, A., Albers, S. (Hrsg.), 2000.
14. Timmers, P.: Business models for electronic markets, in: Electronic Markets, 8(2):3-8, 1998.
15. Timmers, P.: Electronic commerce : strategies and models for business-to-business trading, Wiley, 2000.
16. Weiss, G. (Editor): Multiagent systems: a modern approach to distributed artifical intelligence, The MIT Press, Cambridge, Massachusetts, 1999.
17. Wooldridge, M., Jennings, N.R.: Intelligent agents: Theory and practice. Knowledge Engineering Review, 1995.
18. Zirpins, C., Weinreich, H., Bartelt, A., Lamersdorf, W.: Advanced Concepts for Next Generation Portals, DEXA 2001, Workshop WBC, accepted for publication, 2001.

Integration of Goods Delivery Supervision into E-commerce Supply Chain

Anke Thede[1], Albrecht Schmidt[1], and Christian Merz[2]

[1] Telecooperation Office, Universität Karlsruhe, 76131 Karlsruhe, Germany
{anke, albrecht}@teco.edu
http://www.teco.edu/~anke/awaregoods.html
[2] SAP AG Corporate Research, 76131 Karlsruhe, Germany
christian.merz@sap.com

Abstract. One of the benefits of electronic commerce is the gain of speed and easiness through electronic delivery of commerce data. Only the data specifying the delivery of the physical goods is not integrated into the electronic supply chain and therefore presents an unpleasant interruption of integration. The goal is to find a way to transfer delivery and goods related data electronically to gain rapidity and reliability. This paper focusses on supervisory data of sensitive goods and describes an implementation of a technique to store these data electronically and to integrate their flow seamlessly into the enterprise systems. It also gives an outlook to further utilization and improvements.

1   Introduction

Business to business (B2B) and business to customer (B2C) transactions often involve physical goods to be exchanged between partners. Much of current work in the field of electronic commerce, especially looking at B2B, does not incorporate physical goods. Workflows often do not model the specific difference introduced by physical transport in the commerce process. When it comes to quality control and quality ensurance properties of goods make an important difference compared to documents or data [9,4].

Often specific restrictions and handling requirements apply to the goods when transported or in stock. Typical examples are food, medical products and production chemicals. These products must be kept under certain conditions in order not to get wasted. For supervision, the stocking conditions are monitored and the data is then transferred into the enterprise resource planning system (ERPS) to be checked and controlled. For the transportation process the necessity of supervision and control of the goods' conditions applies in the same way but is a much more delicate and complicated matter.

In this paper we go along an example of chemical products used in the process of semiconductor manufacturing that have to be kept in a certain temperature range in order to stay useable. In case the temperature range is violated the best before date has to be considerably lowered. Or even worse, the characteristics of

L. Fiege, G. Mühl, and U. Wilhelm (Eds.): WELCOM 2001, LNCS 2232, pp. 206–218, 2001.

the chemicals might change in a way that they are no more utilizable and have to be disposed of [5,1].

Upon arrival of such goods the customer wants to determine the state of this material, whether it can be used at all and until when. As employment of bad material might have severe consequences for the whole production chain the worst case has to be assumed in case of doubt. As a consequence, still useable material might have to be discarded due to the lack of sufficiently accurate data.

Assuring the assumed properties of delivered goods is an important quality management (QM) task. The consumer's quality management department has to make sure that only reliable material in good condition is inserted into the manufacturing process, usually within the scope of an incoming inspection [10]. The inspection data must be made available in the ERPS in a way that offers sufficient error resistance, accuracy, speed and security of data handling.

If an incoming inspection does not offer sufficiently accurate data or cannot be executed due to chemical processes the inspection has to be performed already during the transport. However, the process of quality management during transportation is rather decoupled from the ones at the producer and the consumer. Test data can normally not be transmitted immediately into the ERPS but have to be collected and stored by a device transported with the goods. The transfer and the examination are performed upon arrival. Nowadays, the data is often still collected using rather old fashioned tools like analogous thermometers with only a maximum and minimum indicator or paper plots and is therefore not accurate and detailed enough. Moreover, the exchange of data is not automated but the collected information is transferred manually into the consumer's ERPS (see fig. 1). This procedure is time consuming and subject to potential errors and the reliability of the test data is lowered considerably.

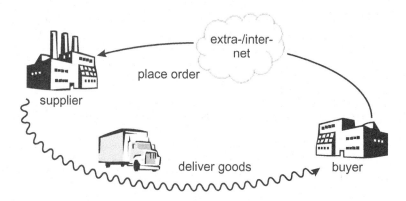

Fig. 1. Current data flow: digital ordering, analogous delivery data

Accuracy, completeness and reliability of data becomes an important issue when it comes to an argument between supplier, consumer and shipping company, one saying that the material was transported according to the specifications and the other one not wanting to accept the load because the data is not reliable enough or too close to specification limits. In this case, an insurance will not care about the consumer's doubt and rely on the raised data even if close to the limits. This is thus to the customer's disadvantage.

Completeness of the inspection data is even more at risk when during transportation the goods are kept in intermediate stocks for some time to continue their journey at a later point. In these cases goods often change between organizations. Considering a typical transport scenario by ship, train and truck, this would involve an international shipping company, a national logistics partner and a local or regional transportation company. When quality supervised goods change between transportation media the measuring devices may be taken off before the material is in the safety of the controlled stock rooms. It may thus reside in non acceptable conditions without there being any supervision. This is beyond the customer's control who can only believe in the reliability of the intermediate stock responsible to sufficiently take care of the goods and measuring devices.

More physical problems are due to the fact that most existing measuring devices are rather heavy and big in size. It is difficult to fix them well to the goods making sure that they are not damaged and do not fall off. Both cases would result in incomplete or incorrect data and the consumer will most probably not be able to accept the shipment. In the observed business cases the choice of the type of device is up to the supplier. The consumer is therefore confronted with various types of devices attached to different parts of the goods. Finding the device and reading out the data correctly constitutes a problem which must not be underestimated.

Inspection data taken during the transport of sensitive physical goods for quality management purposes are nowadays not integrated in the electronic commerce workflow but raised using analogous devices and transferred manually into the ERPS. Consequently, the test data lack accuracy and reliability. The completeness is endangered when the goods change transportation medium or are kept in intermediate stocks. Our goal is to improve these processes and solve the problems by integrating the inspection data into the electronic workflow (see fig. 2).

2   Requirements for the Integration of Inspection Data

From the problems described earlier and the scenarios given a number of requirements for the integration of physical goods in e-commerce processes can be stated. The major issues are concerned with

- the device that collects the data
- the connection to the backend systems
- the protection of the data against manipulation

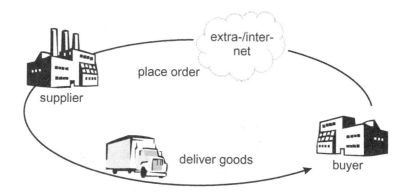

Fig. 2. Ideal e-commerce data flow circuit without interruption

- the format for data representation
- the software needed for the integration
- the realization of non-interrupted measurements
- making measurement data available during transport

The integration presumes a digital measurement device attached to the goods to measure the respective conditions. This already offers enhanced accuracy of the test data as loss during data transfer can be avoided. Transferring the data into the customer's ERPS can be done either by transmitting them directly using a remote communication method or by using a digital data logger to store the data and transfer them upon arrival. The first method requires a virtually continuous, wireless connection between all the means of transport and the customer's ERPS. This is complicated and expensive to implement but offers the most effective control over the goods' conditions. It does not only offer integration but also improves the overall process and the possibilities of quality management of transported goods. It can be considered a further step to the second one which is easier to realize and closer to the method applied nowadays, i.e. analogous data loggers.

Independently of the type of data transmission the device and the whole system have to fulfill several requirements. To overcome the lacking completeness of the inspection data the device should be able to continue working also during intermediate stocking periods or reloading. This means that firstly, the device has to be sufficiently small and lightweight not to fall off the goods it is attached to and not to obstruct handling the load. Secondly, it has to be able either to transmit data also when in stock or to log a sufficient amount of data to cover the whole transportation period from the supplier to the consumer. Calculating a shipping time of 3 months and a measurement interval of 15 to 30 minutes this would result in 4.320 to 8.640 stored values.

Additionally, the data identifying the different transport units has to be stored on the device as well. This is necessary to implement the automatic transfer of the measurements to the consumer's backend system. This information is added to every unit of measurement data transferred to the customer's ERPS.

In case something goes wrong during the transport the device becomes a target to potential manipulation to cover up the problem. Therefore it has to offer sufficient security mechanisms which make manipulation impossible or at a minimum recognizable. For a transmitting device the danger affects basically the transmission medium and protocol. For a wireless medium, manipulation is especially easy. Authentication and encoding can be used together with an appropriate protocol. For a data logger, this concerns mainly the logger and the stored data. Manipulation can be prevented on the software side by offering only a very restricted set of functions the device can execute, by restricting the set of authorized communication peers and identifying them through passwords or similar mechanisms or by encoding the communication. On the hardware side, the pieces have to be secured against violation or exchange. Additional control can be gained by logging specific events like reading out the measurement values or execution of other operations and by controlling the integrity of the device's data (e.g. total amount of values must correspond to measurement interval and measurement starting time).

Starting the device's measurements must happen when it is already fixed on the load. This is important to prevent that measurement values originate that yet do not reflect the conditions of the respective goods. As the exact time of the transport's start can usually not be determined the device must receive an order. This implies that the common materials on the transport mediums or the containers must not influence the communication ability of the device.

Software is needed to perform the communication with the device and the ERPS. At the supplier's site, the device has to be initialized before the transport. This comprises parameterization of the measurement according to the delivery conditions, storing the material identification and starting the measurement. At the customer's site, the software has to receive the measurement values from the device, either all at once or just a subset. It then has to transfer the values into the ERPS where they are assigned to the corresponding inspection lot according to the material identification.

It is furthermore practical to provide a possibility to check the measurements during the transport. If specification limits are violated at an early point of the transport the goods can immediately be returned to the supplier rather than still delivered to the customer. This can be accomplished by a piece of software which only receives values from the device and displays them in a table or graphically.

A very important point is the definition of the format in which the data are transferred. The data have to be understood by the supplier's as well as the customer's system, the format must thus be flexible to adapt to different requirements and still easy to implement and interpret. This applies to electronic commerce data in general. Consumer and supplier must assure that their systems communicate over a well defined interface avoiding any misinterpretation and falsification of the transmitted data. The interface must allow connection of many different backend systems and transmission of diverse data structures and must thus be widespread and flexible.

False data and transfer errors have to be detected and corrected either manually or automatically by the system. Also the handling of the involved devices as well as the user interfaces of the corresponding software have to be designed in a very easy to use and error resistant way as not only well-trained quality managers but also less skilled workers may have to interact with the system and carry out involved tasks.

3   An Architecture

In this section, we want to develop further details of a solution's architecture derived from the requirements given in the last section. As already adumbrated, a solution consists of:

- a measuring device that accompanies the transported goods
- a software that works together with the supplier's ERPS and also can communicate with the device (reading delivery parameters from the supplier's system and initializing the measuring device before the transport)
- a software at the customer's site that can communicate with the accompanying device and feedback the data acquired during the transport into the customer's ERPS.

We have a closer look at these components to show how they can be realized so that they meet the requirements stated above.

3.1   The Accompanying Device

The device that is transported with the physical goods must offer the following functionality:

- store data for identification and description of the goods (or a pointer to this data, e.g. URL)
- monitor the parameters that have to be supervised in order to assure the quality during the transport (e.g. temperature, shock, acceleration, orientation, magnetism etc.)
- store and transmit the measurements, where storage can signify a limited or unlimited number of values and transmission can be during the transport of a portion of values as well as all values at once upon arrival.

Devices such as digital data loggers for measuring a wide range of different parameters and storing the data are available off-the-shelf in great variety from a large number of companies. They usually dispose of a certain amount of memory to hold the stored values as well as the measurement parameters, a processing unit and a sensor. For communication with other computers they provide a communication interface, mostly for serial cable connection or serial infrared transfer. Size, weight and shape vary as well as other properties like estimated battery life, alarm function when exceeding thresholds and configuration possibilities. Data loggers usually come with a stand alone PC program for configuration and starting the measurements as well as reading the values from the logger and displaying them.

However, most devices do not offer extra memory for storing material description or other delivery data. They do not provide security mechanisms or the possibility to mark special events during the transport by time stamps and an event description. These features have thus to be added to a chosen logger.

For transmission of measurements during the transports similar devices exist or can be adapted accordingly to which a wireless connection can be established. As this is a long range connection usually mobile phone networks (e.g. GSM) are used. As these connections are cost intensive and establishing takes some time it is convenient to log a certain amount of data on the device and only transmit this data at longer intervals. Often, the transport media are already equipped with a system for remote connections for event tracking purposes. In this case, the device could just establish a short range connection to this system which then forwards the data.

3.2   The Software Architecture

An essential focus designing the software for backend system communication lies in choosing the most general, future oriented and widely spread interface to be able to use it with all kinds of systems. The interface must allow local as well as remote communication and must consist of a data format that is easy to transmit and to store, that allows modification of erroneous data and that offers flexible definition of data structures. Storing the data is necessary to add some failure resistance to the transfer which prevents the data from getting lost in case of communication errors.

As these requirements apply to e-commerce data transfer in general, the deployment of the Extensible Markup Language (XML) [3] as the data storage format and the Hypertext Transfer Protocol (HTTP) as the communication protocol seems to be the most promising possibility. This combination meets the above requirements without any exception and with some minor enhancements is merged in the Simple Object Access Protocol (SOAP) for which support is already integrated in a large number of systems. By this decision, the process can be integrated in a Web Server infrastructure and is therefore open for the integration with any backend system working on this basis. It also allows the interoperability with service discovery approaches such as UDDI. As the customer's part of the software constitutes the main part of the system responsible for the integration we take a closer look at a corresponding software architecture. The task of the consumer's software is to communicate with the device to read the measuring values and goods identification and transfer these data into the customer's backend system. It has to produce feedback output about the success or failure of the transfer and take according actions.

It is possible either to use software fully integrated with the ERPS rather than a separate software that communicates over a communication interface (e.g. XML/HTTP). The advantage is the good control over the data which after being transferred to the customer's site travel only inside the system. Data representation and integrity does not play a significant role as the representation with XML can be adapted to any internal data format. The advantage of a separate piece is that with the widespread XML/HTTP communication interface it can be used with many different backend systems. As our goal is to work out a general solution we concentrate on the independent system.

The tasks can be accomplished by one single piece of software running on a PC which is connected to the device communicating with the measuring device. Depending on the kind of communication this computer should be situated close to the goods receipt area. As the workers around are not necessarily computer experts the aim is to automate the task as far as possible.

The program must automatically establish a communication link to any device in reach and read the transmitted data. These data are either in a device-dependent format or already in XML. The program transforms the data in XML, stores them in a file and transfers them via an HTTP connection into the customer's ERPS. Storing the data in a file offers security against communication failures and also provides a possibility to view the data independently of the backend system. Using an XSL style sheet and an XML/XSL capable web browser the data can be viewed from any system in the network or even fed into another program for graphical preparation and display.

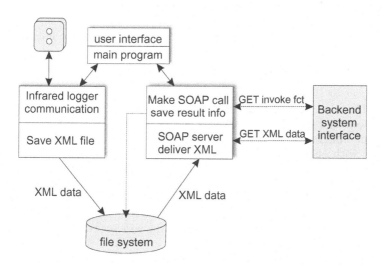

Fig. 3. Software architecture

A software architecture for linking a data logger via an infrared interface can be seen in fig. 3. It constitutes a separate module for communication with the device and saving the transmitted data in an XML file. This allows for adapting the interface for communication with the device according to the specific requirements. Another module realizes the data transfer to the ERPS via XML/HTTP. The user interface is contained in a third module to be easily adapted to the needs of different user groups with special tasks and skills. The user interface mainly serves for displaying the status of the data transmission as well as any problems or errors. As the system works automatically and user input can be avoided the user interface can be realized using XML/XSL as well. This offers flexibility for defining different interfaces and an easy network access also in secured environments (e.g. firewalls).

4   The Implementation of a Prototype

To show the benefits of using a system that integrates the quality management data of physical goods we implemented a prototype following the described architecture. The prototype was developed in conjunction with Infineon Technologies AG, Germany, as buyer of temperature sensitive chemical products and Shipley, Netherlands, as the corresponding supplier.

As our main goal was the integration of the existing quality management processes into the e-commerce workflow rather than an overall improvement of the QM we chose to use a data logger as measuring device. A device able to transmit the values immediately and remotely into the ERPS is more complicated and expensive and would have more difficulties to be accepted by the corresponding parties as it is a larger step away from the system they are used to.

It was required to integrate the system with SAP R/3 which is Infineon's ERPS. R/3 provides the SAP BusinessConnector, a tool for linking external applications via an HTTP/XML interface, and from the most current release 4.6 also offers full and integrated support for SOAP [11].

The Device. As data logger we chose the "Minidan", a miniature data logger produced by Esys GmbH, Germany [2]. The Minidan is a data logger available for recording temperature as well as other parameters. It can hold up to 16.000 values with an accuracy of 0.5 to $0.0135°C$. It has the shape of a cube with an edge length of 31mm and a weight of 28g including battery. It contains an infrared interface for PC connection. The advantage compared to a serial cable connection is the missing socket avoiding additional edges and offering a very resistant and water proof construction. Considering the rather small amount of data to be transferred the loss of speed of the wireless connection compared to cable is not important.

The battery of the Minidan lasts for two to ten years, depending on the intensity of usage. The logger was modified as already explained earlier to offer space for 976 bytes of extra information and to be able to store a time stamps and a description to mark special events (e.g. when starting and reading out the logger).

The Supplier's Part. The task of the supplier's software part is to write the delivery data of the transport goods to the data logger and to initialize its parameters according to the delivery specifications between the supplier and the consumer. This is done by a stand alone software on a backend computer as preparation of the transport. To start the measurements when the logger is already fixed on the transport goods another separate handheld device was developed. This device disposes of an infrared interface and issues the start command to any data logger in reach. LEDs serve to indicate the success or failure of the starting.

The Consumer's Part. The software at the consumer's site was developed according to the general architecture presented earlier.

It consists of a program running on a PC close to the goods receipt area being equipped with an infrared interface. Upon reception of the goods the data loggers are taken off and put in front of to the PC's interface. The software automatically detects any logger and invokes the reading of the measurement values and the goods' description. The data is stored in an XML file in the local or remote file system. Via a web server having access to these files the XML data can be linked to a corresponding XSL style sheet and be viewed in an XML/XSL capable browser.

The XML file is then transferred via HTTP into the backend system which takes care of assigning the values to the corresponding inspection lot. The HTTP response contains a return code indicating whether the data could successfully be related to the order entries. If so, the data logger is initialized and ready to be sent back to the supplier for the next deployment.

If an error occurs the system determines whether it is of a temporary nature or not. Temporary would be e.g. if the corresponding inspection lot is locked by another user who is likely to unlock it soon. Therefore the system automatically retries to transfer the data after a certain period. However, if this fails for a certain number of times or if the error is permanent (eg. wrong data, association to lot impossible) the cube and the associated XML data file are marked as erroneous and a notification is sent to the quality management responsible. It is his task to locate the error and correct the XML data file manually. The transfer process can then be re-invoked. The user interface showing the status and error messages is implemented in XML and different XSL style sheets adapted to different user groups. The display visible to the worker is shown in fig. 4, a more detailed version exists for the quality manager.

Automating the reading process as well as the transferring and error handling as far as possible serves to avoid user input. Workers should be prevented from having to interact with the system and thus from having to be specially trained. User input is always a very likely source of problems or errors and must thus be restricted to the absolutely necessary. As remote access to the program data

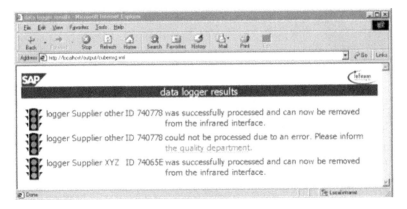

Fig. 4. Simple user interface for workers

and status is easily feasible error correction can be done remotely by quality managers rather than by workers directly on the PC.

5   Conclusion and Future Outlook

The aim of this project was to examine and implement an integrated solution for transporting and supervising goods in an e-commerce environment. Special care laid on the examination of the involved QM processes and the improvement of the accuracy, completeness and reliability of the inspection data. A temperature logger was adapted to specific quality ensurance requirements and software was written for managing the data logger and connecting it to the existing e-commerce systems. XML and HTTP was used for defining the interfaces going along with current e-commerce trends. The system is currently installed and used for supervision of chemical products. Users on both the supplier's and the customer's side are very optimistical about the advantages and the progress this system offers and think that there is a great potential for improving business and quality management processes on the basis of this approach.

5.1   Future Outlook

Many further enhancements of this solution are possible.

A paper delivery note is still issued for every goods' transport. To offer utmost integration this could be included in a general digital goods descriptor which is automatically initialized with the e-commerce system data and is added to every kind of transport. It would contain all goods-related data and therefore comprise supervisory measurements as well.

Checking of the logged data and taking according actions is in our case still time based. As already mentioned, the device can be equipped to be able to send the measurement data directly to a controlling system. An alternative is an event based solution. This would enable the device to send out a message on special events (e.g. via GSM to a mobile phone or via radio frequency (bluetooth) to some device on the transport medium). Above all errors like exceeding a temperature limit can in both cases be recognized at once. Actions can be taken at the earliest point and the wasting of the goods can be prevented rather than only recognized later. The quality of the goods thus increases and becomes more deterministic. This corresponds to the concept of "aware goods", i.e. goods that supervise themselves and take care that they are kept in a good condition.

Further improvement and automation for aware goods can be gained by installing a wireless communication device at the entry of the goods receipt area. As soon as a truck passes the device connects to all measuring devices accompanying the load and reads out the available information. The incoming material can be checked and accepted by the system which is fed back to the goods receipt responsible. The goods receipt can also automatically be entered in the ERPS. Knowledge about the existence of supervising devices and even the electronic delivery note become transparent for most persons involved in the process.

Tracking of goods could be included in a general goods descriptor. Supply chain management [7] would be facilitated and schedules can be optimized when the current location of delivered goods is trackable at any time. With good supervision the goods' quality can be assured and stock space can be utilized more efficiently. It is known exactly when goods will arrive and that they will most probably be in good state, thus material can be ordered a short period before being used and reserve material can be reduced to a minimum (just-in-time concept [6]). The flexibility and speed of e-commerce compared to traditional commerce can be maximally exploited.

A tracking device associated to the goods rather than the transport medium allows for easier tracking when goods change medium or are kept in intermediate stocks. Effectively, the palettes are to be tracked, not the truck they are on.

Acknowledgements. We would like to thank Robby Rochlitzer, Esys GmbH, Berlin, Germany and Matthias Schlaubitz, Infineon Technologies AG, Dresden, Germany for their good inspiration and cooperation in designing and implementing this project and for their detailed information about the involved processes.

We also would like to thank Christian Decker for his first prototypical implementation of a system for accessing the Minidan and for transferring the data into the SAP R/3.

References

[1] Berk, Joseph, Berk, Susan: Quality Management for the Technology Sector. Butterworth-Heinemann (2000)
[2] Esys GmbH: Entwicklungslizenz für Minidan^{TEMP}. (2000) http://www.esys.de
[3] Harold, E., Means, W.: XML in a Nutshell. O'Reilly. January 2001.
[4] Jablonski, S., Böhm, M., Schulze, W.: Workflow-Management - Entwicklung von Anwendungen und Systemen. dpunkt.verlag, Heidelberg (1997)

[5] Johnson, G.: Semiconductor E-Commerce: Driving Supply Chain Efficiencies. Research Report (2001)

[6] Kamiske, G., Brauer, J.-P.: Qualitätsmanagement von A bis Z. Carl Hanser Verlag München Wien. 1999.

[7] Kerridge, S., Slade, A., Kerridge, S., Ginty, K.: Supplypoint: Electronic Procurement Using Virtual Supply Chains - an Overview. In EM - Electronic Markets. Vol.8, Nr.3 (1998)

[8] Lamersdorf, W., Merz, M.: Trends in Distributed Systems for Electronic Commerce. Lecture Notes in Computer Science, Vol.1402, Springer Verlag (1998).

[9] Merz, Michael: Electronic Commerce - Marktmodelle, Anwendungen und Technologien. dpunkt.verlag (1999)

[10] Reinhart, G., Lindemann, U., Heinzl, J.: Qualitätsmanagement. Springer-Verlag Berlin Heidelberg. 1996.

[11] SAP AG. mySAP Lifecylce Management, Quality Management. 2001.

Scalable Regulation of
Inter-enterprise Electronic Commerce

Naftaly H. Minsky* and Victoria Ungureanu**

Rutgers University, New Brunswick, NJ 08903, USA,
{minsky,ungurean}@cs.rutgers.edu

Abstract. In the current electronic-commerce literature, a commercial transaction is commonly viewed as an exchange between two autonomous principals operating under some kind of contract between them—which needs to be formalized and enforced. But the situation can be considerably more complex in the case of *inter-enterprise* (also called business-to-business, or B2B) commerce. The participants in a B2B transaction are generally not autonomous agents, since their commercial activities are subject to the policies of their respective enterprises.

It is our thesis, therefore, that a B2B transaction should be viewed as being governed by three distinct policies: the two policies that regulate the activities of the two principals, while operating as representatives of their respective enterprises, and the policy that reflects the contract between the two enterprises. These policies are likely to be independently developed, and may be quite heterogeneous. Yet, they have to *interoperate*, and must all be brought to bear in regulating each B2B transaction. This paper presents a mechanism for formulating such interoperating policies, and for their scalable enforcement, thus providing for regulated *inter-enterprise* electronic commerce.

1 Introduction

In the current electronic-commerce literature, a commercial transaction is commonly viewed as an exchange between two autonomous principals operating under some kind of contract between them. The formulation and enforcement of such contracts are among the main problems presently facing this field. But the situation can be considerably more complex, and more challenging, in the case of *inter-enterprise* commerce (also called business-to-business, or B2B commerce). This is because the participants in a B2B transaction are generally not autonomous agents but are subject to the policies of their respective enterprises.

It is our thesis, therefore, that a B2B transaction should be viewed as being governed by three distinct policies: the two policies that regulate the activities of the two principals, while operating as representatives of their respective enterprises, and the policy that reflects the contract between the two enterprises.

* Work supported in part by NSF grants No. CCR-9710575 and No. CCR-98-03698
** Work supported in part by DIMACS under contract STC-91-19999 ITECC, and Information Technology and Electronic Commerce Clinic, Rutgers University

L. Fiege, G. Mühl, and U. Wilhelm (Eds.): WELCOM 2001, LNCS 2232, pp. 219–232, 2001.

This state of affairs can be illustrated by the following example: Consider a pair of enterprises E_1 and E_2 that trade with each other under a contract defined by policy P_{12} below:

> **Policy P_{12}:** *A business transaction between E_1, the client enterprise in this case, and E_2, the vendor, is initiated by a purchase order (PO) sent by some agent x_1 of E_1 to an agent x_2 of E_2, specifying the merchandise and the desired delivery time t. The exchange of merchandise and payment between the two agents is subject to the following provisions:*
> - *payment should accompany the PO;*
> - *the buyer, x_1, can cancel his order before the specified delivery time t, and will be reimbursed 90% of the payment he made, while 10% of it will go to x_2.*
> - *if the merchandise has been supplied by x_2 by time t, and the order has not been canceled by x_1, then the seller will get his payment and the buyer will get his merchandise; otherwise, the buyer x_1 would be fully refunded.*

Also, suppose that enterprise E_1 has the following policy, P_1, regarding such purchases:

> **Policy P_1:** *Agents in E_1 are allowed to purchase from E_2 in accordance with contract P_{12}, if the following conditions are met:*
> - *x_1 must have a budget assigned to it by a designated* `budgetOfficer`*.*
> - *a purchase order (PO) can be issued only if the balance in x_1 budget exceeds the scrip amount included in the offer. If this is the case, x_1's budget is reduced accordingly.*
> - *if the merchandise requested by x_1 is not delivered for whatever reason, its budget is increased by the refunds received under the contract between E_1 and E_2.*

And suppose that enterprise E_2 has its own policy, P_2, regarding responses to purchase orders:

> **Policy P_2:** *Agents in E_2 are allowed to respond to purchase orders in accordance with contract P_{12}, but the arrival of purchase orders and of payments, as well as the delivery of the purchased goods, must be monitored by a designated agent called* `auditor`*.*

It is clear that any purchase transaction between these two enterprises must conform to all three policies above. The problem is how can such three distinct policies be brought to bear on a single transaction?

One may attempt to deal with this problem by compiling a textual *composition* of the three policies into a single one, and then subject all transactions between the two enterprise to this composition. This technique has been proposed, for access-control policies, by several authors [4,2]. But textual compositions won't do for B2B commerce, for the following reasons: First, the two enterprises are likely to consider their policies P_1 and P_2 confidential, and may be reluctant to reveal them to a single composer. Second, these policies would be usually formulated separately, by different organizations, and without any knowledge of each other; therefore, it might be difficult to ensure that they are compatible with each other and composable. Third, a hard textual composition would be an impediment to the independent evolution of the policies of individual enterprises.

So, we need a mechanism that allows different enterprises to interoperate dynamically, under a mutually agreed contract, without sacrificing the confidentiality of their internal policies, and without losing their ability to make changes in these policies at will. We already addressed certain aspects of this problem, using a message exchange mechanism called Law-Governed Interaction (LGI) [6, 7]. In particular, a technique for establishing intra-enterprise policies, like P_1 and P_2 above, has been presented in [1]. And the issue of interoperability between enterprises has been addressed in [10].

But these techniques suffer from several difficulties. Chief among them is that although LGI itself is strictly decentralized, the mechanism proposed in [10] relies on a single agent to enforce the contract over all transactions between any pair of enterprises. Such a centralized enforcer might become a bottleneck, and a dangerous single point of failure when the number of the transactions grows. This, and another difficulty with the previous LGI-based mechanism are addressed in this paper.

The rest of the paper is organized as follows. We start, in Section 2, with a brief description of the concept of LGI, and then describe extensions to LGI designed to solve our interoperability problem. In Section 3 we demonstrate the proposed techniques by formulating the three intertwined example policies as *laws* under LGI, and by showing how they are enforced in a scalable manner. We conclude in Section 4.

2   Law-Governed Interaction (LGI) — An Overview

Broadly speaking, LGI is a message-exchange mechanism that allows an *open group* of distributed agents to engage in a mode of interaction *governed* by an explicitly specified policy, called the *law* of the group. The messages thus exchanged under a given law $\mathcal{L}$ are called $\mathcal{L}$-messages, and the group of agents interacting via $\mathcal{L}$-messages is called a *community* $\mathcal{C}$, or, more specifically, an $\mathcal{L}$-community $\mathcal{C}_{\mathcal{L}}$.

By the phrase "open group" we mean (a) that the membership of this group (or, community) can change dynamically, and can be very large; and (b) that the members of a given community can be heterogeneous. In fact, we make no assumptions about the structure and behavior of the agents[1] that are members of a given community $\mathcal{C}_{\mathcal{L}}$, which might be software processes, written in an arbitrary language, or human beings. All such members are treated as black boxes by LGI, which deals only with the interaction between them via $\mathcal{L}$-messages, making sure

---

[1] Given the popular usages of the term "agent," it is important to point out that we do not imply by it either "intelligence" nor mobility, although neither of these is being ruled out by this model.

it conforms to the law of the community. (Note that members of a community are not prohibited from non-LGI communication across the Internet, or from participation in other LGI-communities.)

For each agent x in a given community C_L, LGI maintains, what is called, the *control-state* CS_x of this agent. These control-states, which can change dynamically subject to law L, enable the law to make distinctions between agents, and to be sensitive to changes in their state. The semantics of control-states for a given community is defined by its law, and could represent such things as the role of an agent in this community, and privileges and tokens it carries. For example, under law L_1 to be introduced in Section 3, as a formalization of our example P_1 policy, the term budget(val) in the control-state of an agent denotes that this agent has been assigned a budget in amount of val.

The rest of this section is organized as follows. We start in Section 2.1 with a brief discussion of the concept of law, emphasizing its local nature, and with a description of the decentralized LGI mechanism for law enforcement. Then, in Section 2.2 we discuss the changes required in LGI for it to support inter-enterprise electronic commerce. We do not discuss here several important aspects of LGI, including its concept of *exceptions*, its treatment of certificates, the deployment of L-communities, the expressive power of LGI, and its efficiency. For these issues, and for implementation details, the reader is referred to [7,1].

2.1   Laws and Their Enforcement

Generally speaking, the law of a community C is defined over a certain types of events occuring at members of C, mandating the effect that any such event should have—this mandate is called the *ruling* of the law for a given event. The events subject to laws, called *regulated events*, include (among others): the *sending* and the *arrival* of an L-message; and the *coming due of an obligation* previously imposed on a given agent. The operations that can be included in the ruling of the law for a given regulated event are called *primitive operations*. They include, operations on the control-state of the agent where the event occured (called, the "home agent"); operations on messages, such as forward and deliver; and the imposition of an obligation on the home agent.

Thus, a law L can regulate the exchange of messages between members of an L-community, based on the control-state of the participants; and it can mandate various side effects of the message-exchange, such as modification of the control states of the sender and/or receiver of a message, and the emission of extra messages, for monitoring purposes, say.

On The Local Enforceability of Laws: Although the law L of a community C is *global* in that it governs the interaction between all members of C, it is enforceable *locally* at each member of C. This is due to the following properties of LGI laws:

- L only regulates local events at individual agents,
- the ruling of L for an event e at agent x depends only on e and the local control-state CS_x of x.

– The ruling of $\mathcal{L}$ at x can mandate only local operations to be carried out at
  x, such as an update of $\mathcal{CS}_x$, the forwarding of a message from x to some
  other agent, and the imposition of an obligation on x.

The fact that the same law is enforced at all agents of a community gives LGI
its necessary global scope, establishing a *common* set of ground rules for all
members of $\mathcal{C}$ and providing them with the ability to trust each other, in spite of
the heterogeneity of the community. And the locality of law enforcement enables
LGI to scale with community size.

Distributed Law-Enforcement: Broadly speaking, the law $\mathcal{L}$ of community $\mathcal{C}$ is
enforced by a set of trusted agents called *controllers*, that mediate the exchange
of $\mathcal{L}$-messages between members of $\mathcal{C}$. Every member x of $\mathcal{C}$ has a controller $\mathcal{T}_x$
assigned to it ($\mathcal{T}$ here stands for "trusted agent") which maintains the control-
state $\mathcal{CS}_x$ of its client x. And all these controllers, which are logically placed
between the members of $\mathcal{C}$ and the communications medium, as illustrated in
Figure 1, carry the *same law* $\mathcal{L}$. Every exchange between a pair of agents x and
y is thus mediated by *their* controllers $\mathcal{T}_x$ and $\mathcal{T}_y$, so that this enforcement is
inherently decentralized. However, several agents can share a single controller,
if such sharing is desired.

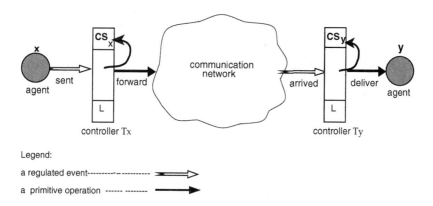

Fig. 1. Enforcement of the law.

Controllers are *generic*, and can interpret and enforce any well formed law.
A controller operates as an independent process, and it may be placed on any
machine, anywhere in the network. We have implemented a *controller-service*,
which maintains a set of active controllers. To be effective in a widely distributed
enterprise, this set of controllers need to be well dispersed geographically, so
that it would be possible to find controllers that are reasonably close to their
prospective clients.

On the Basis for Trust between Members of a Community: For a member of an $\mathcal{L}$-community to trust its interlocutors to observe the same law, one needs the following assurances: (a) messages are securely transmitted over the network; (b) the exchange of $\mathcal{L}$-messages is mediated by controllers interpreting the *same law* $\mathcal{L}$; and (c) all these controllers are *correctly implemented*. If these conditions are satisfied, then it follows that if y receives an $\mathcal{L}$-message from some x, this message must have been sent as an $\mathcal{L}$-message; in other words, that $\mathcal{L}$-messages cannot be forged.

Secure transmission is carried out via traditional cryptographic techniques. To ensure that a message forwarded by a controller $\mathcal{T}_x$ under law $\mathcal{L}$ would be handled by another controller $\mathcal{T}_y$ operating under the *same* law, $\mathcal{T}_x$ appends a one-way hash [9] H of law $\mathcal{L}$ to the message it forwards to $\mathcal{T}_y$. $\mathcal{T}_y$ would accept this as a valid $\mathcal{L}$-message under $\mathcal{L}$ if and only if H is identical to the hash of its own law.

As to the correctness of controllers, we assume here that every $\mathcal{L}$-community is willing to trust the controllers certified by a given certification authority (CA), which is specified by law $\mathcal{L}$. And, every pair of interacting controllers must first authenticate each other by means of certificates signed by this CA. In our case of B2B commerce, for example, it is likely that law $\mathcal{L}_1$, which is the formal expression under LGI of policy P_1, would require the use controllers maintained by enterprise E_1, and certified by a CA managed by that enterprise—and similarly for law $\mathcal{L}_2$. Also, it is likely that law $\mathcal{L}_{12}$, which is the formal expression of the contract between the two enterprises, would require the use of controllers maintained by an organization, and certified by a CA, trusted by both enterprises.

2.2   Providing for Regulated Interoperability between Enterprises

We start, in Section 2.2, with the features added to LGI to support direct interoperability between communities operating under different laws, with no contract between them (this work is a refinement of a concept introduced in [10]). Then, in Section 2, we introduce the concept of *virtual agent*, which is necessary for the scalable enforcement of inter-enterprise contracts.

Interoperability under LGI. By "interoperability" we mean here, the ability of an agent x operating under law $\mathcal{L}$ to exchange messages with and agent x' operating under law $\mathcal{L}'$. To support interoperability we introduce the following concepts into LGI: (a) *portal*, which is the specification within a given law $\mathcal{L}$, of a different law $\mathcal{L}'$ that $\mathcal{L}$ can interoperate with; (b) an *export/import* mechanism used for carrying out interoperation between different laws.

Portals. To enable interoperability between communities governed by laws $\mathcal{L}$ and $\mathcal{L}'$, each of these laws needs to specify a portal for the other. The portal in law $\mathcal{L}$, in particular, would have the form

```
portal(p', hL', c'),
```

where p' is the local name of this portal, to be used within law $\mathcal{L}$; hL' is the one-way hash of law $\mathcal{L}'$, which serves as its identifier; and c' is the CA employed by law $\mathcal{L}'$ for the certification of the controllers authorized to interpret it. Portals are included in the *Preamble* section of the law, as in Figure 3. The set of all such clauses in a given law is called the initial portal table of the law. This table can be changed dynamically, in a manner left out of this paper due to space limitations.

Export/Import: The actual transfer of a message m from an agent x operating under law $\mathcal{L}$ to an agent x' operating under law $\mathcal{L}'$, is carried out via a primitive operation, export, and via an event, imported, as follows:

An operation

```
export(x,m,[x',p']),
```

must be invoked by x under law $\mathcal{L}$, where p' is the local name for the portal of $\mathcal{L}'$ (defined in $\mathcal{L}$). This operation will initiate a handshake with the controller serving agent x' under law $\mathcal{L}'$; if the protocol completes successfully[2], then the following event will be triggered at x':

```
imported([x,p],m,x'),
```

where p is the name of the portal for law $\mathcal{L}$, defined in $\mathcal{L}'$.

Enforcement of Inter-enterprise Contracts via Virtual Agents. The mechanism proposed in [10] for enforcing contracts over inter-enterprise inter-actions employed a *single* mediator for *all* interactions between any agent x_1^i of enterprise E_1 and any agent x_2^j of E_2. This mediator, operating under the given contract law $\mathcal{L}_{12}$, must be created before the contract is enacted, and must be maintained for the lifetime of the contract. Such centralized enforcement of inter-enterprise contracts can easily become a bottleneck, when the number of transactions between a pair of enterprises grows, and it should not be employed unless it is truly necessary.

Centralized contract enforcement might, indeed, be necessary when the contract imposes dependencies between different inter-enterprise transactions. But no centralization is required if the contract at hand treats each inter-enterprise transaction independently of others—as is the case with the example contract P_{12} in Section 1.

Such a contract could be enforced scalably under LGI, if different transactions are mediated by different agents trusted by both enterprises. In the case of P_{12}, in particular, a transaction initiated by a purchase order sent by x_1^i to x_2^j could be mediated by an agent x^{ij} operating under policy P_{12}, as illustrated in Figure 2.

A mediator such as x^{ij} must be created dynamically, when a transaction is initiated, possible by agents, such as x_1^i, which operates under a different law;

---

[2] The protocol completes successfully if the information provided by controllers serving x and x' matches the information given by the portals p' and respectively p.

and it needs to be removed when the transaction terminates. We refer to such agents as *virtual agents*.

Virtual agents differ from regular LGI-agents by the way they are created; and by the fact that a virtual agent does not have an actor (such as a person, or a program) to drive it, but is driven by messages from other agents, such as x_1^i and x_2^j, that participate in the transaction under its jurisdiction. The creation of such light weight and ephemeral agents is discussed below, and their use is illustrated in the following section.

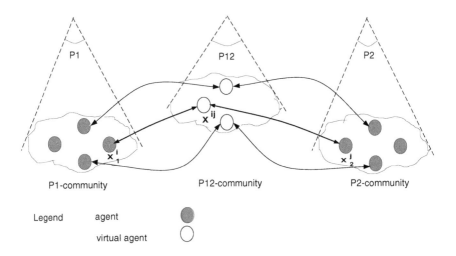

Fig. 2. Interoperation between communities using virtual agents.

The Creation of Virtual Agents: An agent x operating under law $\mathcal{L}$, with controllers certified by certification authority c, can create a virtual-agent x' under a possibly different law $\mathcal{L}'$, with controllers certified by a potentially different certification authority c', by invoking the primitive operation:

```
create(vAgent(N'),home(T'),portal(P'),arg(A')).
```

Here, T' is the name of the controller which is to host the new agent; N' is the "private name" of this particular agent, which will distinguish it from other agents hosted by controller T'; P' is the name of the portal, which identifies: (a) the law $\mathcal{L}'$ under which this agent is to operate, and (b) the CA to be used for the authentication of controller T'; finally, A' is an arbitrary list of arguments that is to be communicated to the newly created agent.

The very first event in the life of the newborn agent would be:

```
created(by(I,P),arg(A')).
```

Here, I is the id of the creator; P is the name of the creator's portal, which must be defined in law $\mathcal{L}'$ that governs the newborn; and A' is the argument list contained in the create operation that created this object.

What happens when this event occurs depends, of course, on law $\mathcal{L}'$ that governs the newborn. For example, under law $\mathcal{L}_{12}$ displayed in Figure 5, it is Rule $\mathcal{R}1$ (discussed in detail in the following section) which determines the effect of a *created*-event at it.

3   A Case Study

We now show how the three policies P_1, P_2, and P_{12}, introduced in Section 1, can be formalized, and thus enforced, under LGI. We note that P_1 and P_2 do not depend on each other in any way. Each of these policies provides for export to, and import from, the contract policy P_{12}, but they have no dependency on the internal structure of P_{12}.

After the presentation of these three policies we will illustrate the manner in which they interoperate by describing the progression of a single purchase transaction. We conclude this section with a brief discussion.

Law $\mathcal{L}_1$ — The Formalization of Policy P_1. Formally, under LGI, the community regulated by this law consists of the employees allowed to make purchases, and the designated agent budgetOfficer, who provides budget to employees. The law of this policy is presented in Figure 3. The law consists of two parts: preamble and rules. The preamble section describes the initial control state of the various agents operating in the community and lists the acceptable communication portals. In this example, the initial control state consists of a term budget(0), denoting that budgets of every agent are initially zero. And law $\mathcal{L}_1$ provides for communication only via portal pt12, the portal for the contract law.

The second part of the law consists of five rules, each followed by an explanatory comment (in italics). We discuss here only the first two rules handling budget allocation. (The rest of the rules will be presented as part of the description of a purchase transaction.) Under law $\mathcal{L}_1$, an agent designated as a budgetOfficer can increase the budget of any agent x_1 by an arbitrary amount Amt by sending a message giveBudget(Amt) to it. The sending of such a message is authorized by Rule $\mathcal{R}1$, which forwards the message to its destination. By Rule $\mathcal{R}2$, when this message arrives at x_1, the budget of x_1 will be incremented by Amt.

Law $\mathcal{L}_2$ — The Formalization of Policy P_2. This law, displayed in Figure 4, defines one acceptable portal, pt12, and thus allows for interoperability only with the contract community. The community regulated by this law consists of employees allowed to respond to POs and the designated agent auditor.

The Contract Law $\mathcal{L}_{12}$. This law, which formalizes the contract policy, described informally in Section 1, is displayed in Figure 5. The preamble of $\mathcal{L}_{12}$ defines

$\mathcal{P}$*reamble:*
    initialCS([budget(0)]).
    authority(contractAuthority,publicKey).
    portal(pt12, hashOfContractLaw,contractAuthority).
    alias(budgetOfficer," budgetOfficer@e1.com").

$\mathcal{R}$1. sent(budgetOfficer, giveBudget(Amt), X1) :- do(forward).
    A giveBudget *message sent by the* budgetOfficer *is forwarded immediately.*

$\mathcal{R}$2. arrived(budgetOfficer,giveBudget(Amt),X1) :-
        budget(Val)@CS, do(incr(budget(Val),Amt)), do(deliver).
    The arrival of an giveBudget(Amt) *message causes the increase by* Amt *of the*
    value Val *held in the* budget *term; the message is also delivered to the receiver*
    X1, *to notify him of the increase.*

$\mathcal{R}$3. sent(X1,M,X2) :- M==purchaseOrder(Specs,Scrip,T),
        budget(Val)@CS, Val > Scrip,
        do(dcr(budget(Val),Scrip)), select(N,C,X12),
        do(create(vAgent(N),home(C),portal(pt12),arg([M,X2]))),
        do(+proxy(Specs,X2,X12)).
    A purchase transaction between X1 *and* X2 *is initiated only if* Scrip, *the amount*
    the X1 *is willing to pay for the merchandise, is less than* Val, *the value of the*
    sender's budget. If this is the case, the budget is decreased accordingly and a
    request to create a virtual agent N@C *is issued.*

$\mathcal{R}$4. sent(X1,M,X2) :- M==cancel(Specs),
        proxy(Specs,X2,X12)@CS,do(export(X2,M,[X12,pt12])).
    A cancel *message is exported immediately to the virtual agent* X12.

$\mathcal{R}$5. imported([X12,pt12],M,X1) :-
        proxy(Specs,X2,X12)@CS, do(deliver(X2,M,X1))
        if M==refund(Specs,Amt) then do(incr(budget(Val), Amt)).
    A message, imported from X12 *via portal* pt12, *is delivered to the destination. If*
    the message represents a refund for Amt, *then the budget is increased by* Amt.

Fig. 3. The law $\mathcal{L}_1$ of enterprise E_1

two portals pt1 and pt2, allowing for interoperation with two communities: the
$\mathcal{L}_1$-community (via pt1), and the $\mathcal{L}_2$-community (via pt2). And we will describe
in the next paragraph how the rules of this law materialize the contract.

The community which operates under this law consists of virtual agents only.
Each such virtual agent is created when a PO is emitted by a client, and is
maintained for the duration of the purchase transaction. As we shall see, a virtual
agent x_{12} acts as a trusted mediator between a client agent x_1 and a vendor agent
x_2, records the terms of the PO, and carries out the provisions of the contract.

Preamble:
    initialCS([]).
    authority(contractAuthority,publicKey).
    portal(pt12,hashOfContractLaw,contractAuthority)).
    alias(auditor," auditor@trust.com").

$\mathcal{R}$1. ```imported([X12,pt12],M,X2) :-
            if M==[purchaseOrder(Specs,Price,T),X1] then
            do(+proxy(Specs,X1,X12))
            do(deliver),
            do(deliver(X2,M,auditor))).```
    A message imported from the contract portal is delivered to the auditor *and to the home agent.*

$\mathcal{R}$2. ```sent(X2,M,X1) :- M==supply(Specs,Ticket),
            do(deliver(X1, M,auditor)),proxy(Specs,X1,X12)@CS,
            do(export(X2,M, [X12,pt12])).```
    When a message is sent by an agent from the vendor enterprise to a client agent, the message is delivered to the designated auditor. *A copy of the message is exported to* X12 *under the contract portal.*

Fig. 4. The law $\mathcal{L}_2$ of enterprise E_2

The Progression of a Purchase Transaction. We explain now how these three laws function together, by means of a step-by-step description of the progression of a purchase transaction initiated by a

    ```purchaseOffer(specs,scrip,t)```

message sent by agent x_1 of enterprise E_1 (the vendor) to an agent x_2 of E_2 (the client).

1. The sending by x_1 of a PO to x_2 denotes the beginning of a new purchase transaction between the two parties and is handled by law $\mathcal{L}_1$ (see Rule $\mathcal{R}$3 of $\mathcal{L}_1$) as follows. If the budget of x_1 is smaller than the amount specified by scrip, then this PO is simply ignored. Otherwise a request is issued to create a virtual agent under the contract-law $\mathcal{L}_{12}$. The arguments passed to the newly created agent are the original PO, together with x_2, the identity of the vendor agent.
2. As a result of this request, a new virtual agent, to be called here x_{12}, is spawned. And immediately, a created event, which is handled by Rule $\mathcal{R}$1 of $\mathcal{L}_{12}$, is triggered at x_{12}. This rule distinguishes between two cases. If the creation request did not come through pt1, the authorized portal of $\mathcal{L}_1$, then the ruling calls for the immediate removal of the virtual agent. Otherwise, the agent is maintained and will serve, as we shall see, as a trusted intermediary between the two parties. In the latter case, the following additional actions are called for:(a) the terms of the order are recorded in the control state of the virtual agent by a term order; (b) an obligation to end the transaction
    ```

$\mathcal{P}$*reamble:*
```
    initialCS([]).
    authority(e1Authority,pk1).
    authority(e2Authority,pk2).
    portal(pt1, hashOfE1Law, e1Authority).
    portal(pt2, hashOfE2Law, e2Authority).
```

$\mathcal{R}$1. ```created(by([X1,PT1]),arg([purchaseOrder(Specs,Scrip,T),X2])) :-
            if (PT1 !=pt1) then do(remove)
            else
                (do(+order(X1,Specs,Scrip,X2)),
                do(imposeObligation(endTransaction,T)),
                do(export(X1,M,[X2,pt2])))).```

A virtual agent is maintained only if the request comes through pt1, the portal
of enterprise E_1. If this is the case, the arguments are processed as follows: (a)
the terms of the order are recorded in the control state of the virtual agent; (b)
an obligation to end the transaction is set to fire at delivery time; and (c) the
original purchaseOrder is exported to the vendor X2.

$\mathcal{R}$2. ```imported([X2,pt2],supply(Specs,Ticket),X12) :-
            order(X1,Specs,Scrip,X2)@CS,
            do(+goods(Ticket)).```

When a supply message is imported by the virtual agent, X12, the ticket
denoting the ordered merchandise is stored in its control state by a term goods.

$\mathcal{R}$3. ```imported([X1,pt1], cancel(Specs), X12) :-
            order(X1,Specs,Scrip,X2)@CS,
            do(export(X12, refund(Specs,Scrip*0.9),[X1,pt1])),
            do(export(X12,cancelled(Specs,Scrip*0.1),[X2,pt2])),
            do(remove)```

A cancel imported before the delivery time is processed as follows. The client,
X1, is refunded the amount paid minus a 10% penalty. The vendor, X2, is notified and receives scrip amounting to 10% of the order price. Finally, the virtual
agent, X12, not longer needed is removed.

$\mathcal{R}$4. ```obligationDue(endTransaction) :- order(X1,Specs,Scrip,X2)@CS,
            if goods(Ticket)@CS then
                (do(export(X12, supply(Specs,Ticket),[X1,pt1])),
                    do(export(X12,payment(Specs,Scrip),[X2,pt2])))
                else do(export(X12, refund(Specs,Scrip),[X1,pt1]))
            do(remove).```

The obligation endTransaction fires at delivery time. The following operations
are triggered by this event. If term goods(Ticket) is present in the control state,
meaning that the vendor supplied the goods, then a supply message containing
the Ticket is exported to the client X1, and a payment message containing Scrip
is exported to the vendor X2. Otherwise, the client is fully refunded. In both cases
the virtual agent, is destroyed.

Fig. 5. The law $\mathcal{L}_{12}$ of the contract between E_1 and E_2

is set to fire at delivery time; and (c) the original PO is exported to the vendor x_2.

3. When a `purchaseOrder` message exported by x_{12} is imported into x_2 via `pt12`, the authorized contract portal, it is immediately delivered to the vendor x_2 and to the `auditor` (Rule $\mathcal{R}1$ of $\mathcal{L}_2$).

4. According to law $\mathcal{L}_2$, agent x_2 can respond to a PO by a `supply(specs,ticket)` message[3], where `ticket` denotes the requested merchandise. By Rule $\mathcal{R}2$ of $\mathcal{L}_2$, the sending of such a message triggers two operations: (a) the message is exported to x_{12} and (b) a copy of the message is delivered to the `auditor`.

5. An import of the `supply(specs,ticket)` response into the virtual agent causes the merchandise to be temporarily stored into the control state in a term `goods` (Rule $\mathcal{R}2$ of $\mathcal{L}_{12}$).

6. Under the contract between the two enterprises a client is allowed to cancel an order before the specified delivery time. We will assume for now that the client exercised its right and sent a `cancel` message to the vendor. By Rule $\mathcal{R}4$ of $\mathcal{L}_1$ such a message is immediately exported to the virtual agent, x_{12}, for disposition.

7. In accordance with the contract law, a `cancel` message imported into the virtual agent *before the delivery time* triggers the execution of the following operations: A `refund` message carrying `scrip` amounting to 90% of the price paid is exported to the client. A `cancelled` message is exported to the vendor to notify him of the outcome. Finally, the virtual agent, x_{12}, no longer needed is removed (Rule $\mathcal{R}3$ of law $\mathcal{L}_{12}$).

8. However, if x_1 does not cancel the order, then the obligation `endTransaction` fires at the virtual agent at the specified delivery time[4].The ruling for this event mandates the following actions: If term `goods(Ticket)` is present in the control state, meaning that the vendor supplied the goods, then a `supply` message containing the `ticket` is exported to the client x_1, and a `payment` message containing `scrip` is exported to the vendor x_2. Otherwise, x_1 is fully refunded. In both cases, the virtual agent, is destroyed. (Rule $\mathcal{R}4$ of $\mathcal{L}_{12}$).

9. Finally, the import of a `refund` message into x_1 causes the budget of x_1 to be increased by the amount specified in the message (Rule $\mathcal{R}5$ of $\mathcal{L}_1$).

Discussion. This case study makes the following simplifying assumptions: (1) all three policies use the same set of messages, and (2) the enterprises policies P_1 and P_2 allows for interoperation only with P_{12}. These assumptions are not intrinsic to the proposed model and were adopted only in order to make the example as simple as possible.

---

[3] To keep the example simple we do not describe here the case when the vendor declines a PO

[4] If the client cancelled in time then, by Rule $\mathcal{R}3$ of law $\mathcal{L}_{12}$ the virtual agent is removed, and thus the obligation dose not fire any longer

4 Conclusion

We have argued that any attempt to regulate inter-enterprise electronic commerce must recognize the fact that such commerce is inherently subject to a combination of several heterogeneous policies: the internal policies of the interacting enterprises, and the policy that expresses the contract between them. To ensure that every inter-enterprise transaction conforms to such a combination of policies, we employed the LGI mechanism—that supports a formal and enforced concept of a policy—extending it in two ways. First, we introduced the *export/import* mechanism, and the concept of *portal*, which allows agents operating under different policies to interoperate. Second, we introduced the concept of *virtual agent*, which can be created dynamically, at the beginning of an inter-enterprise transaction, to handle this transaction subject to the contract-law between the enterprises. What is new about this concept of virtual agent, relative to the conventional concept of a *trusted intermediary* [3,5,8], is: (a) its dynamic and ephemeral nature, which contributes to scalability; and (b) while operating under the contract-law, a virtual agent interoperates with agents operating under the laws of the individual enterprises.

References

1. X. Ao, N. a Minsky, and V. Ungureanu. Formal treatment of certificate revocation undr communal access control. In *Proceedings of the IEEE Symposium on Security and Privacy*, pages 116–129, Oakland, California, May 2001.
2. C. Bidan and V. Issarny. Dealing with multi-policy security in large open distributed systems. In *Proceedings of 5th European Symposium on Research in Computer Security*, pages 51–66, September 1998.
3. S. Glassman, M. Manasse, M. Abadi, P. Gauthier, and P. Sobalvarro. The Millicent protocol for inexpensive electronic commerce. In *Fourth International World Wide Web Conference Proceedings*, pages 603–618, December 1995.
4. L. Gong and X. Qian. Computational issues in secure interoperation. *IEEE Transctions on Software Engineering*, pages 43–52, January 1996.
5. S. Ketchpel and H. Garcia-Molina. Making trust explicit in distributed commerce transactions. In *Proceedings of the International Conference on Distributed Computing Systems*, pages 270–281, 1996.
6. N.H. Minsky. The imposition of protocols over open distributed systems. *IEEE Transactions on Software Engineering*, February 1991.
7. N.H. Minsky and V. Ungureanu. Law-governed interaction: a coordination and control mechanism for heterogeneous distributed systems. *TOSEM, ACM Transactions on Software Engineering and Methodology*, 9(3):273–305, July 2000.
8. M. Roscheisen and T. Winograd. A communication agreement framework for access/action control. In *Proceedings of the IEEE Symposium on Security and Privacy*, Oakland, California, May 1996.
9. B. Schneier. *Applied Cryptography*. John Wiley and Sons, 1996.
10. V. Ungureanu and N.H. Minsky. Establishing business rules for inter-enterprise electronic commerce. In *Proc. of the 14th International Symposium on DIStributed Computing (DISC 2000); Toledo, Spain; LNCS 1914*, pages 179–193, October 2000.

Author Index

Aberg, Johan 164
Adomavicius, Gediminas 180
Alonso, Gustavo 1
Angelim, Sérgio 26
Anido-Rifón, Luis 14

Bartelt, Andreas 193
Buchmann, Alejandro 13
Buttyán, Levente 114
Byde, Andrew 152

Csirik, János A. 139

Eymann, Torsten 63

Gärtner, Felix C. 101
García-Reinoso, Jaime 14
Golle, Philippe 75
González-Castaño, Francisco J. 14

Heuser, Stephan 11
Hubaux, Jean-Pierre 114

Kügler, Dennis 127

Lamersdorf, Winfried 193
Lazcano, Amaia 1
Leyton-Brown, Kevin 75
Lillibridge, Mark 75
Littman, Michael L. 139

Maciuszek, Dennis 164
Meira, Silvio R.L. 26
Merz, Christian 206
Minsky, Naftaly H. 219
Mironov, Ilya 75

Pagnia, Henning 101
Piccinelli, Giacomo 39

Rodríguez-Hernández, Pedro S. 14

Santos, Simone C. dos 26
Schmidt, Albrecht 206
Schuba, Marko 88
Schümmer, Till 51
Shahmehri, Nahid 164
Singh, Satinder 139
Stefanelli, Cesare 39
Stone, Peter 139

Thede, Anke 206
Trastour, David 39
Tuzhilin, Alexander 180

Ungureanu, Victoria 219

Vales-Alonso, Javier 14
Vogt, Holger 101

Wrona, Konrad 88

Zavagli, Guido 88

Lecture Notes in Computer Science

For information about Vols. 1–2136
please contact your bookseller or Springer-Verlag

Vol. 2122: H. Alt (Ed.), Computational Discrete Mathematics. VII, 173 pages. 2001.

Vol. 2137: I.S. Moskowitz (Ed.), Information Hiding. Proceedings, 2001. VIII, 412 pages. 2001.

Vol. 2138: R. Freivalds (Ed.), Fundamentals of Computation Theory. Proceedings, 2001. XIII, 542 pages. 2001.

Vol. 2139: J. Kilian (Ed.), Advances in Cryptology – CRYPTO 2001. Proceedings, 2001. XI, 599 pages. 2001.

Vol. 2140: I. Attali, T. Jensen (Eds.), Java on Smart Cards: Programming and Security. Proceedings, 2001. VIII, 255 pages. 2001.

Vol. 2141: G.S. Brodal, D. Frigioni, A. Marchetti-Spaccamela (Eds.), Algorithm Engineering. Proceedings, 2001. X, 199 pages. 2001.

Vol. 2142: L. Fribourg (Ed.), Computer Science Logic. Proceedings, 2001. XII, 615 pages. 2001.

Vol. 2143: S. Benferhat, P. Besnard (Eds.), Symbolic and Quantitative Approaches to Reasoning with Uncertainty. Proceedings, 2001. XIV, 818 pages. 2001. (Subseries LNAI).

Vol. 2144: T. Margaria, T. Melham (Eds.), Correct Hardware Design and Verification Methods. Proceedings, 2001. XII, 482 pages. 2001.

Vol. 2145: M. Leyton, A Generative Theory of Shape. XVI, 554 pages. 2001.

Vol. 2146: J.H. Silverman (Eds.), Cryptography and Lattices. Proceedings, 2001. VII, 219 pages. 2001.

Vol. 2147: G. Brebner, R. Woods (Eds.), Field-Programmable Logic and Applications. Proceedings, 2001. XV, 665 pages. 2001.

Vol. 2149: O. Gascuel, B.M.E. Moret (Eds.), Algorithms in Bioinformatics. Proceedings, 2001. X, 307 pages. 2001.

Vol. 2150: R. Sakellariou, J. Keane, J. Gurd, L. Freeman (Eds.), Euro-Par 2001 Parallel Processing. Proceedings, 2001. XXX, 943 pages. 2001.

Vol. 2151: A. Caplinskas, J. Eder (Eds.), Advances in Databases and Information Systems. Proceedings, 2001. XIII, 381 pages. 2001.

Vol. 2152: R.J. Boulton, P.B. Jackson (Eds.), Theorem Proving in Higher Order Logics. Proceedings, 2001. X, 395 pages. 2001.

Vol. 2153: A.L. Buchsbaum, J. Snoeyink (Eds.), Algorithm Engineering and Experimentation. Proceedings, 2001. VIII, 231 pages. 2001.

Vol. 2154: K.G. Larsen, M. Nielsen (Eds.), CONCUR 2001 – Concurrency Theory. Proceedings, 2001. XI, 583 pages. 2001.

Vol. 2155: H. Bunt, R.-J. Beun (Eds.), Cooperative Multimodal Communication. Proceedings, 1998. VIII, 251 pages. 2001. (Subseries LNAI).

Vol. 2156: M.I. Smirnov, J. Crowcroft, J. Roberts, F.Boavida (Eds.), Quality of Future Internet Services. Proceedings, 2001. XI, 333 pages. 2001.

Vol. 2157: C. Rouveirol, M. Sebag (Eds.), Inductive Logic Programming. Proceedings, 2001. X, 261 pages. 2001. (Subseries LNAI).

Vol. 2158: D. Shepherd, J. Finney, L. Mathy, N. Race (Eds.), Interactive Distributed Multimedia Systems. Proceedings, 2001. XIII, 258 pages. 2001.

Vol. 2159: J. Kelemen, P. Sosík (Eds.), Advances in Artificial Life. Proceedings, 2001. XIX, 724 pages. 2001. (Subseries LNAI).

Vol. 2161: F. Meyer auf der Heide (Ed.), Algorithms – ESA 2001. Proceedings, 2001. XII, 538 pages. 2001.

Vol. 2162: Ç. K. Koç, D. Naccache, C. Paar (Eds.), Cryptographic Hardware and Embedded Systems – CHES 2001. Proceedings, 2001. XIV, 411 pages. 2001.

Vol. 2163: P. Constantopoulos, I.T. Sølvberg (Eds.), Research and Advanced Technology for Digital Libraries. Proceedings, 2001. XII, 462 pages. 2001.

Vol. 2164: S. Pierre, R. Glitho (Eds.), Mobile Agents for Telecommunication Applications. Proceedings, 2001. XI, 292 pages. 2001.

Vol. 2165: L. de Alfaro, S. Gilmore (Eds.), Process Algebra and Probabilistic Methods. Proceedings, 2001. XII, 217 pages. 2001.

Vol. 2166: V. Matoušek, P. Mautner, R. Mouček, K. Tauser (Eds.), Text, Speech and Dialogue. Proceedings, 2001. XIII, 452 pages. 2001. (Subseries LNAI).

Vol. 2167: L. De Raedt, P. Flach (Eds.), Machine Learning: ECML 2001. Proceedings, 2001. XVII, 618 pages. 2001. (Subseries LNAI).

Vol. 2168: L. De Raedt, A. Siebes (Eds.), Principles of Data Mining and Knowledge Discovery. Proceedings, 2001. XVII, 510 pages. 2001. (Subseries LNAI).

Vol. 2169: M. Jaedicke, New Concepts for Parallel Object-Relational Query Processing. XI, 161 pages. 2001.

Vol. 2170: S. Palazzo (Ed.), Evolutionary Trends of the Internet. Proceedings, 2001. XIII, 722 pages. 2001.

Vol. 2172: C. Batini, F. Giunchiglia, P. Giorgini, M. Mecella (Eds.), Cooperative Information Systems. Proceedings, 2001. XI, 450 pages. 2001.

Vol. 2173: T. Eiter, W. Faber, M. Truszczynski (Eds.), Logic Programming and Nonmonotonic Reasoning. Proceedings, 2001. XI, 444 pages. 2001. (Subseries LNAI).

Vol. 2174: F. Baader, G. Brewka, T. Eiter (Eds.), KI 2001: Advances in Artificial Intelligence. Proceedings, 2001. XIII, 471 pages. 2001. (Subseries LNAI).

Vol. 2175: F. Esposito (Ed.), AI*IA 2001: Advances in Artificial Intelligence. Proceedings, 2001. XII, 396 pages. 2001. (Subseries LNAI).

Vol. 2176: K.-D. Althoff, R.L. Feldmann, W. Müller (Eds.), Advances in Learning Software Organizations. Proceedings, 2001. XI, 241 pages. 2001.

Vol. 2177: G. Butler, S. Jarzabek (Eds.), Generative and Component-Based Software Engineering. Proceedings, 2001. X, 203 pages. 2001.

Vol. 2180: J. Welch (Ed.), Distributed Computing. Proceedings, 2001. X, 343 pages. 2001.

Vol. 2181: C. Y. Westort (Ed.), Digital Earth Moving. Proceedings, 2001. XII, 117 pages. 2001.

Vol. 2182: M. Klusch, F. Zambonelli (Eds.), Cooperative Information Agents V. Proceedings, 2001. XII, 288 pages. 2001. (Subseries LNAI).

Vol. 2183: R. Kahle, P. Schroeder-Heister, R. Stärk (Eds.), Proof Theory in Computer Science. Proceedings, 2001. IX, 239 pages. 2001.

Vol. 2184: M. Tucci (Ed.), Multimedia Databases and Image Communication. Proceedings, 2001. X, 225 pages. 2001.

Vol. 2185: M. Gogolla, C. Kobryn (Eds.), «UML» 2001 – The Unified Modeling Language. Proceedings, 2001. XIV, 510 pages. 2001.

Vol. 2186: J. Bosch (Ed.), Generative and Component-Based Software Engineering. Proceedings, 2001. VIII, 177 pages. 2001.

Vol. 2187: U. Voges (Ed.), Computer Safety, Reliability and Security. Proceedings, 2001. XVI, 249 pages. 2001.

Vol. 2188: F. Bomarius, S. Komi-Sirviö (Eds.), Product Focused Software Process Improvement. Proceedings, 2001. XI, 382 pages. 2001.

Vol. 2189: F. Hoffmann, D.J. Hand, N. Adams, D. Fisher, G. Guimaraes (Eds.), Advances in Intelligent Data Analysis. Proceedings, 2001. XII, 384 pages. 2001.

Vol. 2190: A. de Antonio, R. Aylett, D. Ballin (Eds.), Intelligent Virtual Agents. Proceedings, 2001. VIII, 245 pages. 2001. (Subseries LNAI).

Vol. 2191: B. Radig, S. Florczyk (Eds.), Pattern Recognition. Proceedings, 2001. XVI, 452 pages. 2001.

Vol. 2192: A. Yonezawa, S. Matsuoka (Eds.), Metalevel Architectures and Separation of Crosscutting Concerns. Proceedings, 2001. XI, 283 pages. 2001.

Vol. 2193: F. Casati, D. Georgakopoulos, M.-C. Shan (Eds.), Technologies for E-Services. Proceedings, 2001. X, 213 pages. 2001.

Vol. 2194: A.K. Datta, T. Herman (Eds.), Self-Stabilizing Systems. Proceedings, 2001. VII, 229 pages. 2001.

Vol. 2195: H.-Y. Shum, M. Liao, S.-F. Chang (Eds.), Advances in Multimedia Information Processing – PCM 2001. Proceedings, 2001. XX, 1149 pages. 2001.

Vol. 2196: W. Taha (Ed.), Semantics, Applications, and Implementation of Program Generation. Proceedings, 2001. X, 219 pages. 2001.

Vol. 2197: O. Balet, G. Subsol, P. Torguet (Eds.), Virtual Storytelling. Proceedings, 2001. XI, 213 pages. 2001.

Vol. 2198: N. Zhong, Y. Yao, J. Liu, S. Ohsuga (Eds.), Web Intelligence: Research and Development. Proceedings, 2001. XVI, 615 pages. 2001. (Subseries LNAI).

Vol. 2199: J. Crespo, V. Maojo, F. Martin (Eds.), Medical Data Analysis. Proceedings, 2001. X, 311 pages. 2001.

Vol. 2200: G.I. Davida, Y. Frankel (Eds.), Information Security. Proceedings, 2001. XIII, 554 pages. 2001.

Vol. 2201: G.D. Abowd, B. Brumitt, S. Shafer (Eds.), Ubicomp 2001: Ubiquitous Computing. Proceedings, 2001. XIII, 372 pages. 2001.

Vol. 2202: A. Restivo, S. Ronchi Della Rocca, L. Roversi (Eds.), Theoretical Computer Science. Proceedings, 2001. XI, 440 pages. 2001.

Vol. 2204: A. Brandstädt, V.B. Le (Eds.), Graph-Theoretic Concepts in Computer Science. Proceedings, 2001. X, 329 pages. 2001.

Vol. 2205: D.R. Montello (Ed.), Spatial Information Theory. Proceedings, 2001. XIV, 503 pages. 2001.

Vol. 2206: B. Reusch (Ed.), Computational Intelligence. Proceedings, 2001. XVII, 1003 pages. 2001.

Vol. 2207: I.W. Marshall, S. Nettles, N. Wakamiya (Eds.), Active Networks. Proceedings, 2001. IX, 165 pages. 2001.

Vol. 2208: W.J. Niessen, M.A. Viergever (Eds.), Medical Image Computing and Computer-Assisted Intervention – MICCAI 2001. Proceedings, 2001. XXXV, 1446 pages. 2001.

Vol. 2209: W. Jonker (Ed.), Databases in Telecommunications II. Proceedings, 2001. VII, 179 pages. 2001.

Vol. 2210: Y. Liu, K. Tanaka, M. Iwata, T. Higuchi, M. Yasunaga (Eds.), Evolvable Systems: From Biology to Hardware. Proceedings, 2001. XI, 341 pages. 2001.

Vol. 2211: T.A. Henzinger, C.M. Kirsch (Eds.), Embedded Software. Proceedings, 2001. IX, 504 pages. 2001.

Vol. 2212: W. Lee, L. Mé, A. Wespi (Eds.), Recent Advances in Intrusion Detection. Proceedings, 2001. X, 205 pages. 2001.

Vol. 2213: M.J. van Sinderen, L.J.M. Nieuwenhuis (Eds.), Protocols for Multimedia Systems. Proceedings, 2001. XII, 239 pages. 2001.

Vol. 2214: O. Boldt, H. Jürgensen (Eds.), Automata Implementation. Proceedings, 1999. VIII, 183 pages. 2001.

Vol. 2215: N. Kobayashi, B.C. Pierce (Eds.), Theoretical Aspects of Computer Software. Proceedings, 2001. XV, 561 pages. 2001.

Vol. 2216: E.S. Al-Shaer, G. Pacifici (Eds.), Management of Multimedia on the Internet. Proceedings, 2001. XIV, 373 pages. 2001.

Vol. 2217: T. Gomi (Ed.), Evolutionary Robotics. Proceedings, 2001. XI, 139 pages. 2001.

Vol. 2218: R. Guerraoui (Ed.), Middleware 2001. Proceedings, 2001. XIII, 395 pages. 2001.

Vol. 2220: C. Johnson (Ed.), Interactive Systems. Proceedings, 2001. XII, 219 pages. 2001.

Vol. 2221: D.G. Feitelson, L. Rudolph (Eds.), Job Scheduling Strategies for Parallel Processing. Proceedings, 2001. VII, 207 pages. 2001.

Vol. 2232: L. Fiege, G. Mühl, U. Wilhelm (Eds.), Electronic Commerce. Proceedings, 2001. X, 233 pages. 2001.

Vol. 2233: J. Crowcroft, M. Hofmann (Eds.), Networked Group Communication. Proceedings, 2001. X, 205 pages. 2001.